The Confidence Myth

CW01509053

Ginka Toegel

The Confidence Myth

How Women Leaders can Break Free from Gendered Perceptions

Ginka Toegel
IMD Business School
Lausanne, Switzerland

ISBN 978-3-031-97304-8   ISBN 978-3-031-97305-5   (eBook)
https://doi.org/10.1007/978-3-031-97305-5

© The Editor(s) (if applicable) and The Author(s), under exclusive license to Springer Nature Switzerland AG
2025

This work is subject to copyright. All rights are solely and exclusively licensed by the Publisher, whether the
whole or part of the material is concerned, specifically the rights of translation, reprinting, reuse of illustrations,
recitation, broadcasting, reproduction on microfilms or in any other physical way, and transmission or
information storage and retrieval, electronic adaptation, computer software, or by similar or dissimilar
methodology now known or hereafter developed.
The use of general descriptive names, registered names, trademarks, service marks, etc. in this publication does
not imply, even in the absence of a specific statement, that such names are exempt from the relevant protective
laws and regulations and therefore free for general use.
The publisher, the authors and the editors are safe to assume that the advice and information in this book are
believed to be true and accurate at the date of publication. Neither the publisher nor the authors or the editors
give a warranty, expressed or implied, with respect to the material contained herein or for any errors or
omissions that may have been made. The publisher remains neutral with regard to jurisdictional claims in
published maps and institutional affiliations.

This Palgrave Macmillan imprint is published by the registered company Springer Nature Switzerland AG.
The registered company address is: Gewerbestrasse 11, 6330 Cham, Switzerland

If disposing of this product, please recycle the paper.

To the thousands of extraordinary women who have participated in my programs, I hold deep admiration for your excellence and enduring gratitude for the wisdom you have so generously shared

Preface

Let's assume there is a catalyst so powerful that it could alter our lives, propelling us toward realms of achievement and fulfillment once thought beyond reach. This isn't a fairy tale or the allure of some mythical potion. It's real, and it's transformative. If you haven't already guessed, I'm talking about confidence.

Confidence isn't just a nice-to-have; it's essential, especially for women striving to make their mark in a world that often downplays their achievements. For those navigating both professional and personal growth, confidence is indispensable. It's the solid foundation that enables you to realize your aspirations, break barriers, and achieve success. Yet, for many, this vital foundation remains out of reach, and its absence becomes a significant barrier to reaching their full potential.

For over 30 years, I have been teaching leadership across Africa, Asia, Europe, the Middle East, and North and South America. Many of these programs were designed for women executives, and over time, our conversations shifted from "fixing" women's behavior or capabilities to exploring the roles that organizations and society play in shaping women's leadership journeys. This book reflects those three dimensions, with a primary emphasis on women seeking to empower themselves.

At IMD Business School in Switzerland, we have been running the "Strategies for Leadership" program for women executives for more than 20 years. Many of the stories in this book come from participants who shared their experiences during these sessions (all names have been changed to respect privacy). The idea for this book was sparked during one session when I asked participants if confidence was a good quality to have. After the unanimous "yes," I asked another question: "How many of you want more confidence?" A significant number raised their hands. But when I asked if anyone wanted less confidence because they already had enough, not a single hand went up. This led to a revealing discussion. Some participants argued that women lack confidence, while others countered, "We don't lack it; people just think we do." Their curiosity about which perspective was true inspired me to write *The Confidence Myth*.

The mission of this book is to dismantle myths about women's confidence, or rather, the supposed lack thereof. A persistent narrative suggests that women inherently lack the confidence to lead, assert themselves, or advance in their careers as effectively as men do. But what if this belief is not only false but also a barrier preventing us from recognizing women's true potential? By challenging these misconceptions, my goal is to foster a deeper understanding of how women relate to confidence and to empower them to redefine its role in their personal and professional lives.

Why dispel myths about women's confidence? Because these myths don't just describe a skewed reality—they create one. They teach women to doubt themselves, invite others to question their experiences and expertise, and ultimately deny them opportunities. Outdated ideas like "women are naturally less confident"; "confidence means acting like a man"; or "a confident woman is unlikable" are not just incorrect—they are toxic. They keep women locked into second-tier roles, stifling both their potential in business and their personal growth in life.

When women dare to assert themselves, they risk being labeled as bossy. If they hold back, they are written off as weak. This no-win situation forces women to make themselves small and deny who they truly are just to fit society's narrow mold. The bottom line: these myths don't just harm women; they hold everyone back by curbing the innovation and insight that thrive when all voices are heard. Recognizing these harmful narratives is the first step in dismantling them.

The Confidence Myth sets out to rewrite the narrative on confidence, especially for women in business. It's for anyone curious about how the "lack of confidence" myth took hold and who wants to see it challenged. It's for women who have ever doubted themselves and are hungry for practical insights on rebuilding their self-confidence, no matter how tough the hurdles. It's for allies who want to offer support and for skeptics who need the facts laid out.

Managers stand to gain from understanding the latest research on confidence. After all, strong leadership is about recognizing and nurturing every person's potential. Although conversations about confidence are not new, the landscape has changed. Fifteen or 20 years ago, most of us took for granted that women "don't ask" or are "risk-averse." But cutting-edge data now tells a different story, one grounded in solid empirical research, not just anecdotes.

The goal of this book isn't to lament the challenges facing women in their professional lives. Have we reached true parity? No, but real progress has been made. Are we satisfied with how slowly change is happening? Hardly. At the current pace, it may still take decades to eradicate everyday micro-aggressions. As for unconscious biases—we'll never fully erase them, because they are rooted in how the human brain works. Still, awareness is half the battle, and that's where this book comes in.

While *The Confidence Myth* offers explanations and suggestions for beha-vior change, it's crucial to adapt them to your unique context and person-ality. Any adjustments you make should enhance who you are, not compromise your authenticity. Although we often talk about "women" in general, it's vital to remember that women exist at various intersections, and some—for example, women of color—face greater challenges as a result of their overlapping identities. Research shows these groups encounter more microaggressions and biases, increasing the likelihood of confidence issues. Keep in mind that intersectionality matters and that these strategies are not one-size-fits-all.

The book includes many tools to support your journey in understanding the roots of the confidence myth and expressing your authenticity with confidence.

- **Stories of real people**, the challenges they faced, and how they overcame those challenges are highlighted throughout the book.
- **Self-Reflection** features provide questions to help you untangle some of the self-defeating habits you may find yourself repeating, as well as ideas for moving forward with confidence, for example.
- **Take Action** features provide you with a framework to apply many of the solutions offered in this book to your own situation.
- This book is based on a scientific foundation and includes many references to **classic and contemporary research**.

The Confidence Myth is a guide to recognizing and reframing self-doubt, amplifying your voice, and navigating the challenges that often hold women back. You will explore actionable strategies for stopping rumination, silencing your inner critic, owning your achieve-ments unapologetically, and speaking with confidence even in high-stakes moments like salary negotiations or delivering tough feedback.

You'll also learn how to push back against microaggressions and myths like "women talk too much," while confronting more insidious issues such as gaslighting, benevolent sexism, and the "Queen Bee" phenomenon. This book also explores major life transitions such as motherhood and menopause and guides you toward professional help when necessary, ensuring you walk away with a clearer sense of your worth and a blueprint for advancing in every chapter of your life. I hope *The Confidence Myth* will be a useful toolkit for thriving with confidence, authenticity, and authority.

Last but not the least, *The Confidence Myth* reminds us that as leaders, colleagues, mentors, and parents, we're shaping the next generation of leaders, collaborators, and changemakers. By combining genuine support, active sponsorship, and modeling confidence in action, women mentors can make a significant impact on younger colleagues' confidence and professional growth. This, in turn, creates a positive ripple effect, paving the way for more women to thrive in their professional journeys. By nurturing confidence rooted in authenticity and equity—not perfection or conformity—we give our daughters and sons the tools they need to thrive in a world that still has plenty of biases left to dismantle. It's not just about helping them succeed; it's about helping create a better future for everyone.

Acknowledgments Writing *The Confidence Myth* has been an immensely rewarding journey, and I am deeply grateful to the many people who made this book possible.

First and foremost, my heartfelt thanks go to **Mimi Melek**, my brilliant editor, whose insightful feedback, thoughtful questions, and steady encouragement have been instrumental in shaping this book. I am equally grateful to **Liz Barlow**, my publisher at Palgrave, for her unwavering support and belief in this project from the very beginning, and to **Leonie Sittner** for her help and guidance in getting the project finished.

I am deeply grateful to **Jean-François Manzoni**, former President of IMD, who first urged me to share my insights from directing the Strategies for Leadership Program and to put pen to paper. His encouragement was the spark that made this book possible. At IMD, I am fortunate to work alongside inspiring colleagues who constantly challenge and refine my thinking. I am especially grateful to **Delia Fischer**, Chief Communications Officer, for her championing of this work, and to **Paul Milner**, Publishing Lead, for his thoughtful collaboration and commitment to sharing IMD's thought leadership with the world.

A warm thank-you goes to **Ivana Ramos** for her excellent design work. Her creative vision and attention to detail brought this book to life in ways I could not have imagined.

Finally, I want to acknowledge the many colleagues and program participants I've had the pleasure of working with over the years. A special thanks to the *Strategies for Leadership Alumni Community* and its president, **Feena May**, for over a decade of thought-provoking conversations. Your ideas, feedback, and shared experiences have deeply shaped the thinking behind this book. I'm truly grateful for your wisdom and generosity.

Ginka Toegel

Competing Interests The author has no competing interests to declare that are relevant to the content of this manuscript.

Contents

List of Figures

List of Tables

1

Do Women Lack Confidence?

Vignette 1.1: Renata Weibel

Renata Weibel was recently promoted to Chief Strategy Officer at NorthBay Tech Solutions. She had been with the company for 15 years, steadily advancing through roles in product development and skillfully leading negotiations that significantly increased sales and expanded into new markets. But even after all of her contributions to the company, she knew people still made assumptions. One of her peers made a comment during a meeting: "You are not asserting yourself, like most women here," when she defended a request from one of her direct reports. Her boss was a bit surprised when Renata asked for a promotion.

During her first week in the new role, Renata had a big proposal on the table: steering NorthBay into emerging international markets. Some of her colleagues called it risky, but she had done her homework and trusted her ability to pull it off. At the board meeting, she laid out her research, showing revenue projections, potential pitfalls, and how to tackle them step by step. One board member, Martin, raised an eyebrow and said, "That seems like a pretty big leap. Are we sure this is the right time?"

Renata stayed calm. "If we move now," she explained, "we can secure contracts before our competitors step in. I've already mapped out the costs and the team we'll need." Martin flipped through her slides, clearly taken aback by her detailed analysis. By the end of the meeting, most of the board was on her side.

After the meeting, she pulled the CEO aside. "I'll need a bigger budget to make this work," she said, listing the extra hires and resources. The CEO agreed without hesitation, seeing how carefully she had planned. It felt good to be open about what she needed.

© The Author(s), under exclusive license to Springer Nature Switzerland AG 2025
G. Toegel, *The Confidence Myth*,
https://doi.org/10.1007/978-3-031-97305-5_1

Of course, rumors still floated around. One colleague said, "She's too cautious and won't shake things up." That stung, but Renata reminded herself of how well her projects performed and that her worth wasn't defined by other people's doubts.

Ten months later, NorthBay had already broken into a promising new market. At one of the board meetings, Martin even admitted, "Renata's initiative is one of our best strategic moves in years." Staff credited her thorough approach, willingness to stand up for her ideas, and visible drive to succeed.

Skepticism no longer overshadowed her achievements. Consistent results and a strong belief in her own capabilities were her credo. In the end, she thought, all those myths about women in leadership dissolve in the face of real actions and when outcomes come to light.

Renata's story illustrates the concepts of confidence, self-confidence, self-esteem, and self-efficacy. Renata is confident she can pull off projects, and her self-efficacy shines through her meticulous planning and successful project execution. In the boardroom, she taps into her self-confidence to present and defend her expansion strategy. Her self-esteem is rooted in her robust sense of self-worth, which is not defined by other people's doubts.

Renata's story also illustrates some pervasive myths we will try to debunk. One of them is the myth about women's confidence, reflected in her peer's comment: "You are not asserting yourself, like most women here." The confidence myth refers to the widespread but inaccurate belief that women inherently lack confidence compared to men, particularly in professional settings. This flawed assumption of universal gender differences attributes women's lack of career progression primarily to their alleged lack of confidence, rather than to systemic barriers or biases. Considering women's supposed lack of confidence as the primary factor holding them back in their careers places the burden on women and obscures other factors at work in the professional realm and in society.

And there are more of those myths. For example, "Women don't ask," reflected in her former boss's surprised reaction when she asked for a promotion. Or the myth that women are reluctant risk-takers, evident in Martin's comment, "That seems like a pretty big leap."

This chapter will first discuss the concept of confidence before exploring what fuels the "women lack confidence" narrative. Next, we will examine what research reveals about women's confidence and ambitions. The chapter concludes with two additional myths that warrant scrutiny: Women are risk-averse, and women don't ask for what they want, need, and deserve.

1.1 What Is Confidence?

The psychological concept of confidence has been studied extensively over the years. Confidence plays a crucial role in how we perceive ourselves and interact with the world around us. While the terms confidence, self-confidence, self-efficacy, and self-esteem are frequently used interchangeably in everyday conversation, they represent distinct psychological constructs. Understanding the nuances among them can help clarify the contributors to our sense of self and how these constructs influence our ability to navigate life's challenges.

Confidence: A Broad Perspective

Confidence, from the Latin *fidere*, which means "to trust," encompasses a general sense of trust, certainty, or assurance in oneself, others, or situations. It is a state of mind that allows us to approach challenges and opportunities with a positive outlook. Confidence is linked to action. For example, under-confidence can prevent a talented manager from applying for a senior position, which, in turn, makes them less likely to pursue future opportunities. This aligns with how some psychologists define confidence: a mindset that amplifies our thoughts and feelings, facilitating the translation of ideas into actions (Petty, 2015). Confidence is not limited to any one aspect of life. It can be situational or domain-specific, meaning that you may feel very confident in one area of your life but less so in another.

This gap in confidence is not universal but context-specific. For example, you might be confident about making financial projections for your division but less assured about giving a presentation at a company town hall meeting. Confidence can extend beyond the individual and include trust in external factors. For instance, you might have confidence in your team's ability to win a proposal or in a particular product's quality.

Confidence does not only manifest as self-assurance and assertiveness; embracing vulnerability is also a form of confidence. For example, admitting a knowledge gap and seeking expertise from a team member reflects confidence in your ability to recognize personal limitations, value others' skills, and prioritize collective success over individual ego. Only confident people admit mistakes and own their vulnerability. Often, those who lack confidence hide behind a mask.

Self-Confidence: A Personal Shield

Self-confidence is trust in your own abilities, capabilities, and expertise. It is an internal sense of trust in yourself that allows you to take on challenges, pursue goals, and navigate social situations with ease. Imagine you're about to give a presentation at work. The butterflies in your stomach start to settle as you remind yourself of all the times you've successfully spoken in public before. That's self-confidence—belief in your own abilities. You can think of self-confidence as a personal shield that protects against self-doubt.

Self-confidence is often visible in a person's behavior, body language, and decision-making. Unlike confidence, it is always self-directed and stable across different situations. However, it can still fluctuate based on experiences and feedback. There are two types of self-confidence: specific self-confidence and general self-confidence.

Specific self-confidence is the confidence a person has in their ability to perform a particular task or behavior in a specific situation (Oney & Oksuzoglu-Guven, 2015). Specific self-confidence is context-dependent, which means it can vary across different domains or activities. For example, a person might have high specific self-confidence in their ability to analyze a financial document but low specific self-confidence in public speaking. Remember Renata Weibel? She had specific self-confidence in her ability to conduct revenue projections and analyze potential pitfalls.

General self-confidence is a more stable, trait-like characteristic that reflects an individual's overall belief in their ability to succeed across various situations and tasks. It's not tied to any specific context but rather reflects a person's general sense of self-assurance and belief in their capabilities. General self-confidence is relatively consistent across different areas of life and is close to the concept of confidence when relating to the self. For example, a person with high general self-confidence believes they can handle whatever comes their way: a new job, a difficult conversation, or learning a new skill.

Self-Efficacy: The Task-Specific Belief in One's Abilities

Self-efficacy, a concept introduced by social psychologist Albert Bandura, refers to an individual's belief in their capacity to execute behaviors necessary to produce specific, desired results. Self-efficacy is task-specific and relates to a person's perceived ability to succeed in particular situations or accomplish specific tasks (Bandura, 2001). In the introductory case, Renata's self-efficacy is evident in her meticulous planning and successful project execution.

Unlike self-esteem, which is a global self-evaluation, self-efficacy can vary greatly across different domains of life. High self-efficacy in one life domain doesn't necessarily translate to high self-efficacy in another. For instance, a marketing expert might have high self-efficacy in conducting marketing research but low self-efficacy in public speaking.

Self-efficacy influences how people approach goals, tasks, and challenges, affecting their motivation, effort, and perseverance. To a large extent, it is shaped by past experiences. The positive effect of self-efficacy on performance is well-documented, but extremely high self-efficacy can lead to complacency and reduced effort, potentially resulting in poorer performance (Vancouver et al., 2002). Self-efficacy can be likened to a toolbox with different tools for different tasks, some well-used and others rarely touched.

Self-Esteem: The Global Evaluation of Self-Worth

Self-esteem refers to an individual's overall sense of self-worth and value. It is a more global and enduring evaluation of the self compared to confidence or self-confidence (Judge et al., 2003). Self-esteem encompasses how much a person likes, approves of, and values themselves as a person, regardless of their abilities or achievements.

Confidence and self-confidence often relate to specific abilities or situations, while self-esteem is a more comprehensive self-assessment that includes various aspects of a person's identity, such as appearance, personality, and overall competence. People need more than a high level of self-confidence to like themselves (Hollenbeck & Hall, 2004). High self-esteem is associated with positive self-regard and resilience in the face of setbacks, while low self-esteem can lead to self-doubt and negative self-talk. For instance, someone with high self-esteem may still feel valuable even if they fail at a task because their self-worth isn't tied to performance. Self-esteem is often developed early in life but can be influenced by experiences and personal growth throughout adulthood.

While generally considered negative, low self-esteem can sometimes motivate people to work harder and achieve more to compensate for perceived shortcomings (Brockner, 1983). Contrary to popular belief, very high self-esteem isn't always positive; it can lead to narcissism, aggression, and unrealistic expectations (Baumeister et al., 1996). Self-esteem can be metaphorically described as a deep-rooted tree that provides stability and nourishment to a person's self-image.

The Interplay of Confidence, Self-Confidence, Self-Efficacy, and Self-Esteem

The concepts of confidence, self-confidence, self-efficacy, and self-esteem are distinct yet interconnected. Confidence provides a general sense of trust and assurance, while self-confidence zeroes in on our belief in our own abilities. Self-esteem offers a global evaluation of our worth, and self-efficacy focuses on our perceived capability to succeed in specific tasks or situations. There is some evidence that self-efficacy and self-esteem are important components of self-confidence, which appears to be a much broader concept (Kane et al., 2021).

Recognizing the unique role each concept plays allows us to more effectively target areas for improvement and build a more robust sense of self. For instance, you might have high self-efficacy in your professional skills but struggle with overall self-esteem. Recognizing this distinction allows for more focused personal development efforts.

At the same time, these concepts do not exist in isolation. They interact and influence each other, creating a dynamic interplay that shapes a person's overall self-concept. Cultivating one area often leads to positive effects in others, creating a positive, self-perpetuating cycle of personal growth.

Table 1.1 Four confidence concepts

Concept	Characteristics	Examples
Confidence	A general sense of trust or certainty Can be situational or domain-specific Extends beyond the self	Belief in your team's ability to introduce a new competitive product Belief in your team's ability to succeed
Self-confidence	A belief in one's own abilities and judgments Visible in behavior and decision-making Can be specific or general	Volunteering for presentations Ease in approaching new social situations
Self-efficacy	A task-specific belief in one's ability to influence outcomes Varies across domains Influences the goal approach and perseverance	Believing in your ability to do a financial analysis, but not public speaking
Self-esteem	Overall sense of self-worth Global and enduring self-evaluation Includes various aspects of identity	Maintaining positive self-regard despite setbacks Valuing yourself regardless of external factors

Table 1.1 summarizes the characteristics of the four confidence concepts and provides some examples for each. In this book, I will focus predominantly on self-confidence and self-efficacy.

These concepts are interconnected but have distinct characteristics. Confidence is the broadest, applying to both the self and others. Self-confidence is more focused on personal abilities. Self-efficacy is even more specific, relating to competence in particular tasks or domains. Self-esteem is the most comprehensive self-evaluation, encompassing overall worth and identity.

Self-Reflection 1.1: Self-Confidence, Self-Esteem, and Self-Efficacy

- Which of your experiences have contributed the most to your self-confidence, and how can you create more opportunities like these in the future?
- Are there any recurring negative thoughts about yourself that affect your self-esteem? What would help you start challenging these beliefs?
- How does the way you tend to respond to setbacks or failures affect your self-confidence?
- In which areas of life do you feel highly competent? How can you use these strengths to boost your self-confidence in other areas?
- Are there people or situations in your life that consistently undermine your self-esteem? If so, what boundaries could you set to protect your sense of self-worth?
- How often do you acknowledge and celebrate your personal accomplishments, and how might doing it more often influence your self-confidence?
- When working on new goals, do you think primarily about potential successes or possible failures? How might shifting this perspective impact your belief in your ability to succeed?
- What actions or routines could you incorporate into your daily life to strengthen your self-confidence, self-esteem, and self-efficacy?

1.2 What Feeds the "Women Lack Confidence" Narrative?

For a long time, the dominant narrative in business has been that women lack self-confidence, which is given as the reason why few women have reached top positions. While there might have been some truth to this decades ago, in the twenty-first century, significant changes in society, education, and organizational structures demonstrate that women do not lack the confidence to advance in many life domains. As a result, recent research does not support a *consistent* gender difference in self-reported self-confidence. To be clear, there's still work to be done, but the blanket statement that "women lack confidence" is no longer valid. So why does this outdated adage persist? There are several possible misleading explanations: meta-perception, sex differences, socialization, and differences in communication style.

Meta-Perception and Self-Perception

One explanation for the persistence of this narrative could be the difference between self-perception and meta-perception—what we think about ourselves versus what we believe others think about us. In general, women do not lack self-confidence, but they may doubt that others recognize and value their capabilities and contributions. But does this really matter? This distinction is crucial because our identity is shaped not only by how we see ourselves but also by how we believe others perceive us and how we measure up to our peers. Research has shown that women tend to under-predict their performance ratings from superiors compared to their male colleagues (Sturm et al., 2014). Furthermore, while men are preoccupied with comparing themselves to others and with their own self-views, women tend to place greater emphasis on others' perceptions of them (Roberts, 1991). This difference in focus can contribute to the misperception that women lack confidence, when in reality, they may simply be more attuned to external evaluations.

Meta-perceptions, or beliefs about how others perceive us, undoubtedly impact our behavior. For instance, if a woman in a senior management position believes she has the qualifications for a CEO position but doubts that decision-makers would view her as suitable for the role, she might deem it futile to apply in the first place. These meta-perceptions can hold women back by influencing their decision to act, or not to act. When women refrain from trying for promotions due to negative meta-perceptions, they interrupt the cycle of learning and experience that is crucial to growing confidence. This cycle of inaction based on negative meta-perceptions can reinforce the very narrative about a lack of confidence that we are challenging.

Another factor contributing to the lack of self-confidence narrative is the distinction between being self-confident and *appearing* self-confident. Perceived confidence is crucial, as it enhances an individual's ability to exert influence within their organization (Guillén et al., 2018). While women may feel confident internally, how they appear to others might not always reflect this. For instance, introverted women might be less vocal in meetings and avoid looking people in the eye—both behaviors are often misinterpreted as a lack of confidence. While this may be true in some cases, this attribution tends to be overgeneralized.

Complicating matters further for women, but not men, is the link between influence and perceptions of warmth. Women are expected to be perceived not only as confident but also as caring and prosocial. As one study notes, "While self-confidence is gender-neutral, the consequences of appearing self-confident are not," because "the 'performance plus confidence equals power and influence' formula is gendered" (Guillén, 2018, p. 3). Consequently, confident men find it easier to meet expectations, while confident women leaders may face penalties for not conforming to gender role stereotypes. This double standard further perpetuates the misconception about women's confidence levels in professional settings.

Sex Differences

The persistence of the "fixing women's confidence" narrative has been partially sustained by claims about fundamental differences between men and women. These claims emphasize that, compared to men, women possess intrinsically distinct characteristics in terms of natural inclinations, mindsets, and behaviors. The more we accentuate hypothetical contrasts between men and women, the more we risk portraying these differences as fixed and predetermined rather than fluid and changeable. This narrative significantly affects how organizations approach inequity in the workplace. For a long time, organizations have emphasized fixing women's perceived lack of confidence, inability to ask and negotiate, risk-aversion, and many other behaviors and attitudes that women supposedly needed to "fix."

Of course, there are biological differences between women and men, but they do not fully explain differences in behavior or attitudes in the workplace. Take, for example, the claim of "dimorphism" or sex differences in the brain. In a 2005 Science publication, Simon Baron-Cohen et al. proposed that the male brain, compared to the female brain, exhibits a higher neuronal count and density, along with increased intra-hemispheric white matter (Baron-Cohen et al., 2005). This pattern, they argue, suggests increased connectivity within each hemisphere and reduced connectivity between them. These differences, in turn, may predispose the male brain toward systemizing (e.g., analyzing or problem-solving), while the female brain tends more toward empathizing—that is, the ability to recognize and respond to emotions in others.

A recent meta-study debunks this myth. As leading researcher Lise Eliot concludes, "Male/female brain differences appear trivial and are population-specific. The human brain is not 'sexually dimorphic'" (Eliot et al., 2021, p. 667). Many of the differences often attributed to sex are actually more accurately explained by variations in brain size. For example, gray-to-white matter ratio or inter-hemispheric vs. intra-hemispheric connectivity don't necessarily distinguish male brains from female brains, but rather larger brains from smaller brains. This means that a man with a smaller brain may have more in common neurologically with the average woman than with men who have larger brains. Similarly, a woman with a larger brain may share more neural characteristics with the average man than with women who have smaller brains. To illustrate this point, imagine lining up all human brains from smallest to largest. You would find a significant overlap between male and female brains, with plenty of women having larger brains than many men, and vice versa. The differences within each sex group would be more striking than the differences between the averages of the two groups.

There are, of course, sex differences in the hormone system. Estrogen supports bonding and connection while counteracting conflict and risk-taking. Testosterone, on the other hand, can fuel a drive for status, making it an important factor in shaping social hierarchies by motivating behaviors such as aggression and dominance that help people compete for and maintain higher standing (Eisenegger et al., 2011). Men have about ten times more testosterone circulating in their system than women do. A study of male traders in the City of London, who traded interest rate futures, revealed that higher levels of testosterone stimulate risk-taking, and winning triggers the release of more testosterone into the body (Coates & Herbert, 2008). Experimental studies have also confirmed that increases in testosterone influence financial risk-taking (Apicella et al., 2014). Interestingly, testosterone levels in men decrease when they spend more time with their children (Gettler et al., 2011). So, do hormonal differences alone explain the variability in self-confidence when making financial decisions? As you will see later in this chapter, scientific evidence does not support the claim of gender differences in risk-taking, for example.

Stereotypes and Gender Disparities in Leadership

Attributing the imbalance of men and women in leadership roles to sex differences perpetuates traditional and stereotypical ideas about how men and women should behave and the roles they are best suited for in business and society. These beliefs keep things the way they've always been in terms of gender roles and don't help companies change how they operate. For example, relegating women to supportive roles or passing them over for promotion to leadership roles perpetuates the stereotype that men have what it takes to be leaders, while women are better suited to supportive roles. While this stereotypical perspective of sex differences might seem outdated, it provides the easiest and fastest way to process information. The human brain naturally prefers familiar patterns and resists change, so maintaining gender stereotypes feels comfortable and requires less mental effort. When people notice men and women acting in ways that fit traditional gender roles, they often use a mental shortcut. Instead of considering the circumstances that might be influencing behavior, they tend to jump to the easiest conclusion—that the person they are observing is acting this way simply because that's who they are as men or women. Mental shortcuts are quick and easy, but they are often inaccurate.

Many of the differences in leadership positions and status we see between men and women at work aren't due to inherent personality traits but rather to unequal treatment and inequity in opportunities. Imagine you are playing a game where certain players are not told what the rules are or are given less information, as often happens to women in the workplace. With restricted access to important information and limited connections, it becomes harder for women to express interest in an opportunity, negotiate effectively, or even know about prime opportunities for promotion.

This lack of opportunity and access is only one side of the story, though. Research by Exley and Kessler (2022) highlights how women's self-perception can influence workplace outcomes. Their study shows that, even when men and women perform equally well on math and science tasks (fields commonly stereotyped as "male"), women consistently rate themselves less favorably, whether they are promoting themselves to potential employers or simply judging their skills in private. This gap in self-evaluation is not merely a result of different approaches to self-promotion; it reflects a deeper difference in how men and women perceive their own abilities, a pattern that appears as early as middle school. Interestingly, the gap disappears for tasks tied to verbal ability, which suggests that negative stereotypes around math and science are a key reason for the disparity. Combined with unequal access to information and opportunities, these skewed self-evaluations further limit women's ability to thrive in certain professional settings.

One area where significant gender disparities exist in the workplace is the quality of performance feedback provided by managers. One study, which analyzed 1000 feedback comments from 146 mid-career leaders and conducted an experiment with 159 managers, revealed striking differences in the quality of feedback given to men and women, despite similar quantities of feedback overall. Men received 60% more actionable feedback than women, with comments more frequently referencing specific skills or achievements (Doldor et al., 2021). Women received 2.5 times more feedback about their personality and communication style, which often included vague suggestions to be more confident. The feedback to men encouraged them to set the vision, proactively leverage politics, be assertive, and develop confidence in specific skills. All of those comments are actionable. Meanwhile, women were encouraged to focus on delivery, cope with politics, and be cooperative and deferential. Women's lack of confidence was considered a general flaw, but their managers provided no actionable recommendations. These biases were exhibited by both male and female managers, suggesting that gender stereotyping is a pervasive hurdle that transcends the gender of the feedback provider. This disparity in feedback quality has significant implications for women's confidence and career advancement, as vague feedback makes it more challenging to identify specific areas for improvement, and personality-focused feedback reinforces gender stereotypes.

The Role of Socialization and the Mindset Theory

Research on the role of the socialization process has contributed to the "women lack confidence" narrative as well. In the 1980s, psychologist Carol Dweck developed the Mindset Theory, which suggests that people's views of the source of their success can be placed on a continuum, with innate abilities on one end and hard work on the other (Dweck, 2006). People with a growth mindset believe their intelligence, personality, or character can be developed; they view failure as an opportunity to grow, thrive on challenges, and enjoy trying new things. As a result, people with a growth mindset stretch themselves and take more risks. Assuming that growth requires effort, they actively seek feedback, learn from criticism, and reach higher levels of performance. People with a fixed mindset, on the other hand, believe that their potential is determined at birth. Setbacks affect their self-concept ("I'm a complete failure"), and because they don't believe they can exceed their potential ("I'm just not good at this"), they avoid challenges, become defensive when criticized, or give up altogether. Not surprisingly, these individuals are unable to reach their full potential.

Dweck suggests that in the early school years, girls have longer attention spans and more advanced verbal and social skills. As a result, as they receive more praise for being excellent students, they start craving the approval of parents and educators. Girls don't learn how to fail; they learn how to perfect things. Avoiding risks and not making mistakes becomes their strategy to achieve their goals. But failing and trying harder next time are essential to confidence-building. Boys, on the other hand, tend to get significantly more criticism at an early age for their conduct. They receive it not only from adults but also from peers, which Dweck suggests makes them more resilient toward negative feedback at later life stages. Certain types of praise, particularly person-focused ("You are so smart!") rather than effort-focused ("Excellent, you invested a lot of effort!"), can actually decrease motivation and performance (Mueller & Dweck, 1998).

Self-Reflection 1.2: Applying the Mindset Theory

Reflecting on your upbringing may help you understand whether certain circumstances in your early life contributed to a lack of confidence. In her book *Mindset*, Carol Dweck points out specific links between parental style and mindset. Consider the questions below as a good starting point for exploring the roots of confidence issues:

1. Reflect on the praise you received in childhood. Did your parents or teachers emphasize your intelligence, or did they highlight your effort and perseverance? In what ways do you believe this shaped your self-view?
2. Recall your earliest memory of failing. What went through your mind at that moment? Did you attribute the setback to a lack of ability, or did you consider other factors?
3. Think of a significant person in your life (e.g., parent, teacher, friend) who avoids risks and struggles to admit mistakes. How does this person's reaction to setbacks influence your own approach to challenges and failures?
4. Consider a difficult transition in your life that shook your confidence. What made this period so challenging, and do you recognize any recurring patterns of self-doubt or loss of confidence in your life?

5. Remember a moment when you had the opportunity to truly shine. What thoughts or concerns surfaced for you—about your own abilities, potential judgment from others, or fear of failure? How did those worries affect your actions?

6. Reflect on times when someone outperformed you. Did you immediately assume they were simply smarter or more talented? How has this perception influenced your motivation or self-esteem?

(Adapted from Dweck, 2006)

The mindset theory is very compelling, but replication studies have failed to confirm Dweck's findings. A recent article in the journal *Intelligence* discussed all three factors: measured intelligence, intelligence mindset, and gender. Since most of the previous studies had only been conducted with children and adolescents, it tested whether, as adults, women have more of a fixed mindset than men, and whether women with higher measured intelligence are more likely to hold fixed mindsets. The researchers found no evidence that women held fixed mindsets more than men and no support for the claim that holding more of a growth mindset results in greater academic persistence (Macnamara & Rupani, 2017). They concluded that neither gender nor intelligence is consistently associated with mindset.

In summary, when subjected to closer scrutiny, the generalization that women lack self-confidence, as well as some of its explanations, are not supported by research. This suggests the need for a more nuanced understanding of confidence and its development across genders.

Differences in Communication Style

If socialization and a fixed mindset can't explain the "women lack confidence" narrative, perhaps it can be explained in terms of differences in how men and women communicate. We make judgments about the confidence of people around us based on the way they communicate and present themselves. Much of our behavior, including our individual linguistic styles or characteristic speaking patterns, has its roots in our childhood experiences. Children typically tend to play in same-sex groups; girls prefer to play in small groups or only with a best friend, while boys prefer larger groups with a leader, where they are motivated to signal status. Girls tend to share secrets and emphasize connection rather than status. In general, girls who signal superiority are disliked and labeled as "bossy." Boys tend to give orders, entertain the group by telling jokes and stories, and talk up their knowledge and abilities. Girls tend to downplay their authority, while boys try to top each other.

Based on these observations, the sociolinguist Deborah Tannen provides a powerful analysis of who gets heard and why. She explains that school-age children learn different ways of speaking by observing their same-sex peers (Tannen, 1995). Girls learn conversational rituals that emphasize rapport, while boys learn rituals that focus on status. As boys grow up in their social groups, they look for "opportunities to put others down and take the one-up position for themselves" (p. 144). Girls, on the other hand, take the one-down position, "assuming that the other person will recognize the ritual nature of the self-denigration and pull them back up." In an interview for *Harvard Business Review*, Tannen stated that not much has changed since she published her article in 1995, and rapport rituals for girls and status rituals for boys are still relevant (Tannen, 2019).

Vignette 1.2: Status and Power

Status refers to the social position or rank an individual holds within a group or society. It measures the social prestige and respect granted to a person based on various factors. Status can be ascribed, meaning it is assigned at birth or based on factors beyond an individual's control (e.g., race, gender, family background), or achieved, meaning it is earned through personal efforts, accomplishments, or choices (e.g., education, occupation, wealth). It influences how individuals are perceived and treated by others, affecting their social interactions and opportunities.

Power, on the other hand, is the ability to control resources and influence others' behavior, even against their will. It involves the capacity to make decisions and shape outcomes; control rewards and punishments; the right to require obedience; and access to informational resources. Power also stems from others' respect, identification, or attraction, as well as the belief that the powerholder possesses superior abilities (Magee & Galinsky, 2008).

While power and status are often correlated, they can exist independently. For example, a manager might have the power to hire and fire employees but lack the respect of their team. Conversely, status can exist without power. People may be highly respected or admired for their expertise, achievements, or personal qualities without having formal authority or control over resources. Preconceived notions about gender roles can affect how women are perceived in leadership positions, potentially impacting their status even when they hold powerful positions.

Many women today hold senior positions, but the expectations of how people in authority should speak are still based on men performing the leadership role. Based on their early socialization, women are reluctant to sing their own praises, thinking this will make a negative impression. Instead, they assume that others will notice, give credit, and reward their contributions and hard work. The early patterns of boys' and girls' behavior may persist into adulthood, potentially influencing the ways men and women interact socially. While women try to minimize status differences and concern themselves with saving face for others (particularly when managing down), their male counterparts are driven by a desire to maintain the one-up position. Not surprisingly, in this context, when women ask questions, it might be misinterpreted as a sign of lacking confidence.

Men and women often exhibit different communication styles in the workplace, which can impact organizational dynamics. While women tend to be perceived as asking more questions, being relationship-oriented, and empathetic in their communication, men are generally perceived as more direct, assertive, and task-oriented. Women tend to apologize more frequently than men, which contributes to their being perceived as less

Table 1.2 Women's communication styles

	Style of speaking	Unintended impact
Giving credit	Uses "we" instead of "I" when discussing achievements, because "I" can come across as overly self-promotional.	Speaker may not receive recognition for their achievements and be reluctant to share ideas in the future.
Displaying humility	Understates their assurance rather than confronting doubts about future performance, because confident behavior may be seen as too arrogant.	The speaker's perceived lack of confidence can lead to doubts about their competence, causing others to overlook their good ideas.
Asking questions	Asks questions to engage the other side and to stimulate knowledge sharing.	The speaker may be perceived as lacking knowledge; if inquiry is suppressed, valuable information can go undiscovered.
Apologizing	Apologizes readily to demonstrate consideration and empathy for others.	The speaker may appear less authoritative or commanding.
Being indirect	Uses indirect language instead of being straightforward when instructing subordinates, because being too direct may be seen as domineering.	Subordinates may conclude that the manager is indecisive and unclear in their thinking, leading them to dismiss the manager's directives as unimportant.

confident, as it sounds like they have just admitted fault. When speaking, men don't hesitate to call attention to themselves; they frequently use "I," while women tend to use "we" and focus on rapport and face-saving. As Deborah Tannen suggests, these verbal behaviors make women sound less confident (see Table 1.2). What might be perceived as a lack of confidence is driven by a motive not to be perceived as boastful and therefore disliked.

These preferences manifest in various ways within organizations, and being aware of them can help foster more effective collaboration and reduce misunderstandings. However, it's crucial to recognize that these are generalizations, and individual communication styles may vary significantly, regardless of gender.

1.3 What Research Says About Women's Confidence and Ambition

Interest in gender differences in self-confidence has been longstanding. As early as the mid-1970s, social psychologist Ellen Lenney challenged the notion that women inherently lack confidence. In her review of research on the topic, Lenney highlighted empirical evidence showing that women's self-confidence is significantly influenced by situational factors. For instance, task specificity plays a role: women tended to underestimate their performance in spatial and creativity test sections, but not in others. Additionally, women's self-confidence was lower when clear performance feedback was absent and when social comparison was emphasized (Lenney, 1977). In the latter case, women's self-confidence often depended on whom they were comparing themselves to. Lenney found that women were unlikely to have lower self-confidence when they were provided with unambiguous information about their task abilities.

A recent study provides a more nuanced picture (Zenger & Folkman, 2019). This study found a significant difference in the confidence levels of men and women under the age of 25, a difference that disappears at age 40, as shown in Fig. 1.1.

Research suggests that women's confidence tends to increase with age, continuing to rise even after age 60, when men's confidence typically begins to decline. Between the ages of 25 and 60+, men gain 8.5 percentile points in confidence, compared to 29 percentile points for women. However, note that there is a large confidence gap between men and women earlier in their careers, from ages 25 to 45. These findings might explain younger women's

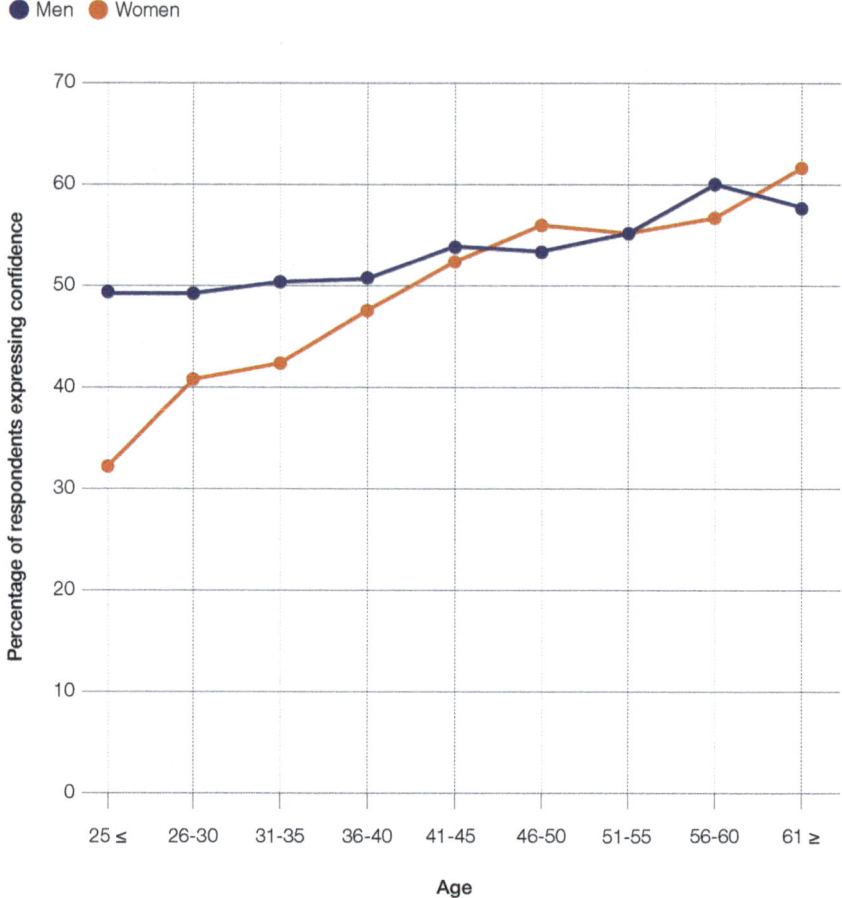

Fig. 1.1 Women's and men's confidence ratings from ages 25–61. Women begin their careers with lower confidence than men but experience a much steeper increase over time. Data from 3,876 men and 4,779 women since 2016 show women's confidence growth outpacing men's by over three times, primarily due to the large initial gap. *Source* Adapted from Zenger & Folkman (2019). Copyright 2019 by Harvard Business Review

reluctance to step up and apply for promotions. As long as women are promoted based on performance while men are promoted based on potential, it will remain challenging for young women to feel prepared for the next career step. Despite these challenges, the long-term trend of women's increase in confidence throughout their careers is encouraging. It suggests that, with experience and personal growth, women can overcome initial barriers and develop into highly effective leaders.

Research evidence shows that men get promoted basically on what could be, thus benefiting from perceptions of potential, while women have to demonstrate concrete performance (Player et al., 2019). A comprehensive study of 29,809 management-track employees at a major North American retail chain revealed that women outperform men in current job performance, yet are rated lower in perceived future potential (Benson et al., 2024). This study also revealed significant gender disparities in performance evaluations and promotion practices. Despite receiving higher job performance ratings, women were consistently given lower potential ratings compared to their male counterparts. This discrepancy in potential ratings accounted for about half of the observed gender gap in promotions. Importantly, these lower potential ratings for women were not accurate predictors of future performance or retention. In fact, women consistently outperformed their male colleagues who had received the same potential ratings. However, despite this demonstrated superior performance, women continued to receive lower potential ratings in subsequent evaluations. These findings suggest a persistent and systemic underestimation of female employees' potential, contributing to persistent gender gaps in leadership and career advancement.

However, there could be a silver lining to the higher scrutiny women face before promotion. This increased scrutiny may motivate women to invest more in their personal development, which can pay dividends later in their careers. This could partially explain why women rate themselves as more effective leaders in the later stages of their careers, as shown in Fig. 1.2.

The disparity in promotion criteria (performance vs. potential) highlights a systemic issue that organizations need to address. By creating more equitable promotion practices, companies could accelerate the growth of confidence in younger women and help them reach their full leadership potential earlier in their careers.

Often, it's not self-confidence but the perceived job fit and satisfaction that significantly impact women's decisions to accept promotions, suggesting that human resource departments should be mindful of the messages conveyed in job descriptions that may inadvertently discourage women applicants. Women sometimes rationalize themselves out of job opportunities, particularly leadership roles, through a process known as job crafting (Hernandez, 2018). Job crafting is a proactive process where employees redesign and modify aspects of their jobs to better align with their personal strengths, needs, and values (Wrzesniewski & Dutton, 2001). Job crafting encompasses task crafting (e.g., modifying the number, scope, or type of job tasks); relational crafting (e.g., changing the quality or amount of interaction

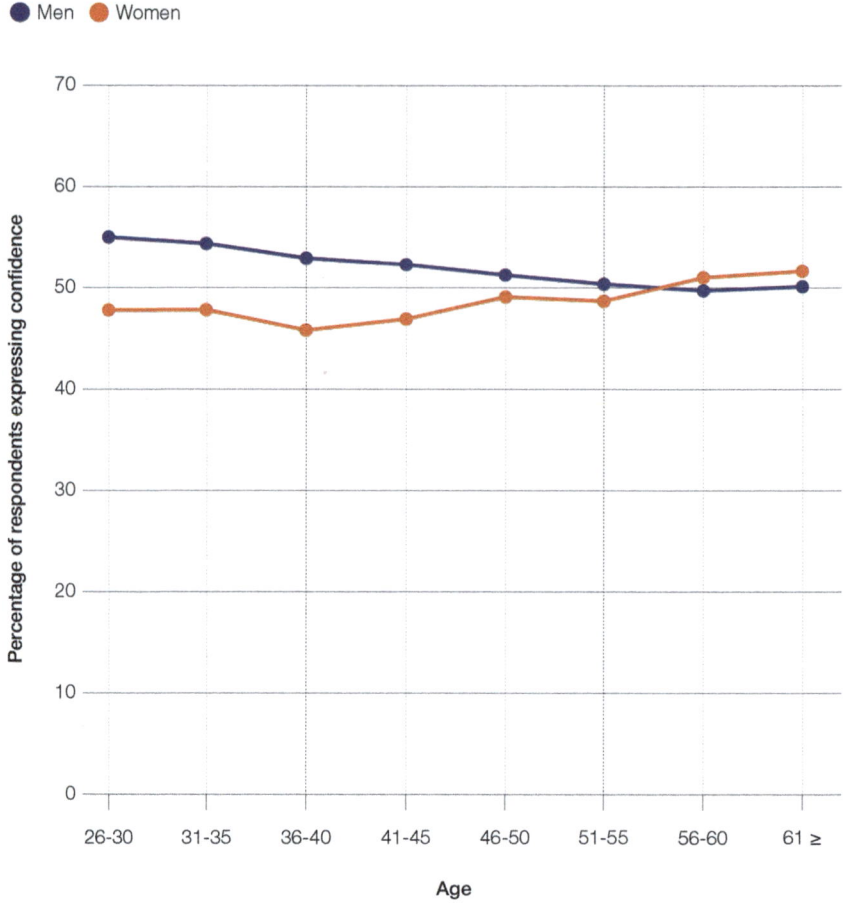

Fig. 1.2 Women's self-ratings as leaders rise later in their careers. Data from 40,184 men and 22,600 women show a gradual decrease in men's self-evaluation. This trend contrasts with the common perception that men maintain consistently high levels of self-confidence throughout their careers. As men gain more experience and face various challenges in their professional lives, they become more realistic or perhaps even more critical of their own capabilities. *Source* Adapted from Zenger & Folkman (2019). Copyright 2019 by Harvard Business Review

with others at work); and cognitive crafting (e.g., altering one's perception or mindset about the job). By engaging in job crafting, employees take an active role in customizing their work experience, potentially finding greater meaning and purpose in their roles without changing jobs.

As job crafting involves individuals shaping the meaning they attach to their work, it can lead women to perceive a promotion as a barrier to personal fulfillment and family time, which could result in a poorer fit and lower satisfaction. Women with a strong gender identification are especially prone to this perception, viewing leadership roles as less suitable for their lives and, as a result, rejecting them.

Catherine Tinsley and Robin Ely's research concludes that "sexes aren't so different after all." Their research found that the difference between women's and men's self-esteem or confidence has an effect size of 0.10, which is trivial from a statistical point of view (Tinsley & Ely, 2018; see Fig. 1.3). An effect size is a way to describe how big or meaningful a change or difference is in a study. Instead of just telling us whether a result is "significant," it shows us *how much* of a difference there is. It helps us understand whether a result is real, but also if it's practically meaningful in the real world.

A large effect size (0.8 or greater) means the difference or relationship is substantial enough to be noticeable and important in practical terms. A medium effect (0.5–0.79) would be noticeable, and a small effect (0.2–0.49) might be barely noticeable. An effect size smaller than 0.2 is considered to be trivial and of no practical significance. Tinsley and Ely argue that the sex differences in behavior are rooted in organizational structures and practices that create different experiences for men and women. They also point out that the effect sizes of self-confidence (0.10) and propensity to take risks (0.13) are trivial and of no practical significance.

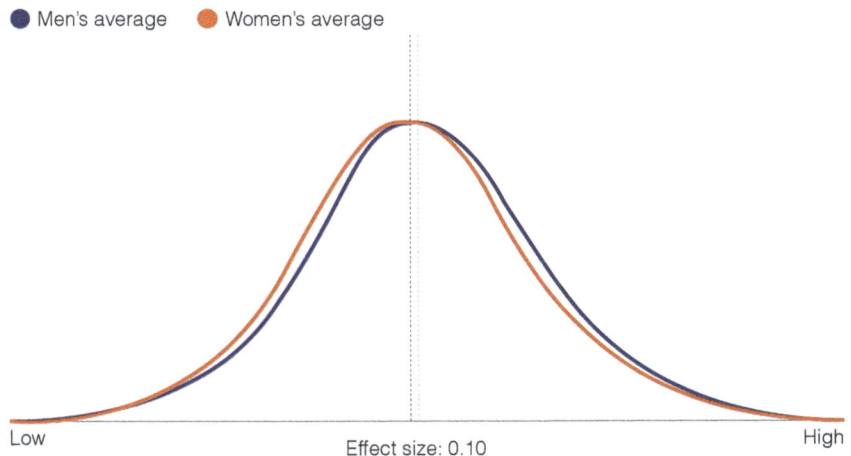

Fig. 1.3 The difference in women's and men's self-confidence is minimal. The effect size of 0.10, as shown for the difference between women's and men's self-confidence in the graph, is trivial and of no practical significance. *Source* Adapted from Tinsley & Ely (2018). Copyright 2018 by Harvard Business Review

Tinsley and Ely's analysis demonstrates that the difference between men's and women's self-confidence is negligible. While there might be a tiny difference between the averages of women's and men's self-confidence, it's so small that it doesn't really mean anything in practical terms. In other words, you couldn't reliably guess someone's level of confidence just by knowing their gender.

Tinsley and Ely's discussion is based on a meta-analysis with two separate studies, which examined gender differences in self-esteem (Kling et al., 1999). A meta-analysis is a statistical method that combines results from multiple studies to draw more reliable conclusions. It offers three key advantages over single studies: increased accuracy due to larger sample sizes and diverse contexts; greater comprehensiveness by showing context-specific results; and higher precision by calculating effect sizes to determine the impact of sex differences. In their meta-analysis, Kling et al. (1999) concluded that, on average, men scored slightly higher than women, but the difference was small.

While self-confidence refers to the belief in one's own abilities and judgments, ambition is the desire to achieve and succeed. Ambitious individuals often set high goals for themselves, work hard to achieve their objectives, and seek opportunities for growth and advancement. Confidence and ambition can be complementary. Confidence can fuel ambition by providing the self-belief necessary to pursue challenging goals. Conversely, achieving ambitious goals can boost confidence.

At age 7, girls already have ambitions. Psychiatrist Anna Fels talks about young girls' ambitions, characterizing them as "a delightfully unapologetic sense of grandiosity and limitless possibility" (Fels, 2004, p. 52). A journalist she interviewed when researching the topic of women's ambitions admitted that, as a 7-year-old girl, she had written the acronym IWBF in her notebook for "I will be famous." Fels states that there are two elements to those ambitions. While the first one relates to mastery of a special skill (e.g., writing, dancing, etc.), the second one is about recognition (e.g., fame, status, praise, etc.). In a similar vein, McKinsey and LeanIn provide evidence in their 2023 annual report (Field et al., 2023) that the women and men in their study were equally ambitious. This appears to be a consistent trend, as their report from five years earlier had already indicated that women attempted to negotiate for promotions at least as frequently as their male counterparts (Thomas et al., 2018). The finding challenges the notion that women are less likely to advocate for their career advancement and suggests that the disparity in promotion rates may be due to factors other than a lack of aspirations on the part of women (see Fig. 1.4).

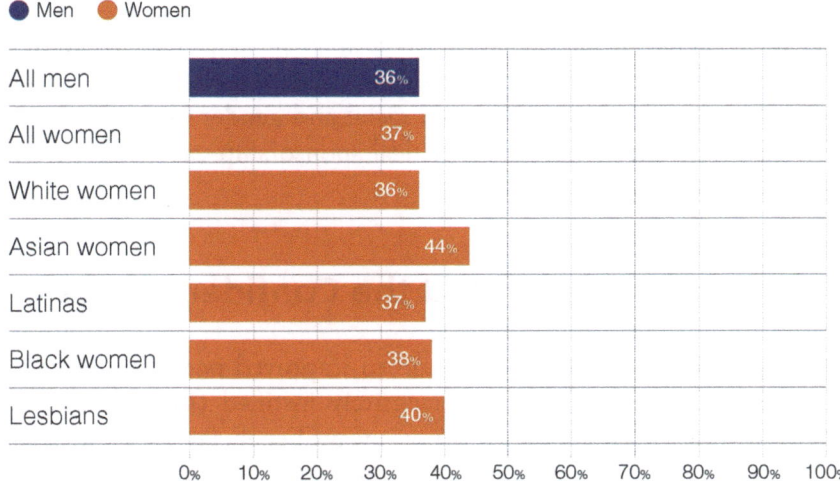

Fig. 1.4 Women ask for promotions more often than men. The 2018 "Women in the Workplace" report by McKinsey and LeanIn indicates variations in career aspirations among different demographic groups, with Asian women demonstrating the highest levels of career ambition. *Source* Adapted from Thomas et al. (2018). Copyright 2018 by McKinsey & Company and LeanIn.org

Furthermore, the study found that, at the director level, women and men were equally interested in senior leadership roles and that young women were particularly ambitious. This might seem like a contradiction, given the recent discussion of young women rating themselves as less confident. However, it's possible to have one without the other. For example, a person might be confident in their abilities but lack the ambition to pursue challenging goals. Alternatively, someone might be highly ambitious but struggle with self-doubt and a lack of confidence.

In the same study, nine out of 10 women under the age of 30 were interested in being promoted to the next level, and three out of four wanted to become senior leaders.

Studies indicate that women of color are highly driven but underrepresented in leadership positions due to marginalization at the intersections of race and gender. The concept of intersectionality recognizes how overlapping identities, such as race and gender, create overlapping systems of disadvantage. Women of color have to contend with both sexism and racism, a situation sometimes referred to as "double jeopardy." This can manifest in everyday workplace challenges like microaggressions, unconscious bias, and exclusion from networks essential for career advancement. Women of color often have ambitions to advance into leadership roles that are as high or higher than those of their white peers. For example, the "Women in the Workplace" report from 2023 suggests that 96% of women of color confirmed that their career is important to them, and 88% aspired to be promoted to the next level. However, racial and gender biases, fewer visible role models, and limited access to critical sponsorship can stifle the realization of these ambitions.

1.4   Overconfidence and the Confidence Myth

In some situations, confidence can lead to improved performance and outcomes, even if that confidence isn't entirely justified (Johnson & Fowler, 2011). However, overconfidence is not always beneficial, as it often fails to accurately reflect actual competence. Studies have shown that individuals' confidence in their knowledge or abilities frequently does not correlate with their true performance or understanding. The Dunning-Kruger effect suggests that people with lower competence are more likely to overestimate their abilities (Kruger & Dunning, 1999). This bias affects individuals' recollections of past performance, influencing their evaluations of future performance.

Research has explored the interaction among the three facets of overconfidence: overestimation, overplacement, and overprecision (Moore & Healy, 2008). Overestimation involves inflating one's actual performance, level of control, or likelihood of success. The second facet, overplacement, is characterized by exaggerating one's performance relative to others—essentially believing one is better than the average. Finally, overprecision is defined as excessive certainty in the accuracy of one's beliefs.

Empirical studies reveal that when reversals of the first two types of overconfidence occur—resulting in what appears to be underconfidence—they tend to manifest across different task categories. For challenging tasks, individuals often overestimate their own performance while mistakenly believing they are worse than others. Conversely, for simpler tasks, people typically underestimate their own performance but overestimate their ranking relative to others. Overprecision appears to be more persistent than the other two forms of overconfidence, often diminishing the magnitude of both overestimation and overplacement effects.

Overconfidence leads to certain behaviors, such as expansive body language, a lower vocal tone, and a tendency to speak early and often in a calm, relaxed manner, which gives the individual the appearance of competence, often resulting in higher social status (Anderson et al., 2012). The desire for status seems to be fundamental, as its level impacts subjective well-being, self-esteem, and mental and physical health (Anderson et al., 2015). Faking confidence doesn't help, as we are capable of spotting it pretty quickly in others.

Researchers explored the tendency of men to unconsciously inflate their performance and to exhibit genuine overconfidence. The findings of these studies suggest that men honestly believed their performance was 30% higher than it actually was (Reuben et al., 2012). This might explain why men have a lower threshold for applying for jobs than women do. Internal research at Hewlett-Packard, for example, suggests that women apply for open jobs only if they think they meet all the required criteria, whereas men respond to the posting even if they meet less than two-thirds of the requirements (Mohr, 2014). Again, as discussed earlier, socialization is a contributing factor to this difference in overconfidence. Girls at school are rewarded for following the rules and, at work, for obtaining the right accreditations to perform a role (Mohr, 2014).

Often, alleged gender differences in self-confidence are used to explain why women remain underrepresented in high-income occupations. To explore this idea, a recent study drew on two main sources: a survey of experts and an analysis of experimental findings on self-confidence from the past 20 years (Bandiera et al., 2022).

What emerged was a clear contradiction between beliefs and evidence. Most experts surveyed believe that men are overconfident and women are underconfident. Yet, when the researchers aggregated the existing experimental data using their statistical model, they discovered two surprising things. First, both men and women tend to be overconfident, rather than one group being overconfident and the other underconfident. Second, the model could not rule out the possibility that men and women may be equally prone to overestimating themselves.

The gap between experts' beliefs and the actual data stands out starkly. For example, the study shows that 72% of the research findings indicate both men and women are overconfident. Only 8% of experts, however, interpreted the literature this way. By contrast, 77% of experts think men are overconfident while women are underconfident, even though only 18% of the actual findings support this view. In other words, the consensus among experts deviates significantly from the patterns identified in aggregated research. This highlights how much influence assumptions and gender stereotypes can have, even in academic discussions about gender and self-confidence. This disconnect contributes to the "women lack confidence" narrative.

1.5   More Myths: Women are Reluctant Risk-Takers, and Women Don't Ask

Taking risks and advocating for yourself in the workplace can significantly impact how others perceive your confidence and competence. While risk-taking and asking for raises or promotions may feel uncomfortable, they seem to be crucial in shaping how others perceive your confidence and, by extension, your potential for career growth.

Risk involves the possibility that something bad will happen. Risk-taking is neither good nor bad, as the repercussions depend on the context in which the risk is taken. Sara Blakely, the founder of Spanx, risked her entire savings of $5000 to start her company, which is now valued at over $1 billion. Author Cheryl Strayed took a risk by embarking on a solo hiking journey along the Pacific Crest Trail, which became the basis for her bestselling memoir *Wild* and the subsequently released box office hit film. Often, the risks we try to avoid are not life-threatening but deeply rooted in fear, one of our most powerful emotions. And we experience so many of those fears: What if they judge me and perceive me as incompetent? What if I make a mistake, or even worse, I fail? What if I feel embarrassed? What if I'm not good enough?

The perception that women are reluctant risk-takers and don't ask for what they want and deserve, such as promotions or pay raises, leads to inequities in promotions and pay. The gender stereotype that women are risk-averse leads to the assumption that women may not make effective leaders because of their reluctance to take risks (Branson, 2006). The reality is that when women make mistakes, they're often judged more harshly than men are for similar errors, which can make them more hesitant to take risks or speak up to share their ideas. Additionally, compared to men, women are more likely to downplay their certainty, while men are more likely to minimize their own doubts (Tannen, 1995).

Does Gender Influence Risk-Taking?

A significant number of studies report gender disparity in risk-taking behavior, with women exhibiting greater risk-aversion compared to men. The traditional studies suggest that stress amplifies this gender difference, decreasing risk-taking in women while increasing it in men due to variations in brain activity related to risk computation and action preparation (Lighthall et al., 2012). A body of research argues that women tend to be more risk-averse and perceive greater risks than men across different domains, particularly in financial decision-making (Croson & Gneezy, 2009). For example, one meta-analysis analyzed data from 15 sets of experiments with the same underlying investment game and found evidence that women tend to make more conservative financial decisions and take fewer investment risks compared to their male counterparts (Charness & Gneezy, 2012). One of the underlying reasons appears to be the fact that women tend to underestimate large probabilities of gains more strongly than men, particularly when the decisions are framed as investments (Fehr-Duda et al., 2006). Women's lower willingness to take financial risks compared to men has also been related to their higher levels of loss aversion and lower levels of financial optimism (Dawson, 2023).

Other studies have reported that women are more concerned about unfair or unequal outcomes when taking social risks that could disadvantage themselves or others. There is a pattern indicating that women typically are more averse to inequality than men in risky situations, which drives gender differences in social risk-taking behavior (Friedl et al., 2020). In addition, gender differences in risk-taking seem to be moderated by cultural factors such as gender roles and socialization.

Much like communication and play styles, gender differences in risk perception emerge early in childhood (Hillier & Morrongiello, 1998). Socialization plays a significant role in shaping gender differences, with girls generally perceiving greater risks compared to boys. As you read earlier, girls are traditionally socialized to be nurturing, to emphasize connections with others, and to prioritize maintaining relationships. Boys, on the other hand, are typically socialized to be more independent, assertive, and dominant, which may lead to lower risk perceptions. Girls' socialization to prioritize interpersonal relationships makes them more sensitive to risks that could disrupt those relationships, while boys' socialization is less focused on social risks and consequences. These socialization patterns reinforce feelings of vulnerability, dependency, and lack of control in women, which can accentuate perceptions of risk and reduce their belief in their ability to manage risks effectively. In comparison, men's socialization emphasizes independence, confidence, and being in control, all characteristics that are associated with lower risk perceptions.

Explanations from Evolutionary Psychology

Evolutionary psychology provides intriguing hypotheses about how gender differences in risk-taking behavior may have evolved due to different reproductive strategies and costs between men and women. In general, men exhibit greater variability in reproductive success compared to women (Friedl et al., 2020). One man can potentially father many offspring, while a woman's reproductive capacity is more limited. This creates an evolutionary incentive for men to take greater risks through competition for mates, status-seeking among other men, and mate acquisition to increase their reproductive potential and pass on their genes.

Women's higher levels of risk aversion can be explained by parental investment asymmetry, which suggests that many male-female differences, including those in humans, arise from how much time, energy, and personal risk each sex invests in parenting compared to finding and keeping a mate. According to this perspective, women invest more time, energy, and resources in pregnancy, nursing, and child-rearing than men, which makes them more risk-averse to protect their own survival and the survival of their offspring (Trivers, 1996). In contrast, men's lower investment in parenthood creates an incentive to take more risks that could increase mating opportunities. Compared to women, men face greater competition for mates. Taking risks related to dominance, resource acquisition, and displays of physical superiority may have increased men's mating success throughout evolution (Buss, 1989). According to evolutionary psychologists, men's riskier behaviors may have been sexually selected by women as signals of genetic advantage, the ability to acquire resources, or a willingness to protect offspring (Ronay & Hippel, 2010; Baker & Maner, 2008). These behaviors are evolutionarily adaptive and allow male risk-takers to pass their genes on to future generations.

In sum, evolutionary psychologists propose that the asymmetric reproductive costs and variance in reproductive success have shaped men to be more inclined toward risk-taking behaviors that could increase mating and reproductive success, while women evolved greater risk-aversion to protect themselves and their offspring. This risk-aversion can be both advantageous and disadvantageous for women in the workplace. While cautious decision-making may help them avoid costly mistakes, it can also limit their opportunities for growth, innovation, and leadership advancement. The ideal solution is to consciously evaluate when risk-aversion is beneficial and when stepping outside comfort zones might stimulate professional growth and success. Needless to say, these evolutionary influences likely interact with cultural and social factors.

A Critical Look at the Research

Many older studies support the idea that women tend to avoid risks, reinforcing the stereotype of gender-based differences. But this is an overly simplistic view, and recent research takes a more critical perspective to challenge these findings. This research highlights that risk-taking is not an inherent individual trait but rather a socially constructed concept influenced by various factors. For example, social pressures such as gender stereotypes and peer influence can shape risk-taking behavior (Rawn & Vohs, 2011). Researchers have observed that the inclination for risk varies based on the situation (Hanoch et al., 2006); for instance, someone might be comfortable with skydiving but hesitant to invest in cryptocurrency. Although these stereotypes are widespread, research suggesting that women are inherently more risk-averse than men lacks strength and consistency (Filippin & Crosetto, 2016). Furthermore, a meta-analysis suggests that the reported gender gap in risk-taking seems to be decreasing over time (Byrnes et al., 1999).

Most of the recent research is rewriting the narrative about gender differences in risk-taking. We have all heard the claims that women tend to be more cautious with their investments. A big part of what has been reported as a gender difference might be more about who tends to have more financial knowledge. When women have the necessary understanding and knowledge about investments, gender disparities in financial risk-taking disappear (Dwyer et al., 2002). A man and a woman with the same level of financial knowledge are likely to have more similar attitudes toward risk than we might expect. This suggests that if we focus on improving financial education for everyone, we are likely to see gender differences in risk-taking shrink even more.

A recent study examined the performance of female analysts and analyzed over 2 million stock forecasts made by 17,240 male and female analysts, covering a total of 13,636 stocks (Kumar, 2010). The conclusion was that female analysts issued bolder and more accurate forecasts, and they possessed better-than-average skills due to self-selection, which led to only the strongest female analysts joining.

Another interesting study concluded that companies with women CEOs and organizations with greater numbers of women executives and directors engage in greater financial risk than those led by men (Ingersoll et al., 2023). It also provided evidence that a firm's risk-taking increases as the number of women executives in the company increases. At the board level, when the number of women directors increased beyond symbolic representation, boards showed a greater readiness to encourage the company to pursue more significant risks. Moreover, the presence of women directors increased the risk-taking of both men and women CEOs. To reach board positions, women have had to embrace risks at various points in their careers. Embracing risks has evolved into a fundamental characteristic and a regular behavioral pattern for these influential leaders. This study concludes that women face a significant "risk tax," which refers to the extra burden of risk-taking behavior that women leaders must undertake to achieve high-level positions and to overcome gender stereotypes.

Recent research demonstrates that the gender difference in risk-taking does not amount to much at all. Its effect size of 0.13 is considered trivial in statistics. In fact, it is so small that, in everyday life, it's almost meaningless, as we already discussed on page 21. This suggests that, in terms of risk-taking, men and women are more alike than different, contrary to the myth that women are risk-averse.

Self-Reflection 1.3: How Open to Risk Are You?

1. To what extent did your upbringing discourage risk-taking behaviors? Did the people around you challenge gender stereotypes?
2. Do you have a role model(s) who has successfully taken risks and inspired you to do the same? Seeing other women in leadership roles who have embraced risk-taking can help break down psychological barriers and self-imposed limitations.
3. Do you have a growth mindset? Individuals with a growth mindset believe their abilities can be developed through effort and are more likely to take risks, viewing setbacks as opportunities for growth.
4. Do you have robust support systems in place (e.g., peer coaches, mentors, and sponsors) within the organization? Women are more likely to take risks when their support systems provide guidance, feedback, and advocacy, particularly around potential backlash associated with risk-taking.
5. How do you frame risk-taking: as reckless and dangerous, or as a strategic and calculated approach to achieving long-term goals? For example, investing in capital expenditures and research and development could be considered strategic risks that lead to long-term revenue potential and innovation.
6. How do you reward yourself for calculated risk-taking, regardless of the outcome? This reinforces the message that risk-taking is valued, and failures are considered learning opportunities rather than setbacks.
7. Risk-taking requires being open to possible failures, while perfectionism is about the feeling of control (Helgesen & Goldsmith, 2018). Is failure an option for you? To what extent do you try to be in control?

The Myth That Women Don't Ask for More

In their 2003 article "Nice Girls Don't Ask", Linda Babcock, Professor of Economics at Carnegie Mellon University, and her co-authors argue that men are more likely than women to negotiate for what they want, and the difference is significant (Babcock et al., 2003). In one of their studies, 57% of male MBA graduates negotiated their initial salary offer, compared to only

7% of female graduates. The reluctance of women to negotiate resulted in tangible financial disadvantages. For example, male MBA graduates in their second study had starting salaries that were, on average, 7.6% higher than their female counterparts. This gender difference in negotiation behavior extended beyond salary discussions. Men generally viewed more situations as potential negotiations and engaged in them more frequently than women did. The reasons for this disparity, according to the authors, are complex, involving socialization (women are often taught to focus on others' needs rather than their own), cultural expectations, and potential penalties women face when they negotiate assertively.

A fascinating new study challenges this long-held belief and reveals some surprising findings (Kray et al., 2024). Researchers examined real-world data from MBA students and alumni of a top US business school, and what they found might surprise you. Contrary to popular opinion, women actually reported negotiating their salaries more frequently than men, not less. But how does this square with earlier research? The authors of this study dug deeper, re-examining past studies, and they uncovered an intriguing trend. While men did indeed negotiate more often than women before 2000, this gap has since disappeared and even reversed itself. Both men and women are now more likely to negotiate, but women seem to have embraced this skill with particular enthusiasm. The outdated belief that "women don't ask" isn't just inaccurate—it's potentially harmful. This misconception can lead to increased gender stereotyping, even in areas unrelated to negotiation. For example, it might result in heightened skepticism about women's leadership abilities.

A meta-analysis explored gender differences in economic negotiation outcomes (Mazei et al., 2015). It found that when both men and women had practice negotiating, the gap in negotiation shrank. When given information about the salary range, women and men performed similarly. Additionally, when people were negotiating for someone else (a friend or family member), the gender difference disappeared. In situations where women didn't expect to face stereotypes or biases—for example, when they had solid negotiation experience or were advocating for another individual—they outperformed men.

The differences between men and women in negotiation change based on the situation, experience, and information available. Successful negotiation is not about being born a natural negotiator; it's about the circumstances and how prepared the negotiator is. This means we can create environments where everyone, regardless of gender, can become skilled at striking a good deal.

Why do we need to look closer at the myth that women don't ask? It's important to critically examine this myth because it can unfairly shape how decision-makers view women's entitlement to raises, promotions, and recognition. When people assume women are not speaking up for themselves, they may interpret it as a signal that women believe they do not deserve more. This myth also feeds into the idea that women lack ambition or avoid challenges at work.

In conclusion, the persistent myths that women lack confidence and ambition, don't take risks, and don't ask for what they want have been debunked by recent research. These misconceptions not only misrepresent women's capabilities and behaviors, but they also perpetuate harmful stereotypes that can hinder career advancement and gender equity in the workplace. Understanding that women do not lack confidence and ambition, that they do take risks when necessary, and that they do ask for raises and promotions at rates similar to men shifts the focus to addressing systemic biases and structural barriers that prevent women from advancing in their careers.

Yet, even as we dispel these damaging myths, we must also acknowledge the ways in which women sometimes undermine themselves in the workplace. In the next chapter, we explore a range of self-defeating behaviors and, more importantly, discuss how to overcome them.

References

Anderson, C., Brion, S., Moore, D. A., & Kennedy, J. A. (2012). A status-enhancement account of overconfidence. *Journal of Personality and Social Psychology, 103*(4), 718.

Anderson, C., Hildreth, J. A. D., & Howland, L. (2015). Is the desire for status a fundamental human motive? A review of the empirical literature. *Psychological Bulletin, 141*(3), 574.

Apicella, C. L., Dreber, A., & Mollerstrom, J. (2014). Salivary testosterone change following monetary wins and losses predicts future financial risk-taking. *Psychoneuroendocrinology, 39*, 58–64.

Babcock, L., Laschever, S., Gelfand, M., & Small, D. (2003). Nice girls don't ask. *Harvard Business Review, 81*(10), 14.

Baker Jr, M. D., & Maner, J. K. (2008). Risk-taking as a situationally sensitive male mating strategy. *Evolution and Human Behavior, 29*(6), 391–395.

Bandiera, O., Parekh, N., Petrongolo, B., & Rao, M. (2022). Men are from Mars, and women too: A Bayesian meta-analysis of overconfidence experiments. *Economica, 89*, S38–S70.

Bandura, A. (2001). Social cognitive theory: An agentic perspective. *Annual Review of Psychology, 52*(1), 1–26.

Bandura, A. (2012). On the functional properties of perceived self-efficacy revisited. *Journal of Management, 38*(1), 13.

Baron-Cohen, S., Knickmeyer, R. C., & Belmonte, M. K. (2005). Sex differences in the brain: Implications for explaining autism. *Science, 310*(5749), 819–823.

Bateman, A. J. (1948). Intra-sexual selection in Drosophila. *Heredity, 2*(3), 349–368.

Baumeister, R. F., Smart, L., & Boden, J. M. (1996). Relation of threatened egotism to violence and aggression: The dark side of high self-esteem. *Psychological Review, 103*(1), 5.

Benson, A., Li, D., & Shue, K. (2024, March 4). "Potential" and the gender promotion gap. *SSRN*: https://dx.doi.org/10.2139/ssrn.4747175

Branson, D. M. (2006). *No seat at the table: How corporate governance and law keep women out of the boardroom* (Vol. 26). NYU Press.

Brockner, J. (1983). Low self-esteem and behavioral plasticity: Some implications. *Review of Personality and Social Psychology, 4*, 237–271.

Buss, D. M. (1989). Sex differences in human mate preferences: Evolutionary hypotheses tested in 37 cultures. *Behavioral and Brain Sciences, 12*(1), 1–14.

Byrnes, J. P., Miller, D. C., & Schafer, W. D. (1999). Gender differences in risk taking: A meta-analysis. *Psychological Bulletin, 125*(3), 367.

Charness, G., & Gneezy, U. (2012). Strong evidence for gender differences in risk taking. *Journal of Economic Behavior & Organization, 83*(1), 50–58.

Coates, J. M., & Herbert, J. (2008). Endogenous steroids and financial risk taking on a London trading floor. *Proceedings of the National Academy of Sciences, 105*(16), 6167–6172.

Croson, R., & Gneezy, U. (2009). Gender differences in preferences. *Journal of Economic Literature, 47*(2), 448–474.

Dawson, C. (2023). Gender differences in optimism, loss aversion and attitudes towards risk. *British Journal of Psychology, 114*(4), 928–944.

Doldor, E., Wyatt, M., & Silvester, J. (2021, February 10). Men get more actionable feedback than women. *Harvard Business Review*. https://hbr.org/2021/02/research-men-get-more-actionable-feedback-than-women

Dweck, C. S. (2006). *Mindset: The new psychology of success*. Random House.

Dwyer, P. D., Gilkeson, J. H., & List, J. A. (2002). Gender differences in revealed risk taking: Evidence from mutual fund investors. *Economics Letters, 76*(2), 151–158.

Eisenegger, C., Haushofer, J., & Fehr, E. (2011). The role of testosterone in social interaction. *Trends in Cognitive Sciences, 15*(6), 263–271.

Eliot, L., Ahmed, A., Khan, H., & Patel, J. (2021). Dump the "dimorphism": Comprehensive synthesis of human brain studies reveals few male-female differences beyond size. *Neuroscience & Biobehavioral Reviews, 125*, 667–697.

Exley, C. L., & Kessler, J. B. (2022). The gender gap in self-promotion. *The Quarterly Journal of Economics, 137*(3), 1345–1381.

Fehr-Duda, H., De Gennaro, M., & Schubert, R. (2006). Gender, financial risk, and probability weights. *Theory and Decision, 60*, 283–313.

Fels, A. (2004). Do women lack ambition? *Harvard Business Review, 82*(4), 50–60.

Field, E., Krivkovish, A., Kügele, S., Robinson, N., & Yee, L. (2023). *Women in the workplace report.* McKinsey & Company and LeanIn.org. https://www.mckinsey.com/featured-insights/diversity-and-inclusion/women-in-the-workplace-2023

Filippin, A., & Crosetto, P. (2016). A reconsideration of gender differences in risk attitudes. *Management Science, 62*(11), 3138–3160.

Friedl, A., Pondorfer, A., & Schmidt, U. (2020). Gender differences in social risk taking. *Journal of Economic Psychology, 77*, 102182.

Gettler, L. T., McDade, T. W., Feranil, A. B., & Kuzawa, C. W. (2011). Longitudinal evidence that fatherhood decreases testosterone in human males. *Proceedings of the National Academy of Sciences, 108*(39), 16194–16199.

Guillén, L. (2018, March 26). Is the confidence gap between men and women a myth? *Harvard Business Review*, 2–5.

Guillén, L., Mayo, M., & Karelaia, N. (2018). Appearing self-confident and getting credit for it: Why it may be easier for men than women to gain influence at work. *Human Resource Management, 57*(4), 839–854.

Hanoch, Y., Johnson, J. G., & Wilke, A. (2006). Domain specificity in experimental measures and participant recruitment: An application to risk-taking behavior. *Psychological Science, 17*(4), 300–304.

Helgesen, S., & Goldsmith, M. (2018, March 28). How women can succeed by rethinking old habits. *Strategy + Business.* https://www.strategy-business.com/article/How-Women-Can-Succeed-by-Rethinking-Old-Habits

Hernandez, M. (2018, January 11), Rationalizing yourself out of a promotion. *MIT Sloan Management Review.* https://sloanreview.mit.edu/article/rationalizing-yourself-out-of-a-promotion/

Hillier, L. M., & Morrongiello, B. A. (1998). Age and gender differences in school-age children's appraisals of injury risk. *Journal of Pediatric Psychology, 23*(4), 229–238.

Hollenbeck, G. P., & Hall, D. T. (2004). Self-confidence and leader performance. *Organizational Dynamics, 33*(3), 254–269.

Ingersoll, A. R., Cook, A., & Glass, C. (2023). A free solo in heels: Corporate risk taking among women executives and directors. *Journal of Business Research, 157*, 113651.

Johnson, D. D., & Fowler, J. H. (2011). The evolution of overconfidence. *Nature, 477*(7364), 317–320.

Judge, T. A., Erez, A., Bono, J. E., & Thoresen, C. J. (2003). The core self-evaluations scale: Development of a measure. *Personnel Psychology, 56*(2), 303–331.

Kane, A., Yarker, J., & Lewis, R. (2021). Measuring self-confidence in workplace settings: A conceptual and methodological review of measures of self-confidence, self-efficacy and self-esteem. *International Coaching Psychology Review*, *16*(1), 67–89.

Kling, K. C., Hyde, J. S., Showers, C. J., & Buswell, B. N. (1999). Gender differences in self-esteem: A meta-analysis. *Psychological Bulletin*, *125*(4), 470.

Kray, L. J., Kennedy, J. A., & Lee, M. (2024). Now, women do ask: A call to update beliefs about the gender pay gap. *Academy of Management Discoveries*, *10*(1), 7–33. https://doi.org/10.5465/amd.2022.0021

Kruger, J., & Dunning, D. (1999). Unskilled and unaware of it: How difficulties in recognizing one's own incompetence lead to inflated self-assessments. *Journal of Personality and Social Psychology*, *77*(6), 1121.

Kumar, A. (2010). Self-selection and the forecasting abilities of female equity analysts. *Journal of Accounting Research*, *48*(2), 393–435.

Lenney, E. (1977). Women's self-confidence in achievement settings. *Psychological Bulletin*, *84*(1), 1.

Lighthall, N. R., Sakaki, M., Vasunilashorn, S., Nga, L., Somayajula, S., Chen, E. Y., Samii, N., & Mather, M. (2012). Gender differences in reward-related decision processing under stress. *Social Cognitive and Affective Neuroscience*, *7*(4), 476–484.

Macnamara, B. N., & Rupani, N. S. (2017). The relationship between intelligence and mindset. *Intelligence*, *64*, 52–59.

Magee, J. C., & Galinsky, A. D. (2008). Social hierarchy: The self-reinforcing nature of power and status. *Academy of Management Annals*, *2*(1), 351–398.

Mazei, J., Hüffmeier, J., Freund, P. A., Stuhlmacher, A. F., Bilke, L., & Hertel, G. (2015). A meta-analysis on gender differences in negotiation outcomes and their moderators. *Psychological Bulletin*, *141*(1), 85.

Mohr, T. S. (2014). Why women don't apply for jobs unless they're 100% qualified. *Harvard Business Review*, *25*, 40–45.

Moore, D. A., & Healy, P. J. (2008). The trouble with overconfidence. *Psychological Review*, *115*(2), 502.

Mueller, C. M., & Dweck, C. S. (1998). Praise for intelligence can undermine children's motivation and performance. *Journal of Personality and Social Psychology*, *75*(1), 33.

Oney, E., & Oksuzoglu-Guven, G. (2015). Confidence: A critical review of the literature and an alternative perspective for general and specific self-confidence. *Psychological Reports*, *116*(1), 149–163.

Petty, R. (2015, March 16). Confidence: What does it do? [Video]. TEDxOhioStateUniversity. https://www.youtube.com/watch?v=cKu-32iyHs0

Player, A., Randsley de Moura, G., Leite, A. C., Abrams, D., & Tresh, F. (2019). Overlooked leadership potential: The preference for leadership potential in job candidates who are men vs. women. *Frontiers in Psychology*, *10*, 391596.

Rawn, C. D., & Vohs, K. D. (2011). People use self-control to risk personal harm: An intra-interpersonal dilemma. *Personality and Social Psychology Review, 15*(3), 267–289.

Reuben, E., Rey-Biel, P., Sapienza, P., & Zingales, L. (2012). The emergence of male leadership in competitive environments. *Journal of Economic Behavior & Organization, 83*(1), 111–117.

Roberts, T.-A. (1991). Gender and the influence of evaluations on self-assessments in achievement settings. *Psychological Bulletin, 109*(2), 297.

Ronay, R., & Hippel, W. V. (2010). The presence of an attractive woman elevates testosterone and physical risk taking in young men. *Social Psychological and Personality Science, 1*(1), 57–64.

Rosenberg, M. (1965). Rosenberg self-esteem scale. *APA PsycTests.* The scale is also available on the following site. https://www.apa.org/obesity-guideline/rosenberg-self-esteem.pdf

Sturm, R. E., Taylor, S. N., Atwater, L. E., & Braddy, P. W. (2014). Leader self-awareness: An examination and implications of women's under-prediction. *Journal of Organizational Behavior, 35*(5), 657–677.

Tannen, D. (1995). The power of talk: Who gets heard and why. *Harvard Business Review, 73*, 138–148.

Tannen, D. (2019). *How women's ways of talking differ from men's* [Interview] (pp. 39–47). Harvard Business School Publishing Corporation.

Thomas, R., Cooper, M., Konar, E., Rooney, M., Noble-Tolla, M., Bohrer, A., Yee, L., Krivkovich, A., Starikova, I., Robinson, K., Nadeua, M.-C., & Robinson, N. (2018). *Women in the workplace.* McKinsey & Company and LeanIn.org. https://wiw-report.s3.amazonaws.com/Women_in_the_Workplace_2018.pdf

Tinsley, C. H., & Ely, R. J. (2018). What most people get wrong about men and women: Research shows the sexes aren't so different. *Harvard Business Review, 96*(3), 114–121.

Trivers, R. L. (1996) Parental investment and sexual selection. In L. D. Houck & L. C. Drickamer (Eds.), *Foundations of animal behavior: Classic papers with commentaries* (pp. 795–838). University of Chicago Press. (Reprinted from B. Campbell (Ed.), "Sexual Selection and the Descent of Man, 1871–1971," Chicago: Aldine, 1972, pp. 136–179).

Vancouver, J. B., Thompson, C. M., Tischner, E. C., & Putka, D. J. (2002). Two studies examining the negative effect of self-efficacy on performance. *Journal of Applied Psychology, 87*(3), 506.

Wrzesniewski, A., & Dutton, J. E. (2001). Crafting a job: Revisioning employees as active crafters of their work. *Academy of Management Review, 26*(2), 179–201.

Zenger, J., & Folkman, J. (2019). Women score higher than men in most leadership skills. *Harvard Business Review, 92*(10), 86–93.

2

Disrupt Self-Defeating Behaviors

Vignette 2.1: Fabiana Cordova

Fabiana Cordova, Director of Programming at Westbridge Broadcasting, was reviewing the latest ratings report when her phone buzzed with a message from her manager, Executive VP of Content, Wing Blum: "Fabiana, we need to talk. Can you come to my office at 2 PM?" Fabiana felt butterflies in her stomach. Despite the recent success of their new morning show, *Sunrise Today*, she couldn't shake the feeling that something was amiss. Was there a critical viewership report for *Sunrise Today* they needed to discuss? Perhaps Wing wanted to talk about last week's executive meeting, where she hadn't contributed any ideas. Maybe it was about the incident with the missed compliance form filing. Or was he dissatisfied with the farewell party for Rudi that she had volunteered to plan?

The events of the past few weeks began to unfold in her mind. Fabiana recalled sitting in her office, staring at the ratings report for *Sunrise Today*. The numbers were impressive—they had unexpectedly surpassed a major competitor. Yet, instead of feeling triumphant, Fabiana felt nervous. As Director of Programming, she had been instrumental in the show's success. She had personally scouted and negotiated the contract for the charismatic host, Ritika. It was Fabiana who had pushed for the innovative format, including the popular cooking segment. However, when Wing burst into her office with a bottle of champagne, exclaiming, "We did it, Fabiana!" she found herself deflecting. "Oh, it was nothing really … it was Ritika who added that cooking segment," Fabiana said, forcing a smile. "I only played a small part." Wing frowned slightly but didn't press the issue. As he left, Fabiana overheard him in the hallway, loudly praising Ritika and the production team for the show's success.

Later that week, during the monthly executive meeting, the CEO asked for ideas to capitalize on *Sunrise Today*'s success. The room fell silent for a moment.

© The Author(s), under exclusive license to Springer Nature Switzerland AG 2025
G. Toegel, *The Confidence Myth*,
https://doi.org/10.1007/978-3-031-97305-5_2

Fabiana had several well-thought-out strategies but thought, "Someone else will probably make a suggestion." Just as she was about to speak up, the Head of Marketing jumped in with a suggestion. Fabiana's ideas remained unshared. After the meeting, Fabiana's colleague, Giorgio, approached her. "I was hoping to hear your thoughts in there, Fabiana. You always have great insights." Fabiana shrugged. "Oh, I didn't want to take up too much space. Besides, Sjur's idea was good."

There was also the incident last week when one of her department managers forgot to file a required broadcasting compliance form on time. Fabiana became consumed with guilt and replayed the incident mentally over and over, asking herself if she should have reminded the manager more frequently or if she could have delegated differently. With a habit of dwelling on mistakes, she could not let it go, even though the issue was rectified within 24 hours with minimal fallout. She confided to a friend, "How stupid of me … I'm not cut out to lead … I should have caught it sooner."

The farewell party for Rudi, which she had volunteered to organize, was also a headache—a task usually handled by administrative staff. Fabiana was exhausted, as it was taking so much of her time and energy, which she desperately needed for developing a new primetime concept.

As she packed up to leave, she noticed the CEO's email about an upcoming town hall, where department heads would present their strategies for the next quarter. Fabiana felt queasy at the thought of speaking in front of the entire company. "Maybe I can just send out a memo instead," she thought, already drafting an email in her mind as she headed to Wing's office, still trying to guess what was on his mind.

2.1   Self-Doubt and the Power of Reframing

Now that you've read about some of the myths that contribute to the perception that women lack confidence, let's take a look at some of the self-defeating behaviors that make it hard to overcome this perception. The popular press often claims that women lack confidence. Sometimes, that perception is reinforced by commonly observed behaviors that seem to signal a lack of confidence. These often unconscious behaviors can manifest in various ways, such as excessive humility; failure to claim credit for achievements; reluctance to apply for promotions or new opportunities; invisibility in group settings or in meetings; and perfectionism leading to procrastination and missed deadlines. As you just read, Fabiana, a successful and innovative executive, downplayed her achievements, gave credit for *Sunrise Today*'s success to the host instead, and hesitated to speak up in a meeting, thinking someone else would have a better idea. From boardrooms to classrooms, women often grapple with these persistent behavioral patterns related to self-doubt.

These behaviors aren't the result of character flaws or innate personality traits; they are learned responses, often rooted in societal expectations, past experiences, or anxiety. Rationalizing them—for example, attributing them to personality, "I'm an introvert and can't speak up"—is the wrong strategy. The good news is that, with awareness and effort, these self-sabotaging habits can be unlearned. This chapter will explore these behaviors, their origins, and, most importantly, discuss strategies to overcome them.

Vignette 2.2: Tucci Ivowi

Tucci Ivowi, a successful businesswoman from Ghana, CEO and founding member of the Ghana Commodity Exchange, shares a poignant example that illustrates the common experience of second-guessing oneself and feeling insecure about one's abilities, especially in professional settings. Tucci, at that point in time a newly hired brand manager, attended a training program on the fundamentals of the coffee business for marketing and sales professionals. The presenter asked a simple question about the difference between soluble coffee and roast-and-ground coffee. Despite knowing the answer, Tucci hesitated to respond due to self-doubt and a fear of looking foolish. Her internal monolog was, "Am I good enough? … Will I make a fool of myself?" Tucci rationalized her silence, thinking someone else with more experience would respond. It turned out she did know the correct answer (Ivowi, 2021).

Sadly, this is not an isolated incident but a recurring pattern throughout many women's careers. Tucci's story is an example of how self-doubt can prevent people from showcasing their knowledge and skills, even when they are highly capable. As her career progressed, she realized that "the benefit of raising my voice outweighs the emotional cost of my silence" (Cohn, 2021).

Research indicates that approximately 70% of people experience episodes of significant self-doubt at least once in their lives (Gravois, 2007). In fact, moderate levels of self-doubt and anxiety can be mobilizing factors, as they trigger heightened self-awareness and promote unbiased processing of self-relevant information, which serves to enhance performance when facing new challenges such as a new job. Anxiety can be functional; it serves as a signal that you will need greater attention, cognitive energy, persistence, and courage to build new skills and mobilize the necessary resources to overcome the challenge. Anxiety and your physiological reaction to it send the message that this is something you need to take seriously. Persistent self-doubt, however, can be debilitating, paralyzing both thought and action.

Instead of responding with self-doubt, we have the power to change what we tell ourselves and frame this anxiety in a different way by making it our ally. Instead of thinking, "I'm so nervous," you can frame it as, "I'm excited to share my ideas!"; "I'm excited to learn"; "I appreciate the opportunity to do something new"; "I know this experience will make me wiser"; "What a great chance to demonstrate my superpowers."

How we frame a challenge, or even our own feelings of self-doubt, influences our behavior in response to the challenge. Reframing involves taking a different perspective on a problem or question to reveal new solutions or insights. Health psychologist Kelly McGonigal argues that how we frame stress, either as harmful or beneficial can dramatically impact both psychological perceptions and physiological responses, potentially influencing long-term health outcomes (Jamieson et al., 2012; Keller et al., 2012; McGonigal, 2013). For example, a longitudinal study in the United States tracking 30,000 people over eight years found that those who experienced high stress and framed it as harmful had a 43% increased risk of dying (Keller et al., 2012). However, people who experienced stress but did not view it as harmful did not show increased mortality. Researchers estimated that over the eight-year span of the study, about 20,000 people per year died prematurely due to the belief that stress is harmful, not from stress itself. When people were primed to view stress positively, their physical stress response changed. Instead of constricting (a reaction associated with cardiovascular disease), their blood vessels remained relaxed, similar to responses during positive emotions like joy and courage. Research also suggests that participants who were taught to view their stress response as helpful (e.g., "My heart is pounding in preparation for action," or "I'm breathing heavily to supply more oxygen to my brain") showed less anxiety, more confidence, and a healthier cardiovascular profile (Jamieson et al., 2012). All these findings illustrate the power of framing our mindset, because how we think about stress and anxiety has a significant impact on our physical and mental well-being.

Self-doubt is universal and we all experience it from time to time in myriad contexts. How you view the challenges you face, even when you fail, affects how you navigate the different spheres of your life—as a boss, an employee, a parent or a child, as a friend and a student. Mastering reframing is an essential skill for growth and success in all parts of life. This chapter explores how to reframe and overcome self-defeating thought patterns and behaviors such as rumination and self-blame, avoiding visibility, communication pitfalls, and taking on menial tasks.

2.2 Stop Rumination and Self-Blame

Two harmful thought patterns, rumination and self-blame, can set the stage for self-defeating behaviors such as downplaying achievements, not applying for promotions, or staying silent in meetings. These destructive thought patterns chip away at self-confidence, making it more likely that people who engage in them will undervalue themselves and their contributions. For example, Fabiana blamed herself for the incident involving the compliance form and continued to ruminate over it.

Imagine you're trying to fall asleep, but your mind won't stop replaying something you said in a meeting or worrying about something you should have done differently. This endless loop of negative thinking is called *rumination*. While it's natural for everyone to overthink now and then, some of us get stuck in these cycles more frequently or for longer periods, which can take a toll on our emotional well-being. Rumination is closely linked to psychological disorders such as depression and anxiety. It is also one of the reasons why women tend to experience more depressive symptoms than men (Nolen-Hoeksema, 1999). When you are lost in an endless loop of overthinking, it's hard to see the bigger picture or find constructive ways to break the cycle and move forward. Recognizing *why* you ruminate can help you break free from this self-destructive cycle.

In addition to replaying the same unsettling thoughts again and again, rumination can also lay the groundwork for another self-defeating thought pattern: self-blame. The more we dwell on perceived mistakes and regrets, the more likely we are to spiral from repetitive thinking into harsh self-criticism and assume total responsibility for every negative outcome, whether it's truly ours to own or not.

Self-blame is a way of explaining negative events by consistently attributing faults and failures to oneself. Healthy self-reflection can stimulate growth and accountability, but self-blame goes beyond this. It often involves harsh self-criticism, an inability to recognize external factors, and persistent feelings of guilt or shame, even for situations that may be outside a person's control. Key characteristics of self-blame include repetitive and negative self-talk (e.g., "It's always my fault"); overemphasis on personal flaws or mistakes; minimizing or dismissing external factors (e.g., circumstances, other people's actions); and a tendency to see oneself as unworthy because of perceived failures.

Sources of Rumination and Self-Blame

Many factors contribute to falling into rumination. The self-reflection questions will help you identify possible sources.

Self-Reflection 2.1: Identify the Sources of Rumination

- Do you tend to see yourself (and the world) in a pessimistic light? It's easy to keep replaying your problems and feel stuck in them.
- In cultures that praise productivity and perfection, we likely feel guilty or inadequate if we fall short. This can spark those unrelenting "I should have…" or "Why didn't I…" thoughts. Do you always expect flawless results, which lead you to relentless self-evaluation? Do you find yourself dwelling on the tiniest mistakes or worrying that you are not measuring up?
- Did you grow up around people who constantly rehashed negative events or fixated on mistakes? You may have learned that's "just how you deal with problems." Do people in your family tend toward anxiety, which triggers repeated worries, making it tough to break free from the cycle?
- Does rumination feel like problem-solving, even though it often just keeps you circling around the same thoughts without finding relief? When life feels overwhelming, it might seem easier (or safer) to think and rethink rather than to take a risk or make a change.
- Adverse experiences can make you hyperaware of potential threats. Do you endlessly review distressing thoughts in an effort to protect yourself from future pain?
- Sometimes we don't fully understand what we're feeling or why. Could rumination be a clumsy attempt to label or figure out the emotion? Without trusted friends, family, or professionals to talk to, you might try to handle everything internally, only to find yourself stuck in a loop of repetitive, negative thinking.
- In general, feedback is useful. But sometimes, people provide feedback that is not constructive or is based on very superficial knowledge of the facts. What do you do in those cases? Are you able to view those negative comments just as opinions and ignore them, or do you tend to ruminate?

Women are more likely to fall into self-blame for many reasons, including societal expectations to maintain harmony and avoid conflict, perfectionism, family dynamics that assign blame, and a tendency for rumination. Women are subjected to gender stereotypes starting at a young age. Many girls are raised to nurture, and they grow up encouraged to take on more emotional responsibility as caretakers and peacemakers and to maintain harmony in relationships. When something goes wrong, they might turn inward and blame themselves to maintain harmony or avoid conflict. Women who have learned that it's "wrong" to challenge others or stand up for themselves as children might fear causing problems as adults. Rather than risk a confrontation, they might silently take the blame, thinking it's the "easier" path.

The pressure and drive to be perfect can result in self-blame when things go wrong. As women have advanced in business, their roles outside of work have not diminished. According to the Free Time Gender Gap Report (Varela & Moridi, 2024), working women spend double the hours per week, compared to working men, on combined childcare and household work. Society often praises them for juggling multiple roles (mother, wife or partner, daughter, professional, friend) and never dropping the ball. Trying to live up to an impossible standard with ever-increasing demands can lead you to assume any slip-up is completely your fault. A flawless performance in every sphere (school, work, family, relationships) is not humanly possible. Whenever reality doesn't match these high expectations, you may see it as your failure.

Similar to a drive for perfectionism, growing up in a critical family environment where people pointed out your mistakes can lead to the internalization of a harsh, judgmental inner voice. This internal critic often mirrors the language and tone of childhood authority figures, creating patterns of self-criticism that can persist well into adulthood (Stone & Stone, 1993). The constant exposure to criticism during the formative years shapes neural pathways and emotional responses, making self-judgment an automatic response to challenges or perceived failures. The formation of negative cognitive patterns that persist into adulthood can lead to rumination, or you might automatically blame yourself because that's what you are used to hearing.

Finally, people who have a habit of ruminating can be vulnerable to self-blame, especially if they are constantly looking for a reason why things went wrong. Psychological conditions such as anxiety or depression can turn your thoughts negative. You might feel that you need to find a reason to explain why you feel down, so you decide, "It must be me."

Self-Reflection 2.2: Maladaptive Thinking and Self-Blame

Think about the last time you blamed yourself for a negative event. Let's explore whether you made any thinking errors as you reflected on the event.

- Did you fall into the trap of hindsight bias? This refers to an illusion where knowing the outcome of an event distorts our memory of what we think we knew at the time.
- Do you blame yourself for overlooking cues that foreshadowed what would happen?
- Do you falsely blame yourself for causing the negative event?

- Do you exaggerate your role in the event? As humans, we tend to magnify our own roles.
- Do you ruminate about how you could have prevented the event? If one of your direct reports is fired for unethical behavior, many factors may have contributed to it, and failing to anticipate the problem might not entirely be your fault.
- Are you a people-pleaser who holds herself to an unrealistic standard? A reasonable approach is to ask yourself, "What would I expect from a friend if they went through a similar situation?"
- Are you confusing feelings with evidence? Just because you *feel* guilty does not mean that you *are* guilty.

Overcoming Rumination and Self-Blame

This section will explore how to break free from the damaging grip of rumination and self-blame. Ultimately, rumination doesn't have to be a lifelong burden. By understanding and addressing the factors that drive your overthinking, you can learn new ways to cope and find healthier approaches to facing life's ups and downs.

Here are a few approaches people find helpful: mindfulness practices, emotion regulation techniques, reframing, and techniques borrowed from cognitive behavioral therapy (CBT).

Mindfulness practices train you to notice thoughts without judgment and bring your focus back to the present. Mindfulness works by creating distance from ruminative thoughts through present-moment awareness and nonjudgmental acceptance of thoughts and feelings. This practice helps individuals observe their thoughts without getting caught up in them, reducing their emotional impact. You can set aside regular time each day for mindfulness practice, starting with simple breathing exercises in a quiet space. When ruminative thoughts occur, acknowledge them without judgment and gently redirect your attention to the present moment. Becoming distracted during practice is natural; the key is to return your attention to the present moment without self-criticism. Try a mindfulness exercise yourself.

Take Action 2.1: The Five Senses Exercise

The five senses exercise is a quick mindfulness technique that helps bring awareness to the present moment by systematically focusing on each sense (Ackerman, 2025). Start by finding a comfortable position, placing your feet flat on the ground, and taking a few breaths to settle in.

1. Focus on **sight**: Notice five things you can see, paying attention to details you might normally overlook.
2. Focus on **touch**: Identify four things you can physically feel, such as the texture of your clothing or the breeze on your skin.
3. Focus on **hearing**: Listen for three distinct sounds, which might include background noises like birds chirping or a refrigerator humming.
4. Focus on **smell**: Become aware of two scents in your environment, whether they are pleasant or unpleasant.
5. Focus on **taste**: Notice one taste, which could be a current taste in your mouth or the result of taking a small sip of a drink.

Emotion regulation techniques, such as breathing exercises or journaling, can help you process feelings in a constructive way. The primary mechanism works by directing your attention to modify emotional states. These techniques employ two main strategies:

- Distraction: This involves consciously focusing on different aspects of a situation or recalling thoughts that contradict undesirable emotional states.
- Present-moment awareness: Mindfulness practices help shift attention from ruminative thoughts to current experiences, reducing their emotional impact.

Reframing involves changing how we think about a problem or challenge by adopting different perspectives, reassessing situations to identify positive consequences, or reappraising emotional experiences themselves (Kozubal et al., 2023). Let's say, for example, that you request a meeting with your manager to discuss a difficult challenge, and she doesn't respond. You may start ruminating about why she hasn't responded: "My manager hasn't accepted my request to meet with her. I bet she's getting ready to fire me."

The first step in reframing is to identify the initial negative interpretation. The next step is to examine alternative explanations for the situation. One explanation for this example could be: "She might be very busy." The last step in reframing is choosing a more balanced or constructive perspective. You might think: "My manager hasn't accepted my request to meet with her. Her inbox must be really full after coming back from vacation."

This shift in perspective influences both emotions and behaviors. With the negative interpretation, you might feel fearful and withdraw, avoiding contacting your manager again. With the reframed perspective, you are more likely to respond constructively—in this case, by sending a gentle reminder. Note that for successful reframing, the key is not simply replacing negative words with positive ones, but genuinely considering alternative viewpoints that could be equally valid. This process requires being open to new perspectives and believing in their potential reality.

There are other practical ways to overcome self-blame. You can start by changing how you talk to yourself. People with high levels of self-compassion are kind rather than judgmental toward themselves; they acknowledge that failures are part of the human experience, and by practicing mindfulness, they accept negative emotions without allowing these emotions to define them (Neff & Tóth-Király, 2022). Finally, techniques borrowed from CBT can help you challenge negative thinking and learn healthier patterns. You can read more about CBT and how it can help in depth in Chap. 5.

Melanie Stefan, a postdoctoral researcher at the time, had a brilliant yet unconventional idea that would later spark a movement in academia (Stefan, 2010). Frustrated by the constant pressure to present a flawless image of success, she proposed creating an "alternative résumé of failures." This document would showcase all the setbacks, rejections, and unsuccessful attempts that typically remain hidden behind the polished façade of a traditional resume. Stefan's suggestion wasn't just about airing dirty laundry; she recognized that by sharing our failures, we could destigmatize setbacks, help others feel less alone in their struggles, and provide a more realistic view of an academic career.

The concept resonated deeply with many in the scientific community. Johannes Haushofer, an economist at Stockholm University, took Stefan's idea to heart. In 2016, he made his "Johannes Haushofer CV of Failures" public, detailing rejected papers, unsuccessful grant applications, and positions he didn't get (Haushofer, n.d). Haushofer's CV of Failures became an internet sensation, ironically garnering more attention than his actual academic work.

The movement initiated by Stefan and popularized by Haushofer has helped many to stop self-blaming for failure. As Stefan herself reflected years later, "Every day as a scientist involves failing in various ways, which has made me better at accepting failure and rejection as just part of the scientific process" (Soochan, 2024).

A failure resume can be a powerful tool to transform self-blame and rumination into constructive learning experiences. By documenting setbacks and analyzing them systematically, you can begin to accept failures as both commonplace and necessary for success. As you write, you convert repetitive negative thoughts into organized reflections, shifting your focus away from harmful self-criticism and toward constructive analysis. Ultimately, this practice fosters a growth mindset, helping you learn from mistakes and move forward with greater resilience and self-awareness.

Here are some tips based on insights from CBT, which you will read about in more detail in Chap. 6.

Self-Reflection 2.3: Tips for Overcoming Self-Blame

- Write down any self-blaming thought that comes to mind ("I'm useless"). Then ask yourself, "Is this me talking, or is it fear? Is this really true? What would I say if my friend said this about themselves?" Or just reframe it: "Great! Now I know what to work on . . . "
- Be sure to share responsibilities at home and work. You are not solely responsible for everything that goes wrong.
- Try to reframe absolutist thoughts, such as "I always fail," with more balanced ones, like "I made a mistake, but I also do a lot of things right." Remember that you are not alone, and everyone makes mistakes sometimes.
- Show yourself kindness and self-compassion. Notice when you are hurting, mentally or emotionally, and allow yourself to feel it without judgment. Offer supportive words to yourself, as you would to someone you love. Write yourself a letter in the third person, as if you were a good friend or a loved one (Chen, 2018).
- Practice mindfulness by spending a few minutes each day focusing on your breath or following a guided meditation. When negative thoughts pop up, picture them passing through your mind like clouds—there's no need to chase them or treat them as facts.
- Gradually start setting healthy boundaries. If you often take the blame to avoid arguments or keep others happy, learn to say, "That's not mine to fix," or "I don't think that's fair."

In sum, rumination is a maladaptive thought process that involves going over mistakes or perceived inadequacies again and again. The more we replay those negative thought cycles, the more we start seeing them as "proof" that we are not good enough. Self-blame cements this view by turning "I made a mistake" into "I am a mistake," fueling a deeper sense of personal failing. Over time, these repetitive thought loops erode self-confidence and prevent people from clearly seeing their genuine strengths or accomplishments. As self-worth diminishes, the fear of failing or being found out as incompetent can become paralyzing, leading people to question their achievements and abilities.

Self-defeating behaviors can perpetuate the cycle of maladaptive thought processes. When people feel undeserving, they may shy away from praise or public recognition, further feeding the belief that they have nothing to offer.

The worry of appearing arrogant or the conviction that they "don't really deserve it" keeps them from taking credit for their efforts. Self-blame fuels self-doubts like "I'm not ready" or "I'll fail if I try," leading to missed opportunities for advancement. Insecurity and fear of judgment can inhibit individuals from sharing ideas or speaking up, perpetuating their invisibility. When people don't apply for promotions or remain invisible in group settings, they receive little external validation. They then interpret this lack of recognition as proof that their negative thoughts are correct, which fuels more rumination and self-blame.

2.3   Become Visible, Proactive, and Take Credit

Vignette 2.3: Share Aspirations With Your Manager

A couple of years ago, one of my colleagues came to my office visibly upset. She had learned that a position that she had been hoping to be promoted to had just been advertised. Not only had her manager not approached her about a promotion, but he had not even informed her about the job posting. She said, "I'm the best person for this role and he knows it. An external hire would take years to get to know the organization as well as I do and to reach my level of competency." Her disappointment and anger led her to decide to confront her manager in a routine meeting she was supposed to have with him two hours later. I suggested that she spend the two hours thinking about how to reframe the conversation and approach her manager with a different narrative. I suggested she say, "I'm glad the position I've been waiting for has finally been advertised. I've started working on my application. All these years I've been preparing for it and now I'm going to apply with confidence since I meet all the criteria required." A couple of hours later, she came to my office again with a big smile on her face. "You wouldn't believe it ... My manager apologized because he didn't think of me straight away. He said he realized I was the best candidate because of my intimate knowledge of the organization and the quality of my work. He seemed to be upset with himself for overlooking me." My colleague received the promotion she sought, and she has been appreciated in her new role. She realized that she had failed to share her aspirations with her manager before the position was posted.

What Does It Mean to Be Visible?

In a study at a Silicon Valley technology company, 240 senior leaders were asked to name the most-critical factors for promotion to their level. At the top of the list was visibility (Correll & Mackenzie, 2016). Smith and Cheng-Cimini (2023) suggest that visibility at work means your work is not just noticed but also appreciated, and therefore your achievements are acknowledged. Visibility comes with a number of benefits. First, you become part of the information flow, which means access to more data and analytics. This helps you make more solid decisions and evaluate risks correctly. Second, you are invited to take part in interesting projects, which give you an opportunity to grow. This, in turn, increases your motivation, engagement, and positive attitude toward work because you feel included. And third, it leads to recognition in the form of informal power, promotion, or bonuses, for example, which feeds your determination and courage to become even more visible. Women find it less challenging to be visible in situations that require compassion, empathy, or other traditionally feminine skills. But, of course, that's not enough.

Women need to become visible to key decision-makers. Visibility is crucial to accessing networks of influential leaders who can recommend them for hot assignments—projects that not only stretch their capabilities but also put them in the spotlight. Direct reports often have a clear understanding and appreciation of their manager's capabilities and achievements due to frequent interactions and firsthand observations of their work's impact, but this awareness doesn't always translate upwards in the organizational hierarchy. Higher-level decision-makers, who are typically removed from day-to-day operations, may remain unaware of these accomplishments. This disconnect can significantly hinder a manager's prospects for promotion, as those with the power to advance careers may not recognize the full extent of the manager's contributions and potential. The experience of my colleague illustrates how the excellence of a manager may go unnoticed by those who make promotion decisions, effectively limiting their career progression opportunities.

Women in the workplace often expect their hard work and achievements to be noticed and rewarded without having to actively seek recognition or promotions. The term "Tiara Syndrome" was coined by Carol Frohlinger and Deborah Kolb, founders of the training and consulting firm Negotiating Women, to reflect the mindset where individuals believe that if they perform well and work diligently, their efforts will naturally be acknowledged, much like being awarded a tiara for their achievements. Carol Frohlinger states, "Women expect that if they keep doing their job well someone will notice them and place a tiara on their head. That never happens" (Seligson, 2007). Women who fall into the Tiara Syndrome trap may be overlooked for promotions and raises, as they may not advocate for themselves as strongly as their male peers, who are more likely to self-promote and negotiate for advancement. My colleague refrained from highlighting her hard work and overdelivery, assuming these efforts would naturally catch her manager's attention. This assumption, however, proved misguided, as her manager was preoccupied with numerous other responsibilities.

The questions below will help you reflect on the Tiara Syndrome.

Self-Reflection 2.4: Have You Fallen Prey to the Tiara Syndrome?

- Do you often assume that your hard work will automatically be noticed and rewarded without having to ask for recognition or a promotion?
- Are you hesitant to self-promote or highlight your achievements in professional settings, fearing it might be seen as boastful or inappropriate?
- Is your boss aware of your ambitions? When was the last time you shared your ambitions with them?
- Do you tend to take on additional tasks or responsibilities without negotiating for compensation, title changes, or other forms of acknowledgment?
- When opportunities for advancement arise, do you wait for others to encourage you to apply?
- Are you uncomfortable with negotiating salary, benefits, or role expectations, preferring to accept what's given rather than advocating for recognition of your worth?

The narrative "People should notice when I do a good job" is not as straight-forward as it sounds. We know that self-promotion is positively related to hiring and promotion prospects, as well as pay raises and the allocation of bonuses.

Why, then, do women avoid proactively seeking visibility at work? One of the reasons is that they may perceive it to be a form of self-promotion. They expect their work to be noticed and recognized, assuming that their humility will be appreciated. But humility does not mean silence. Research by Exley and Kessler (2022) suggests that there is a gender gap, with men rating their own performance 33% higher than women who perform at the same level. This gender gap is not driven by women's confidence levels. A study in the British Medical Journal (Lerchenmueller et al., 2019a, b), suggests that, compared to men, women researchers were 21% less likely to engage in self-promotion by using positive labels such as "unique," "novel," "prominent," "excellent," or "unprecedented" to describe their research, which led to less attention to those publications and consequently 13% fewer citations. Good work alone is often not enough to gain recognition; it's crucial to actively draw attention to your achievements so that others can fully appreciate your contributions and value. This gap in self-promotion closes as women rise through the ranks. The fact that women publish their research suggests that they do not lack confidence. They seem to be more concerned with how they are going to be perceived if they promote their work, as others may not perceive their contributions as so substantial that they deserve labels such as "unique," "novel," "prominent," "excellent," or "unprecedented."

You might feel morally superior to those around you who promote themselves, but there is much more at stake here. First, your achievements and recognition also reflect the accomplishments of your team. By not speaking up about your contributions, you indirectly penalize them. By avoiding sharing updates and successes, you decrease the visibility of the whole team. Second, when contributions go unacknowledged, a clear pattern of decline emerges in both individual and organizational performance, not to mention the spill-over of dissatisfaction into other areas of your life.

An effective way to promote yourself is to begin with small steps, for example, concentrating on specific subjects or giving interviews that relate to your specific business. By intentionally sharing insights about your background, the everyday challenges your company encounters, and the larger industry landscape, you can demonstrate leadership and gravitas. By talking about the real problems you are solving and focusing on the work rather than solely on yourself, you highlight your expertise and the value of your contributions without seeming overly self-serving or arrogant.

Don't underestimate the opportunity for visibility that introductions offer. Wojnicki (2022) introduces a simple framework she calls "Present, Past, Future," which could be quite effective. She suggests starting with a statement in the present tense: "Hi! I'm Aisha and I'm a program adviser. My current role is helping prospective candidates decide which program would be the best fit for their current needs."

This statement is followed by one in the past tense that outlines your background and helps you establish credibility: Why should people listen to you? This statement could include your educational credentials, accomplishments in the past, interesting projects you have run, or anything that is relevant to the current conversation.

Here's Aisha's second statement: "My background is in psychology; before joining this team, I was leading a project that explored the effectiveness of virtual training."

The final part of the introduction is future-oriented and should signal your energy and positive attitude toward the work of the group. Make sure that it is authentic, so only use words that are true: "I'm excited because the current discussion maps the opportunities in blending virtual and face-to-face training."

When Visibility Backfires: The Tall Poppy Syndrome

Indeed, there are risks for women who are visible. Women are more severely punished for excessive self-promotion than men. Take, for example, Sheryl Sandberg, former COO of Facebook (now Meta). After publishing *Lean In* in 2013, she became the face of women's ambition in tech, actively promoting her leadership philosophy through extensive media appearances, positioning herself as an expert on women's advancement in the workplace, and frequently highlighting her own success story and achievements. Her high-profile self-promotion led to significant backlash. She was labeled as out of touch with ordinary working women and faced accusations of promoting a privileged perspective.

Fielding-Singh et al. (2018) report that some women opt for the conflict-avoidant strategy of "intentional invisibility," where they tone down their assertiveness and get the job done quietly without drawing attention to themselves, resulting in being liked but underappreciated. The researchers found that women were concerned that visibility would leave them worse off and result in a backlash, as they would be perceived as violating gender norms. The second motive driving intentional invisibility was that increasing visibility is often perceived as self-promoting, which comes across as self-serving. Women in this study sacrificed visibility for behind-the-scenes work, which felt more authentic to them. This approach helped them cope with family pressures as well, as it allowed them to avoid conflicts with partners at home.

The Tall Poppy Syndrome provides another example of how visibility can backfire. This is a social phenomenon where people are criticized, resented, or attacked because of their success or achievements. When successful women are ignored, excluded, silenced, undermined, devalued by having their capabilities downplayed, or gossiped about, a toxic culture is created where they cannot thrive.

The Tallest Poppy Study, conducted by Women of Influence+ (2023), reveals a disturbing pattern of workplace behavior affecting successful women globally. In a comprehensive survey of 4710 women across 103 countries, an overwhelming majority of respondents (86.8%) reported experiencing hostility or penalties due to their professional success and achievements. This phenomenon has significant personal and professional consequences, with 85.6% of women reporting increased stress levels and 73.8% noting negative impacts on their mental health. Two-thirds of respondents suffered from diminished self-confidence.

The professional ramifications are equally concerning. Three-quarters of the women surveyed experienced reduced productivity, while half of them ultimately left their positions due to these experiences. The study also revealed a troubling pattern of career self-limitation, with just over half of the respondents (50.4%) becoming less likely to pursue promotions and 60.5% expressing fear of penalties for displaying ambition.

The hostile behavior came from multiple directions within organizational hierarchies, with male leaders and executives identified as the primary aggressors. However, the researchers found that both male and female colleagues, as well as clients and suppliers, engaged in undermining behaviors. These actions typically manifested as exclusion, microaggressions, achievement minimization, and gaslighting. The study identified several key contributing factors, with jealousy and envy (77.5%) topping the list, followed by sexism and gender stereotypes (74%), personal insecurity (72.7%), organizational culture (62.8%), and competitiveness (55.8%).

Research by Russell Reynolds Associates (Langton et al., 2024) indicates that men tend to remain in CEO positions longer than women. In 2023, the average tenure for female CEOs worldwide was 4.1 years, whereas male CEOs averaged 8.7 years in their roles. What might explain this difference in tenure? The metaphor of tall poppies getting cut down for standing out accurately describes what often happens to women who achieve success, prominence, or high status: they are criticized, resented, or attacked by others. It's not a surprise, then, that women tend to shy away from self-promotion, fearing they will be judged for showing off. As Laura Sanderson, UK lead at Russell Reynolds Associates, points out, " . . . women CEOs are penalized more severely than men . . . for any perceived hubris or limelight seeking."

The Tall Poppy Syndrome and the research on "intentional invisibility" remind us that organizations have a role to play. Rather than placing the burden solely on women, organizations could reframe visibility not as standing in the spotlight alone but as creating meaningful impact and connections that naturally increase recognition and influence within the organization.

Have you experienced the Tall Poppy Syndrome in your career? Reflect on the questions below.

Self-Reflection 2.5: The Tall Poppy Syndrome

- How often do you let someone else have the spotlight, while feeling that your contributions have not been recognized?
- How many times have you let an opportunity for a promotion pass you by because you thought that you were not ready for certain aspects of the new job?
- If your direct reports were asked whether you delegate enough, how would they respond?
- When was the last time you asked for a pay raise?
- How good are you at establishing boundaries, for example, saying "no" without being hugely apologetic, or refusing to do yet another piece of work pro bono?
- What is your online visibility?
- What do you do to become more visible in your network? How are you utilizing your allies to help increase your visibility?
- How comfortable are you with speaking up in professional settings?

Building a Personal Brand

As we discussed, visibility is crucial for career advancement, and one of the most effective ways to enhance your professional visibility is through developing a strong personal brand. A personal brand represents more than just reputation. It is a deliberately crafted professional identity that communicates who you are and what you stand for in the workplace. While everyone naturally develops a reputation through their actions and behaviors, a personal brand emerges from conscious decisions about how you want to be perceived and the values you choose to represent.

Personal brand is not about creating a polished façade, but rather about presenting the most focused version of your authentic professional self. This means aligning your intentions with your actions to influence how others perceive you in your professional sphere. The key distinction lies in intentionality. Your personal brand should reflect your genuine professional identity while strategically positioning your unique characteristics and value proposition to your target audience. It's about making your expertise visible and memorable in a way that differentiates you from others in your field. When done effectively, your personal brand becomes the foundation for how the world sees, understands, and values your professional contribution.

When you think about your personal brand, it might be helpful to gain clarity about your life narrative. You have gone through different experiences. How are they connected? Is there a theme that emerges, one that weaves together the different areas of your life?

Vignette 2.4: Lena

During one of my programs, I had a conversation with Lena, who was trying to develop her personal brand. We started by talking about her childhood, and she described the warmth of family reunions and community potlucks. She recounted how she often took the lead in organizing these gatherings, even as a young girl. Lena's expression turned thoughtful as she recalled a challenging period when she moved to a new school and felt isolated. Then she remembered how she created a "new student welcome committee," realizing this long-ago event ignited her passion for bringing people together. As she continued her story, Lena talked about majoring in Communication, interning at a nonprofit managing social media, and joining a tech startup where she quickly rose to lead community engagement efforts. She then shared a more recent, personal experience. After her partner lost his job, she organized a skill-sharing network in their neighborhood. She explained how this initiative not only helped her family but also strengthened their community. Then we spoke about her current role as a marketing executive at a food-processing company known for innovative, community-focused campaigns. At that point, I asked her, "Is there a theme running through all of these experiences?" After a brief silence, Lena realized how she'd always been drawn to bringing people together and creating engaging experiences—this theme of community building and creative communication was woven through her entire life. The following day, Lena shared with me her personal brand: "I create experiences that connect and engage people."

The Red Sneakers Effect

Imagine walking into a high-powered business meeting of a company in the luxury industry. You're surrounded by executives in crisp suits and polished shoes, but there's one person who stands out—the CEO of a major company, casually dressed in a hoodie, jeans, and bright red sneakers. Instead of being dismissed, this person commands the room's attention and respect. Welcome to the fascinating world of the Red Sneakers Effect.

This intriguing phenomenon was discovered by a team of researchers led by Bellezza (2014), who noticed that sometimes breaking the rules can boost your status. It's not about being rebellious just for the sake of it, though. The key lies in the deliberate choice to deviate from the norm, especially when you're in a position where you could easily conform if you wanted to. We often assume that, to be taken seriously, we need to follow all the rules and fit in. But the Red Sneakers Effect turns this idea on its head. It suggests that sometimes, a carefully chosen act of nonconformity, such as a nonconforming appearance or Power-Point template, can make you appear more confident, competent, and even more powerful.

Of course, context matters. Showing up to your first day at a conservative law firm in flip-flops probably won't win you any favors. The effect works best when you already have some status or when people know that you are familiar with the expected norms. It's about showing that you're secure enough in your position to bend the rules a little. So, next time you are getting ready for an important meeting or event, don't be afraid to be yourself and show your authentic self.

Speaking Up in Meetings

When women speak up more frequently than their colleagues, they often face negative reactions—another example of double standards. This unfavorable response occurs regardless of whether the observers are men or women. Both men and women tend to view talkative women critically, potentially leading to professional setbacks. Brescoll (2012) asked 206 participants to imagine themselves as either the most senior figure or the most junior figure in a meeting, and then asked how much they would talk. Men who pictured themselves in the senior role said they would speak more, while men who imagined themselves in the junior role expected to speak less. However, women who envisioned themselves in a senior position said they would talk just as much as those who saw themselves in a junior role. When asked why, they explained that they didn't want to be disliked or appear too assertive.

Given these reactions, it's not surprising if you are concerned that proposing an idea that is not well thought through might be perceived as foolish by more senior people. You might be held back by concerns that you could feel embarrassed by others' reactions, or even worse, criticized for wasting precious time. The current virtual culture makes it even harder to be noticed and heard and effectively communicate your ideas, as it's difficult to read facial expressions on the screen.

Speaking up in meetings, however, is crucial because it allows women to showcase their skills, knowledge, and leadership abilities. This visibility helps with their career advancement and the building of credibility. By contributing to discussions, women shape outcomes that directly affect them and the organization. Regularly voicing ideas is a useful tool to project self-assurance. This not only raises the profile of women in the workplace but also encourages others to see them as key contributors and leaders.

Actively participating in meetings and speaking up can definitely increase your visibility, but it might require a shift in your mindset (Besieux et al., 2021). For example, you can reframe "My idea may be incomplete" to "My idea could provide a breakthrough on this problem we've been dealing with for months." Thinking of your idea as the first link in a chain that will ultimately lead to a solution might liberate you from self-censoring.

The second reframing, from "It's probably not my place to speak up" to "Silence is not in the best interest of the team," emphasizes the personal role we all play in teams. The major idea behind working in teams is to encourage open interactions between people with diverse backgrounds to maximize the probability that a team member will make a contribution that will ultimately lead to the solution. At the core of team philosophy is the idea that no one has the perfect answer. Team synergy, building on each other's ideas, will lead to the best solution.

The third reframing is from "I want to sound intelligent" to "This is really about the collective intelligence of my team so we can all succeed." You also increase your visibility when you share your reactions to what others say.

Women may choose to remain invisible because of the perfection trap and a fear of making mistakes. And when groups meet, some women go to great lengths to avoid attention. Often, women are reluctant to speak up in meetings and wait until they think they have something really relevant and important to share, as you read about Fabiana's reluctance to share her ideas in the opening vignette. By doing so, they fail to be part of an important process at the beginning of a group's life. When group members first meet, they unconsciously ascribe status based on the extent to which each group member contributes to the achievement of the group's goal. Speaking up, taking initiative (e.g., summarizing the data, writing on the board, etc.), or even just asking a question that stimulates the conversation are "competence cues," which signal leadership potential since those behaviors are associated with being proactive.

Research suggests that anyone can achieve higher status on a team, both at the outset and over time, by shifting their mindset before a first meeting. A study by Galinsky and Kilduff (2013) suggests that we can become more proactive by priming ourselves before the first encounter with a group. For example, remind yourself of a situation when you felt you had power: What did it feel like? Can you visualize it? What were your thoughts? What kind of feedback did you receive afterward? This study provides impressive evidence that those changes in thoughts and feelings can set us up for leadership and impact. Being proactive as the group is forming is essential since status is ascribed early, and group members who achieve high status early are likely to retain it.

Time and time again, participants in the *Strategy for Leadership Program* have told me that they keep silent in meetings because they don't want to be perceived as usurping precious time. This is a legitimate reason to be silent. The question is: do we always need to have an earth-shattering idea, comment, or thought to participate? Sometimes, a question can accelerate a discussion or take it in a very fruitful direction.

Take Action 2.2: Who Speaks and How Much in Meetings

1. The next time you're in a meeting, observe how others participate: How many participants offer groundbreaking ideas or thoughts, and how many contribute with small questions, build on what others have said, acknowledge the contributions of others, clarify, provide a summary, and so on? What the group wants to see is the willingness to contribute and consistent input, even if each contribution is small, for example, asking clarifying questions or offering brief observations that move the discussion forward.
2. Make a decision to speak up—maybe not as the first person, but as the second or third.
3. Avoid unhelpful, self-deprecating openings like, "This is not my area of expertise, but..." Such self-deprecating comments can contribute to a negative impression.
4. If the first meeting for a new project or the first interaction with a group of people makes you reluctant to speak up, follow Galinsky and Kilduff's advice to reframe by thinking about a situation where you perceived yourself as powerful and successful. Write down your feelings, images, and thoughts.

2.4   Communication Pitfalls

You are sitting in a crucial meeting, armed with brilliant ideas that could revolutionize your company's approach. You open your mouth to speak, and you hear yourself saying: "...I'm sorry, but I was just wondering if maybe we could possibly consider..." Sound familiar? If you're wincing in recognition, you're not alone. As women, we often find ourselves caught in a web of communication habits that can feel like quicksand, pulling us down just when we need to stand tall. It's not that we lack ideas or ambition, far from it. Shaped by societal expectations and ingrained habits, sometimes women unknowingly adopt communication styles that undermine their authority, dilute their messages, and diminish their impact. Linguistic choices that might seem innocuous can erode perceived confidence and credibility. Ineffective communication patterns are some of the most pervasive yet overlooked self-defeating behaviors. Next, we'll look at gender differences in communication, including the use of tentative speech forms, overusing "I" statements, using the promotive and prohibitive voice, apologizing, and using humor.

Powerless Speech Styles: Tentative and Indecisive Language

Sociolinguist Robin Lakoff is widely recognized as the pioneer of gender differences in language use, particularly regarding tentative speech forms. In her influential book *Language and Woman's Place*, Lakoff (1975) introduced the concept of "women's language" and discussed linguistic features that she observed were more commonly used by women. Lakoff proposed that women are more likely than men to use tentative speech forms, including hedges (e.g., "sort of," "kind of"); qualifiers or disclaimers (e.g., "I'm not sure, but . . . "); tag questions (e.g., "isn't it?"); and intensifiers (e.g., "so," "very").

Lakoff argued that women use these forms to express uncertainty, avoid assertiveness, and maintain a more "feminine" communication style. This type of communication, however, signals insecurity and a lack of confidence. It is impaired by wordiness, is more difficult to comprehend, and does not command respect. Powerless speech styles should be avoided in formal contexts, high-stakes situations like job interviews, or when making important presentations where credibility and authority are crucial. However, these speech styles can be strategically effective in specific contexts when your goal is to appear collaborative rather than dominant. For example, you can use qualifiers to make statements less abrasive and more inviting, or in a context where warmth and likability are more important than perceived competence. Table 2.1 illustrates the difference between the two styles.

Another language choice that undermines women's status and authority is the use of "indecisive I" statements. Communication consultant and author of numerous books on communication, Phyllis Mindell, argues that starting sentences with "I" when not actually talking about yourself can unnecessarily shift the focus of the sentence to the speaker (Mindell, 2001). It can also imply that the speaker is responsible for problems that aren't theirs or make the speaker appear uncertain or childlike. For example, Tima, a project manager, needs to address delays in her team's work due to a colleague who consistently misses deadlines. Tima would be using an "indecisive I"

Table 2.1 Contrasting powerless and powerful speech

Powerless speech	Powerful speech
Hi! You said you wanted us to talk. Did you want to discuss something?	Hi! You said you wanted us to talk. What's the issue?
I've been alright, just a bit overwhelmed with everything going on, *you know*?	I've been managing, thanks for asking
So, about the team meeting yesterday, it seemed a *little* tense, didn't it? *I wonder if we could perhaps* talk about it?	Regarding the team meeting yesterday, it was quite tense
Well, I think one *of the kinds of* problems is that not everyone is on the same page about the project goals.	One major issue is the lack of alignment on project goals
Could you please do me a favor? *Do you think you could maybe* talk to everyone and see if we can get a consensus?	We need to talk to everyone and establish a consensus
I'm not entirely sure, but *I think* we *really* need to clarify our objectives. *I don't want to step on anyone's toes*, but could you ask why we haven't had a clear direction set yet?	We need to clarify our objectives immediately. Why haven't we set a clear direction yet?
It seems like we need a meeting to sort this out. *Would it be possible for you to maybe* arrange a meeting with the team to discuss our goals?	We need a meeting to resolve this. Please arrange a team meeting to discuss our goals

communication if she said: "I have a concern about our project timeline. I think we're falling behind because I feel John isn't meeting his deadlines." A more effective approach would be to avoid inserting herself into the statement, clearly identifying the issue and its cause without appearing uncertain: "Our project timeline is at risk. The delays are occurring because John isn't meeting his deadlines." Avoiding the "indecisive I" can make the communication more direct and assertive, improving how Tima's concerns are perceived and addressed in a professional setting.

When presenting ideas for change, you can use two different voices (McClean et al., 2018): the promotive voice and the prohibitive voice. The promotive voice sounds more like powerful speech. It is forward-looking and provides positive ideas for improvement, for example, "We could enhance our campaign's reach by integrating more social media platforms." The prohibitive voice identifies current problems or practices that should be stopped, for example, "Our current strategy isn't reaching our target demographic effectively." Research shows that women benefit from framing their ideas more promotively, focusing on future solutions rather than current problems (McClean et al., 2018).

Dominance and Abstraction in Language

The words leaders use impact the perception of their effectiveness. A study by psychologist Dupree (2024) specifically examined the impact of dominant language, defined as words and phrases that convey power, authority, and confidence. Examples of dominant language include terms like "demand," "control," "direct," "assert," "fight," "lead," and so on. For instance, a leader using dominant language might say, "I demand immediate action on this issue" or "We must take control of the situation."

In contrast, nondominant language tends to use words and phrases that are more collaborative and inclusive. The same messages using nondominant language might be phrased as, "I suggest we consider taking action on this issue soon" or "Perhaps we could work together to address this situation." The researchers analyzed the frequency of dominant language words and phrases in political leaders' speeches and social media posts to quantify and compare the prevalence of dominant language across different demographic groups of leaders. This distinction between dominant and nondominant language use revealed the ways in which leaders' communication styles potentially affect perceptions of their leadership.

Interestingly, the study found that white women leaders tend to use more dominant language than their male counterparts, possibly to counter stereotypes that portray them as too submissive for leadership roles. However, this pattern wasn't observed among Black women and Latina leaders, who may be more cautious due to a greater fear of backlash. The consequences of using dominant language varied depending on the leader's race and gender. For instance, media portrayals of women leaders, particularly Black women and Latinas, were more likely to describe them as dominant but cold when they used assertive language. In a simulated social media experiment (Dupree, 2024), constituents rated women leaders, especially Black women, as less likable when they used dominant language, while men of any racial background faced no such penalty. These findings highlight that the effects of dominant language and gender are not uniform across racial groups.

Research indicates that there are gender differences in how entrepreneurs pitch their ventures, with women using less abstract language compared to men (Huang et al., 2021). Concrete language refers to things we can see, touch, or experience directly, while abstract language deals with ideas and concepts like "solution" or "strategic vision." Investors are more likely to back ventures when entrepreneurs present their ideas in abstract rather than concrete terms, as they see this as a sign of the business's potential for growth and expansion. This preference for abstract communication contributes to the gender disparity in entrepreneurial investment, as women's pitches, with more concrete language, make them less likely to attract investment.

Linguistic Gender Stereotypes: Apologizing and Using Humor

Women face different communication-related stereotypes at work that create challenges, particularly when they are in leadership roles. For example, if they adopt more assertive communication styles, they risk being perceived as less warm and likable and more aggressive or unfeminine. On the other hand, when women downplay their contributions or employ hedging language to soften their assertions, they risk being labeled as indecisive and lacking confidence. This double bind extends to both apologizing and using humor. Women are 37% more likely to offer apologies than men, and they also claim to have committed more offenses (Schumann & Ross, 2010). While humor can be a powerful tool for leadership, it's not easy to defy the stereotype that "women aren't funny" (Miron-Spektor et al., 2023).

Let's first focus on apologizing. It appears that men apologize less frequently than women because their threshold for what is considered offensive behavior is higher (Schumann & Ross, 2010). Apologizing often undermines others' perception of your status. Related to the use of tentative speech forms, traditional gender norms and stereotypes dictate that women should be more apologetic and accommodating in their communication style. However, recent research provides a counterintuitive finding that challenges these assumptions.

Apologies that contradict gender stereotypes are perceived to be more effective (Polin et al., 2023). When women use language in their apologies associated with assertiveness and action, they counteract gender stereotypes and increase the effectiveness of their apologies. For example, this could involve providing a clear explanation for the incident and suggesting concrete steps to address the underlying issue. This approach is linked to perceptions of competence and credibility, signaling that the apologizer is capable of addressing and resolving the problem. Instead of conforming to gender norms, which emphasize empathy and emotional understanding, women are more successful when providing apologies that clearly outline their understanding of the issue and their commitment to resolving it.

While genuine apologies can repair relationships and demonstrate emotional intelligence, over-apologizing can send the message that we lack confidence, thereby signaling submission to the listener. Apologizing, especially when you are not at fault, can reinforce a perceived imbalance in which others have more social power.

The stereotype that women lack humor remains remarkably persistent. Some even consider humor to be risky for women, as it may lower the perception of the woman's competence and status. A recent study (Evans et al., 2019) asked participants to watch a video of a store manager named Sam giving a presentation about store performance to regional managers. Before watching, participants read Sam's resume, which showed they were a successful manager with one year of experience running a clothing store. Half the participants saw a video of Sam as a male manager using humor in the presentation, while the other half saw Sam as a female manager using the exact same humor. After watching, participants were asked to rate how disruptive or helpful they found the manager's use of humor during the presentation. The results suggest that when a man and a woman crack jokes in a situation framed as a recruitment interview, their humor is received differently. When the man uses humor, it's more likely to be seen as a behavior that is beneficial to the work environment. One explanation could be that the people in the audience experience the humor as lightening the mood and helping everyone relax. But if a woman were to use the same humor, it's more likely to be perceived as disruptive and inappropriate because it distracts from serious conversation and signals lower commitment. People might even think of the joke as compensation for her lack of experience. As a result, humor could boost the status of men in the workplace and contribute to a view of them as more confident and leadership-material. On the other hand, women's use of humor might lower their status. Women might be perceived as less professional and less capable of leadership roles. Needless to say, these perceptions around who can use humor can have real consequences when it comes to performance evaluations and considerations for promotions or leadership positions.

Sociolinguist Judith Baxter explored how humor is perceived and used in the workplace (Boffey, 2012). She considered humor to be just another resource for leadership. Her research highlights significant disparities in how humor is received in corporate environments, particularly between men and women. Her 18-month study analyzed the speech patterns of men and women in meetings across seven major companies, revealing that over 80% of women's jokes were met with silence, while about 90% of men's jokes elicited laughter. Baxter observed that men often engage in flippant banter and off-the-cuff humor that was well-received and reinforced their leadership roles. Male executives, for example, would use a joke or a sequence of witticisms to banter with a difficult colleague. In contrast, women executives would use the safe option of self-deprecating jokes, mocking themselves instead of mocking others. The self-deprecating approach used by women came across as defensive or even awkward, leading to less favorable reactions. This difference may stem from cultural traditions and gender stereotypes that position men as the jokesters on a stage, while women are expected to assume the supportive role of the audience. Consequently, men are generally more comfortable laughing at their peers, unless those peers are women. The hierarchical nature of corporate boards can further contribute to the differential reception of women's and men's use of humor. Laughter often reflects power dynamics; if women are perceived as lower in the hierarchy, their humor may not receive the same acknowledgment as that of their male counterparts.

The picture is more nuanced when looking at humor used by high-level women, to whom the audience already ascribes expertise, for example, women who are delivering a TED talk. To explore the impact of humor in such presentations, one study analyzed 2407 TED talks and found that using humor increased the speakers' influence, especially for women (Miron-Spektor et al., 2023). Influence was measured by the number of views, how inspiring the talk was (based on audience ratings of persuasiveness and inspiration), and the perceived leadership qualities of the speaker (trained coders rated the perceived leadership, warmth, and competence of the speakers). In the same study, a deeper analysis of 92 highly influential social science talks showed that speakers who used humor were perceived as warm and competent, regardless of the type of humor they used. This research suggests that humor can be beneficial for women in high-status positions and may help them overcome gender stereotypes. The research also highlights humor as a powerful tool for increasing women's influence and delivering successful presentations in the digital age.

Self-Reflection 2.6: Power in Language

- What would members of your team say about the extent to which you use hedges, disclaimers, or tag endings?
- How do you avoid the "indecisive I"?
- Which voice—promotive or prohibitive—dominates your speech?
- To what extent do you use dominant language? Have you experienced any backlash?
- When you pitch, is your language more concrete or abstract?
- In what ways does over-apologizing influence your self-esteem and confidence in both personal and professional settings?

- How can you reframe your language to convey assertiveness instead of resorting to unnecessary apologies? For example, using "thank you" instead of "sorry," or focusing on solutions rather than apologies.
- How do you typically incorporate humor into your professional environment? What positive outcomes and potential drawbacks have you encountered when using humor in the workplace?
- How would you describe the effect of your sense of humor on your workplace interactions and professional reputation? In what ways can humor strengthen or weaken your relationships with colleagues and supervisors?
- Which aspects of humor do you admire most in your professional role models? How can you adapt and incorporate those elements into your own interactions to enhance your effectiveness at work?

2.5   Be Careful With the Menial Tasks at Work

Vignette 2.5: Lola

Lola is a seasoned executive who leads strategic initiatives, manages budgets, and navigates high-level negotiations with ease. Yet, she has been repeatedly asked to select the venue for offsite meetings, which she accepted. It's a small, practical gesture, one that might come from a place of efficiency or even courtesy. However, when such tasks repeatedly fall to her simply because she is a woman, even if she is more likely to accept them, it becomes a subtle yet powerful way of undercutting her authority. The time Lola spends planning company events adds more to her plate, leaving her less time and energy to prepare for board meetings and think deeply about company strategy. There is a cluster of self-defeating patterns around taking on minor responsibilities, which can negatively impact visibility, status, and ultimately stall women's career momentum.

Who Does the Office "Housework?"

Many studies have found that there are gender differences in how work is allocated (De Pater et al., 2010), with women spending more time on nonpromotable tasks than their male colleagues. Sociologist Rosabeth Moss Kanter coined the term "office housework" to describe a subset of nonpromotable tasks that, while necessary for the smooth operation of the organization, are undervalued, often unrecognized, and unlikely to drive revenue. Office housework is invisible because these small, day-to-day tasks often fly under the radar, as they may not appear in job descriptions or performance metrics in a clear, quantifiable way.

Nonpromotable tasks include administrative tasks, such as planning meetings or serving on low-ranking committees (Williams, 2014) that help the team as a whole but don't benefit careers (Grant & Sandberg, 2015); menial or boring jobs that do not require special skills, such as ordering lunch for the team, buying presents for guest speakers, or cards for colleagues to sign; or undervalued assignments, such as organizing office celebrations and mentoring junior employees. What all of these tasks have in common is that everyone should be taking them on, but everyone hopes they will be performed by someone else.

A study in the American Economic Review explored gender differences in accepting and receiving requests for tasks with low promotability (Babcock et al., 2017). Compared to men, women were 48% more likely to volunteer to perform such tasks. The research design ruled out gender-biased explanations, such as the idea that women are better at the task or enjoy it more than men, or that women are altruistic, agreeable, and risk-averse. The real driver of this behavior was the unspoken expectation that women should volunteer more. The same study found that women were 44% more likely than men to be asked to volunteer. Notably, both women and men were equally likely to ask a woman to volunteer rather than a man. Women were also more likely to accept these requests—76% of the time compared to 51% for men. The consequences of taking on these tasks could be substantial (Babcock et al., 2022). When women spend time and effort on dead-end tasks, they have less time and fewer resources to focus on more challenging requests and initiatives that could provide them with visibility and eventually lead to promotions. The researchers estimated that this type of dead-end work for a typical woman employed in a consulting firm, for example, amounted to about 200 h per year, or almost one month.

Why do these tasks disproportionately fall on women? As you read in Chap. 1, in society, we hold gender stereotypes about the kinds of emotions, behaviors, or jobs that are better suited to women and men. Women, for example, are expected to be community-oriented, in other words, caring, approachable, friendly, warm, and supportive. Therefore, compared to men, they are expected to demonstrate more pro-social behaviors (Eagly, 2009). Men, on the other hand, are expected to be assertive, confident, proactive, and in control of the situation. These gender-based stereotypes underlie societal ideas about the division of labor: women should assume supportive, care-giving roles, while men are better suited to leadership roles.

Since office housework is associated with taking care of others rather than taking charge, the unconscious assumption is that it should be performed by women rather than men. Women internalize the expectation that they should volunteer and agree when asked to do prosocial work. They also know that if they do not agree to take on the task, they may face backlash as a result of violating the gender stereotype. Women who refuse to perform office housework often receive fewer recommendations for promotions, and their likability among peers significantly decreases. This backlash effect is a powerful mechanism that reinforces and sustains restrictive gender stereotypes: women who violate gender expectations by being assertive or declining communal tasks are often seen as competent, yet less likable and less deserving of respect.

There is empirical evidence that these expectations lead to different standards for men and women. Women, for example, are held to a higher standard for prosocial behavior. Even worse, there is an unquestioned assumption that tasks involving prosocial behaviors are a part of their job. When men perform the same level of prosocial behavior, they are viewed as taking on an extra task, and this leads to better career outcomes for them. In this way, the relationship between office housework and promotion is positive for men but negative for women (Jang et al., 2021). Needless to say, if women are expected to spend a significant amount of time on nonpromotable tasks, they will progress more slowly in their careers.

A recent study concludes that women often take on menial tasks to keep their male colleagues happy (Koppman et al., 2022). Over the last few decades, women have made significant inroads into many previously male-dominated fields. For example, male engineers increasingly have their work managed and sold by women in management and sales positions. Imagine an advertising agency where the men typically handle creative roles, such as designing and writing copy, while the women are account managers, coordinating with clients. Even though these two groups need each other to get the work done, they are on the same level organizationally, which often leads to clashes over who is in charge or whose priorities come first. Normally, a clear chain of command would settle these disagreements, but when everyone is technically equal, the situation becomes trickier.

According to Koppman et al. (2022), many women in these account manager roles resort to reinforcing traditional gender stereotypes to smooth things over. For example, a woman might bring a sandwich or coffee to her male counterpart to show she cares and subtly encourage him to speed up her project. This gesture resembles playing a "mother" or "cheerleader" role: doing something nurturing to earn goodwill.

The immediate payoff is that the men respond positively, feeling respected and appreciated, which helps move the work along. But in the long run, this approach sets up a hidden hierarchy where women are doing extra emotional or domestic "labor," ultimately putting them at a disadvantage. It reinforces the idea that women's function in the workplace is to "take care of" their male colleagues, undermining their authority and chipping away at the status of women's roles, even when they are at the same level.

In many companies, women of color are allocated an even larger share of the nonpromotable tasks. Ironically, some of the requests related to inclusion place additional burdens on women, especially women of color. For example, I was running a program with a company in a very male-dominated industry, where only 30% of the managerial positions were held by women. The new CEO was serious about changing the organizational culture. Among other initiatives, he requested that women be represented in all internal committees, panels, and decision-making groups. Although his initiative was well-meaning, it had some unintended consequences. To achieve representation, women had to attend multiple committees and meetings, which led to spending significant amounts of time on tasks that were not part of their job, did not contribute to their personal growth, and, as a result, were unmotivating. Women of color experienced an even heavier burden, as they were much more underrepresented in the company than white women.

How would you respond to requests for thankless tasks? Reflect on the questions below to help you make a decision.

Self-Reflection 2.7: Responding to Requests for Menial Tasks

- How much visibility does the task provide you?
- To what extent will the task allow you to use or further develop your skills?
- How likely is it that your performance on the task will be noticed and rewarded by your manager?
- To what extent might working on the task be beneficial in terms of expanding your network?
- How big is the risk of being perceived as a nonteam player if you say no? What might the consequences be?
- What do your trusted advisers and mentors suggest?
- What is the trade-off? How can you turn the request into a negotiation? What is it that you won't have time for if you work on the task (e.g., no time to participate in a training that would lead to an important certification)?
- Do you track the hours you spend on nonpromotable tasks to use as evidence when discussing the matter with your manager?

- Do you often volunteer to do office housework? What makes it difficult for you to say no?
- As a manager, do you expect women team members to perform prosocial behaviors as part of their job?
- As a manager, do you distribute nonpromotable tasks equitably? Some simple techniques, like rotation or drawing straws when allocating office housework, signal equitable treatment.
- Are your male direct reports disproportionately rewarded when they engage in office housework, while your female direct reports are undervalued when they complete the same tasks?

The invisible office housework that benefits organizations persists across different industries, types of organizations, and hierarchies within companies. As long as executives consciously or unconsciously adhere to gender stereotypes that it's predominantly the role of women to engage in community-building and prosocial behavior, we'll witness the inequitable allocation of nonpromotable tasks. This contributes to underutilizing the skills and talents of women in two ways. First, when women are loaded down with nonrevenue generating tasks, their true potential is underutilized. Second, when women regularly perform or are expected to perform menial tasks, they become demotivated, their performance declines, and they may even decide to leave the company, taking their experience and expertise elsewhere. While this problem should be addressed at the organizational level, women can regain control of their time by setting boundaries.

Setting Boundaries: Saying "No"

Vignette 2.6: Saying No

In 2010, four professors in the United States—Laurie Weingart, Lise Vesterlund, Linda Babcock, and Brenda Peyser—started meeting on a regular basis at a restaurant in Pittsburgh to discuss how disappointing it was that much of their time at work was spent on tasks that were not meaningful to them (Babcock et al., 2022). They felt overwhelmed and wanted to take back control over their work lives. Their objective was to strengthen the "no muscle." Any additional work to be taken on had to be balanced by giving up something else. The four professors helped each other prioritize and craft the perfect no-message in a way that would not lead to backlash.

Given the four professors' quest to rebalance their work lives, you might conclude that women should push back and just say "no" to these unrewarded tasks. Unfortunately, this reaction is often followed by backlash. For example, women may face worse performance evaluations, fewer recommendations for promotions, career advancement obstacles, or risk being branded as "difficult," "always complaining," and "selfish." To avoid the backlash, it's important to carefully craft the "no" message. It should raise awareness of the underlying stereotype but also point to a possible solution. Here's an example of how you might turn down a request to work on a nonpromotable task:

"I really appreciate your considering me capable of supporting our team in various ways. I value being a part of this team, and I am always eager to contribute to our shared goals.

However, after giving it much thought, I feel that these tasks might not be the best use of my time and skills, especially considering my current projects and priorities. My concern is that these additional responsibilities might divert my focus from the data analytics project I'm working on, where I believe I can add the most value and drive results for our team.

I am fully committed to our team's success and am more than willing to take on additional tasks when necessary. However, I think it would be beneficial for us to explore ways to distribute these types of tasks more evenly among the team or perhaps identify someone whose skills are better aligned with these requirements. Let me think who might be best suited to help."

Saying "no" effectively in professional settings is a crucial skill that can help set boundaries and increase productivity, but it may be a challenge for many women. As Jane Fonda reflects, "It took me until 60 to discover that 'No' is a complete sentence" (Bosworth, 2011). We often have this concern that we might be perceived as self-centered or stubborn, that the person asking might feel rejected or interpret it as an act of hostility, disloyalty, or disrespect. Joseph Grenny, cofounder of Crucial Learning (2019, pp. 2–5), provides some guidelines for saying "no" in general:

- When you talk to your manager, don't simply say "no." Share your logic and values behind your decision; otherwise, your manager will have to guess what is behind it.
- Acknowledge that others have good reasons for their positions.
- Be confident when communicating, and at the same time, avoid absolute statements such as "The only sensible conclusion is . . . ." Language like "I believe . . . " is much more appropriate.

- When saying "no" to upper management, show respect for their position and share your thinking behind the reason for saying "no." For example: "As my manager, you have asked me to analyze the market for our new product. I gave it some thought, and I have some reservations that I would like to share with you. If you think, however, that those are irrelevant, I'll start working on the analysis. How would you like us to proceed?"

Take Action 2.3: Saying "No"

Choose one day this week to say "no" to all nonessential requests from people around you. There's no need to apologize or explain your behavior. It's their right to ask, and it's your right to say "no." You will discover that saying "no" won't be the end of the world and that you'll have more time and energy for more meaningful work.

Women often find themselves taking on a bigger share of menial tasks at work—things that keep the wheels turning but don't necessarily lead to recognition or career growth. Part of the problem is that these tasks are often expected of women, but it's also true that many women feel pressured to say yes or step in to help. While these contributions are valuable and can help expand your network, they can come at the cost of focusing on more high-profile opportunities. Finding a better balance means not only changing expectations in the workplace but also reminding ourselves to prioritize our own growth and set boundaries when needed.

Breaking free from self-defeating behaviors can be one of the most liberating steps you take in your career. By becoming more visible and proactive and by claiming credit for your contributions, you ensure your hard work doesn't go unnoticed. Overcoming communication pitfalls and silencing the cycle of rumination and self-blame allow you to face challenges with clarity and confidence. Learning to say no to tasks that don't serve your growth may feel uncomfortable at first, but these changes lay the groundwork for self-respect, agency, and lasting resilience in the workplace. By acknowledging and addressing these internal barriers, we can better equip ourselves to navigate difficult conversations. Whether it's delivering bad news, providing feedback, or negotiating salary, transforming challenging discussions into opportunities requires a combination of self-awareness and strategic communication skills.

References

Ackerman, C. E. (2025, March 25). *21 mindfulness exercises and activities for adults.* PositivePsychology.com. https://positivepsychology.com/mindfulness-exercises-techniques-activities/

Babcock, L., Peyser, B., Vesterlund, L., & Weingart, L. (2022). *The no club: Putting a stop to women's dead-end work.* Simon and Schuster.

Babcock, L., Recalde, M. P., Vesterlund, L., & Weingart, L. (2017). Gender differences in accepting and receiving requests for tasks with low promotability. *American Economic Review, 107*(3), 714–747.

Bellezza, S., Gino, F., & Keinan, A. (2014). The red sneakers effect: Inferring status and competence from signals of nonconformity. *Journal of Consumer Research, 41* (1), 35–54.

Besieux, T., Edmondson, A. C., & de Vries, F. (2021, June 11). How to overcome your fear of speaking up in meetings. *Harvard Business Review.* https://hbr.org/2021/06/how-to-overcome-your-fear-of-speaking-up-in-meetings

Boffey, D., (2012, May 19). Why women's jokes fall flat in the boardroom. *The Guardian.* https://www.theguardian.com/money/2012/may/20/boardroom-humour-women

Bosworth, P. (2011). *Jane Fonda: The private life of a public woman.* Houghton Mifflin Harcourt.

Brescoll, V. L. (2012). Who takes the floor and why: Gender, power, and volubility in organizations. *Administrative Science Quarterly, 56*(4), 622–641.

Chen, S. (2018). Give yourself a break: The power of self-compassion. *Harvard Business Review, 96*(5), 117–123.

Cohn, A. (2021, February 15). Don't let self-doubt hold you back. *Harvard Business Review.* https://hbr.org/2021/02/dont-let-self-doubt-hold-you-back

Correll, S., & Mackenzie, L. (2016, September 13). To succeed in tech, women need more visibility. *Harvard Business Review,* 2–6. https://hbr.org/2016/09/to-succeed-in-tech-women-need-more-visibility

De Pater, I. E., Van Vianen, A. E., & Bechtoldt, M. N. (2010). Gender differences in job challenge: A matter of task allocation. *Gender, Work & Organization, 17* (4), 433–453. https://doi.org/10.1111/j.1468-0432.2009.00477.x

Dupree, C. H. (2024). Words of a leader: The importance of intersectionality for understanding women leaders' use of dominant language and how others receive it. *Administrative Science Quarterly, 69*(2), 271–323.

Eagly, A. H. (2009). The his and hers of prosocial behavior: An examination of the social psychology of gender. *American Psychologist, 64*(8), 644.

Evans, J. B., Slaughter, J. E., Ellis, A. P., & Rivin, J. M. (2019). Gender and the evaluation of humor at work. *Journal of Applied Psychology, 104*(8), 1077.

Exley, C. L., & Kessler, J. B. (2022). The gender gap in self-promotion. *The Quarterly Journal of Economics, 137*(3), 1345–1381.

Fielding-Singh, P., Magliozzi, D., & Ballakrishnen, S. (2018, August 28). Why women stay out of the spotlight at work. *Harvard Business Review*. https://hbr.org/2018/08/sgc-8-28-why-women-stay-out-of-the-spotlight-at-work

Galinsky, A. D., & Kilduff, G. J. (2013). Be seen as a leader. *Harvard Business Review, 91*(12), 127–130, 143.

Grant, A., & Sandberg, S. (2015, February 6). Madam CEO, get me a coffee. *The New York Times*, https://www.nytimes.com/2015/02/08/opinion/sunday/sheryl-sandberg-and-adam-grant-on-women-doing-office-housework.html.

Gravois, J. (2007). You're not fooling anyone. *Chronicle of Higher Education, 54* (11).

Grenny, J. (2019, August 5). How to say "no" at work without making enemies. *Harvard Business Review*. https://hbr.org/2019/08/how-to-say-no-at-work-without-making-enemies

Haushofer, J. (n.d.) CV of Failures. https://crlte.engin.umich.edu/wp-content/uploads/sites/5/2020/05/Johannes_Haushofer_CV_of_Failures.pdf

Huang, L., Joshi, P., Wakslak, C., & Wu, A. (2021). Sizing up entrepreneurial potential: Gender differences in communication and investor perceptions of long-term growth and scalability. *Academy of Management Journal, 64*(3), 716–740.

Ivowi, T. (2021, July 28). Do you ever second-guess yourself? *Harvard Business Review*. https://hbr.org/2021/07/do-you-ever-second-guess-yourself

Jamieson, J. P., Nock, M. K., & Mendes, W. B. (2012). Mind over matter: Reappraising arousal improves cardiovascular and cognitive responses to stress. *Journal of Experimental Psychology: General, 141*(3), 417.

Jang, S., Allen, T. D., & Regina, J. (2021). Office housework, burnout, and promotion: Does gender matter? *Journal of Business and Psychology, 36*(5), 793–805.

Keller, A., Litzelman, K., Wisk, L. E., Maddox, T., Cheng, E. R., Creswell, P. D., & Witt, W. P. (2012). Does the perception that stress affects health matter? The association with health and mortality. *Health Psychology, 31*(5), 677.

Koppman, S., Bechky, B. A., & Cohen, A. C. (2022). Overcoming conflict between symmetric occupations: How "creatives" and "suits" use gender ordering in advertising. *Academy of Management Journal, 65*(5), 1623–1651.

Kozubal, M., Szuster, A., & Wielgopolan, A. (2023). Emotional regulation strategies in daily life: The intensity of emotions and regulation choice. *Frontiers in Psychology, 14*, 1218694.

Lakoff, R. (1975). *Language and woman's place: Text and commentaries*. Oxford University Press.

Langton, S., Lanauze-Molines, M.-O. L. R. D., Meynell, L., O'Kelley, R., & Sanderson, L. (2024). *The next CEO: Global CEO turnover index annual report*. Russell Reynolds Associates.

Lerchenmueller, M. J., Sorenson, O., & Jena, A. B. (2019a). Gender differences in how scientists present the importance of their research: Observational study. *BMJ, 367*, l6573. https://doi.org/10.1136/bmj.l657

Lerchenmueller, M. J., Sorenson, O., & Jena, A. B. (2019b, December 20). How women undersell their work. *Harvard Business Review*. https://hbr.org/2019/12/research-how-women-undersell-their-work

McClean, E. J., Martin, S. R., Emich, K. J., & Woodruff, C. T. (2018). The social consequences of voice: An examination of voice type and gender on status and subsequent leader emergence. *Academy of Management Journal*, *61*(5), 1869–1891. https://doi.org/10.5465/amj.2016.0148

McGonigal, K. (2013). How to make stress your friend. *TED Global, Edinburgh, Scotland*, *6*, 13. https://www.youtube.com/watch?v=RcGyVTAoXEU

Mindell, P. (2001). *How to say it for women: Communicating with confidence and power using the language of success*. Penguin.

Miron-Spektor, E., Bear, J. B., & Eliav, E. (2023). Think funny, think female: The benefits of humor for women's influence in the digital age. *Academy of Management Discoveries*, *9*(3), 281–296.

Neff, K. D., & Tóth-Király, I. (2022). Self-compassion scale (SCS). In O. N. Medvedev, C. U. Krägeloh, R. J. Siegert, & N. N. Singh (Eds.), *Handbook of assessment in mindfulness research*. Springer. https://doi.org/10.1007/978-3-030-77644-2_36-1

Nolen-Hoeksema, S., Larson, J., & Grayson, C. (1999). Explaining the gender difference in depressive symptoms. *Journal of Personality and Social Psychology*, *77*(5), 1061.

Polin, B., Doyle, S. P., Kim, S., Lewicki, R. J., & Chawla, N. (2023). Sorry to ask but … how is apology effectiveness dependent on apology content and gender? *Journal of Applied Psychology*, *109*(3), 339–361. https://doi.org/10.1037/apl0001128

Schumann, K., & Ross, M. (2010). Why women apologize more than men: Gender differences in thresholds for perceiving offensive behavior. *Psychological Science*, *21*(11), 1649–1655.

Seligson, H. (2007, February 20). *Ladies, take off your Tiara!* HuffPost. https://www.huffpost.com/entry/ladies-take-off-your-tiar_b_41649#:~:text=us%20an%20email.-,There%20is%20an%20epidemic%20sweeping%20through%20offices%20across%20America%2D%2D,often%20operate%20in%20the%20workplace%2C

Smith, N. D., & Cheng-Cimini, A. (2023, August 18). How to become more visible at work. *Harvard Business Review*. Retrieved from https://hbr.org/2023/08/how-to-become-more-visible-at-work

Soochan, P. (2024, January 26). *Failure in science and the science of failure*. Association for Women in Science. https://awis.org/resource/failure-science-science-failure/

Stefan, M. (2010). A CV of failures. *Nature*, *468*(7322), 467–467.

Stone, H., & Stone, S. (1993). *Embracing your inner critic: Turning self-criticism into a creative asset*. Harper, San Francisco.

Varela, N. V., & Moridi, L. (2024). *The free-time gender gap: How unpaid care and household labor reinforces women's inequality.* Gender Equity Policy Institute. https://doi.org/10.5281/zenodo.13759857

Williams, J. C. (2014, April 16). Sticking women with the office housework. *The Washington Post.* Retrieved from https://www.washingtonpost.com/news/on-leadership/wp/2014/04/16/sticking-women-with-the-office-housework/

Wojnicki, A. (2022, August 2). A simple way to introduce yourself. Harvard Business Review. Retrieved from https://hbr.org/2022/08/a-simple-way-to-introduce-yourself

Women of Influence+ (2023). *The tallest poppy.* https://www.womenofinfluence.ca/tps/

3

Transform Challenging Conversations into Opportunities

Having explored how self-defeating behaviors can thwart women's potential, we now turn our attention to one of the most pivotal arenas in which these behaviors materialize: challenging conversations. Whether delivering bad news, offering feedback, voicing dissent, or negotiating salary, many women find themselves grappling with fears of rejection, conflict, or being perceived as unlikable. In a counterfactual world where such barriers do not exist and where women are universally encouraged to speak candidly and advocate for themselves, these interactions might be far less fraught. Yet, in our present reality, they remain a formidable hurdle. Building on insights from the previous chapter, this chapter presents strategies for reshaping high-stakes dialogs into catalysts for personal and professional growth. By embracing proactive communication techniques and reframing apprehension as opportunity, women can engage in difficult conversations more effectively, ultimately unlocking avenues of influence and fulfillment that might otherwise remain closed.

No one looks forward to having challenging conversations, at work or at home. Going into challenging conversations expecting the worst and, as a result, handling them in ways that undermine your goals presents a self-defeating behavior. For example, if you believe you are "bad" at delivering tough feedback, you might put off these conversations until the very last moment, causing tensions to build and increasing the chances of a heated exchange. If you are anxious about having challenging conversations, you might come across as overly apologetic or defensive, which can unintentionally erode your authority and decrease your listener's willingness to engage.

© The Author(s), under exclusive license to Springer Nature Switzerland AG 2025
G. Toegel, *The Confidence Myth*,
https://doi.org/10.1007/978-3-031-97305-5_3

Over time, repeated negative experiences around certain types of conversations reinforce the idea that "difficult conversations are doomed to fail," making you more likely to avoid them or approach them ineffectively. Good preparation begins with strategically defining what success looks like for you. By clarifying your desired outcome and developing a thoughtful approach to achieve it, you can transform challenging conversations into opportunities for positive change. Consider not just what you want to say, but what specific results you need to achieve.

We'll look at several types of challenging conversations and discuss how to overcome self-defeating behaviors to turn those conversations into opportunities. These challenging conversations include delivering bad news, expressing dissent, providing frank feedback to your boss, discussing salary and promotions, and managing a difficult relationship with your boss.

3.1   Delivering Bad News

When delivering bad news, women sometimes exhibit self-defeating behaviors, such as postponing difficult conversations about performance issues or project failures, softening the message to avoid conflict, apologizing excessively for decisions they didn't make, undermining their credibility through excessive empathy, losing respect due to unclear messaging, or approaching a manager with a problem without considering possible solutions in advance.

When starting a new job, most of us seek advice from colleagues about the unwritten rules of interacting with the new boss. One suggestion you're likely to hear is, "Don't approach the boss with a problem without also offering potential solutions." This advice reflects a widespread preference among managers for direct reports to contribute to solving problems, in addition to identifying them. But how exactly should such a conversation with your manager unfold, and how can you prepare for it?

Amy Gallo, an expert on workplace dynamics and cohost of the award-winning Women at Work podcast, suggests four steps for delivering bad news to your boss (Gallo, 2014): describe the problem, outline alternatives (explain their logic and discuss the pluses and minuses of each one, as well as the implications), share your thinking, and accept responsibility (see Table 3.1).

When you bring a problem to your boss, coming prepared makes all the difference. By laying out the issue clearly, showing that you've thought through different options, explaining your thinking, and taking responsibility,

Table 3.1 The four-step approach to delivering bad news

Steps	Example
Describe the problem	"We've got a serious problem in logistics. Deliveries are way behind, and customers are really ticked off. We're talking double the complaints, 25% longer delivery times, and a ton of bad feedback. It's hurting our reputation and could hit our bottom line. But don't worry, I've got some ideas to fix this mess"
Outline alternatives	"I've come up with three options, and I'd love your take on which one we should go with. We could bring in more hands to help out. It'll definitely speed things up, but it'll cost us, and we might have trouble fitting new people into the team
	Another thought is to shake up our delivery routes. This is a cheap fix and could save us time, but the drivers might not be thrilled about changing their routines. Plus, we're not sure how much it'll actually help in the end
	Or, we could go all in on some fancy tech. Invest in some smart software to do the heavy lifting. It's great for the long run, but it'll be a big investment upfront. We'd need to train everyone too, and there's always the risk of tech headaches"
Share your thinking	"Here's what I'm thinking: Let's hit this problem from two angles. We'll start by tweaking our delivery routes for a quick win, while also gearing up for some tech upgrades down the line. I'll dive into our current routes and get Amro's crew to crunch the numbers on efficiency. We'll roll out these new routes ASAP and keep a close eye on how they affect our delivery times and customer feedback. Jimmy can help get our drivers up to speed so they're not caught off guard
	Meanwhile, Eisa and I will start shopping around for the perfect logistics software. We'll map out all the details: timelines, budget, the whole nine yards. During the last strategy review you mentioned the urgency of finding technology solutions
	What do you think? How does the plan sound?"
Accept responsibility	"This project's success is on me. I'm committed to seeing it through. I'll keep you in the loop with regular updates"

you turn what could be seen as a complaint into a constructive conversation. It might be easier for your boss to accept the solution you propose if you can establish a link to an idea they shared in the past. This way, you remind your boss that they came up with this idea at an earlier time. If this is your usual approach, it will be easier to ask your boss for help when you are looking for solutions.

The four-step approach not only helps solve the problem but also demonstrates that you're someone who thinks things through and cares about achieving results.

3.2   Providing Feedback and Expressing Dissent

When providing feedback to their managers, or engaging in upward communication, women sometimes exhibit self-defeating behaviors, such as diluting important messages to maintain harmony; waiting too long for the "perfect moment"; focusing too much on being likable rather than clear; providing vague rather than specific feedback; or even questioning their right to provide upward feedback. The key is to recognize that effective feedback requires balancing professional assertiveness with clear, specific communication, regardless of gender dynamics. A good relationship is a prerequisite for providing your boss with feedback. If there is no trust, there is a risk that the feedback might be misinterpreted.

Take Action 3.1: Approaching Your Boss with Feedback

- First, ask your boss if it's all right to provide feedback: "Would it be helpful for me to share some observations/thought/insights/feedback I have?"
- State it in a concise way; use only verbs, no adjectives. "During our last conference call, I noticed/observed that you... It made me feel... I'm concerned because... "
- Point out how this behavior prevents your boss from achieving their objectives. For example, "When you cancel meeting agendas at the last minute, it disrupts the team's planning and delays the project deadlines you've set."
- If you have a strained relationship with your boss, try using the appreciative form: "I always appreciate it when you provide me with feedback after I submit a report." The real message here is: "You do not provide me with feedback when I submit a report."

The skills developed in providing effective feedback can serve as building blocks for expressing constructive dissent, as both are forms of upward communication and require balancing assertiveness with organizational awareness. Providing feedback and expressing dissent reflect courage and skill. While feedback typically focuses on specific situations or behaviors that need improvement, dissent challenges broader organizational practices, decisions, or directions. Both involve speaking truth to power, but dissent may carry higher stakes and risks.

We've all been there—your boss suggests an idea or makes a decision that you believe is misguided. Your first instinct might be to nod and keep quiet, but that's not always the best approach. Constructive disagreement can lead to better outcomes and showcase your critical thinking skills. However, it's crucial to choose your battles wisely. Not every disagreement is worth voicing. Ask yourself: Is this issue significant enough to warrant a discussion? Will speaking up lead to a meaningful improvement? If it's a minor issue or a personal preference, it might be better to let it go.

If you have already done contracting (see pp. 82–83), which is establishing a framework for handling disagreements, you can say, "As I shared with you during our contracting, I bring most value when I know that I can raise concerns, even if that may be perceived as disagreement by you."

When you decide to voice your concerns, be sure to manage the timing of your concerns, express your good intentions, be explicit, frame your disagreement as a question, be open to compromise, and follow up after the discussion. Timing is important. Find the right moment to have the conversation and avoid disagreeing with your boss in front of others. Instead, request a one-on-one meeting. Before sharing your dissent, make sure your boss is aware of your good intentions. For example, you might say, "We both care about the effectiveness of our communication channels." You can then continue by showing respect and acknowledging the parts of your boss's idea that you agree with. For example, "I appreciate your ability to see the big picture, and I agree that we need to increase our social media presence." This sets a positive tone and shows you understand their perspective and have considered it. Now you can move on to the content of what you disagree about. To make sure your dissent is not misinterpreted, be explicit about what you mean. For instance, you could say, "When I express concern about our current social media strategy, I'm not suggesting we abandon it entirely. Rather, I'm proposing we refine our approach to better target our core demographic while maintaining our overall increased presence."

Building on the approach of being explicit, you can frame your concern as a question rather than flat-out disagreeing. This method is less confrontational and invites discussion. For example, you might ask, "I'm curious, have we considered how increasing our social media presence might impact our engagement with our long-standing clients who prefer traditional communication channels? Is there a way we can balance both approaches?" When presenting your viewpoint, come prepared with data, examples, or expert opinions that support your position. This shows you've done your homework and aren't just disagreeing based on a hunch.

Whatever you say, confirm that your goal is to find the best solution, so be open to compromise and willing to meet in the middle or incorporate elements of both ideas. Even if the discussion becomes heated, it's important to keep emotions in check. Use "I" statements to express your thoughts without sounding accusatory. For instance, say, "I'm concerned that this approach might exhaust our resources" rather than, "You're not considering how this will affect our team."

If your boss has heard you out but still decides to go in a different direction, respect their decision. You've done your part by voicing your concerns professionally. After the discussion, you can follow up with a brief email summarizing the key points and any agreed-upon actions. This shows your commitment to the team's success, regardless of whose idea is being implemented.

Disagreeing with your boss doesn't have to be confrontational. When done right, it can strengthen your working relationship and contribute to better outcomes for your team and organization. By approaching disagreements with respect, preparation, and a solution-oriented mindset, you position yourself as a valuable, thoughtful team member who's committed to the company's success.

One of the most effective ways to manage disagreements with your boss is to establish a framework for how both of you would handle those disagreements before they even occur. This process, often called "contracting," involves having an upfront conversation about how you will handle differences of opinion. Contracting can significantly reduce the stress and uncertainty around disagreeing with your boss and lead to more productive discussions and better outcomes. Contracting is usually done at the beginning of the working relationship. You can introduce it by saying, "I want to ensure we have a healthy way to discuss different viewpoints when they arise. Could we talk about how we will handle disagreements?" Share your thoughts on how you would like to address disagreements and ask for your boss's preferences. For example: Do they prefer immediate feedback or need time to reflect? Would they rather discuss issues in person, over email, or in a formal meeting? How should urgent disagreements be handled compared to those that are less time-sensitive?

During contracting, you can also make a commitment to hear each other's perspectives before responding. For example, you might suggest the following guidelines:

- Let's commit to hearing each other's full perspectives before formulating our responses.
- Let's use active listening: After one person speaks, the other person summarizes what they have heard to ensure they understand before responding (Weger et al., 2014).

- Let's try the "steel man" approach: We'll each attempt to restate the other's argument in the strongest possible terms before offering our own perspective.

Contracting involves agreeing to focus on facts and data rather than emotions. You can also discuss how to move forward if you cannot reach an agreement. Periodically review how this arrangement is working, and be open to adjusting it as needed.

By contracting for disagreement, you create a safe space for honest communication. It shows your boss that you are committed to constructive dialog and helps prevent misunderstandings about how to approach difficult conversations.

Take Action 3.2: Signaling Disagreement Through Contracting

You can signal respectful disagreement during contracting in different ways:

- "I'd like to offer a different perspective on this."
- "I have some concerns about this approach that I'd like to discuss."
- "I see this situation a bit differently. May I share my thoughts?"
- "I appreciate your viewpoint, and I'd like to explore an alternative angle."
- "I have some reservations about this decision. Could we discuss them?"
- "I respect your decisions, and I also see some potential challenges here."
- "I'd like to play devil's advocate for a moment."

3.3 Dealing with Conflict: Avoiding the Drama Triangle

Have you ever been stuck in a conflict that feels like it's going nowhere? Chances are you've stumbled into what psychologist Stephen Karpman calls the "Drama Triangle," which explains why some conflicts seem to go round and round without ever getting solved (Karpman, 1968). The Drama Triangle creates self-defeating behaviors that keep participants trapped in destructive patterns, such as becoming dependent on rescuers, experiencing guilt when not rescuing, avoiding authentic communication, or perpetuating conflicts without resolution.

Karpman identifies three roles: the Victim, who feels helpless and oppressed; the Persecutor, who criticizes and blames; and the Rescuer, who intervenes to help the Victim, often enabling dependent behavior.

These roles are not static; they are fluid and can shift during interactions. Individuals often have a preferred or default role, but they may move between roles as the conflict unfolds (Conscious Leadership Group, 2021). The drama starts when they begin swapping roles. Let's look at the example of Shih-Han, Ala, and Barbara caught in the drama triangle.

Vignette 3.1: Drama Triangle

Shih-Han, an eager new hire, is working late nights on her first major project. She's drowning in spreadsheets and feeling way out of her depth; this activates a classic Victim mode. Ala is her direct boss, and Barbara is Ala's boss, overseeing it all. Instead of asking Ala for help, Shih-Han vents to Barbara during a chance encounter by the coffee machine. "Ala's expectations are impossible," she sighs. "I'm going to fail!" Barbara, feeling a mix of sympathy and responsibility, assumes the role of the Rescuer and decides to have a word with Ala. She marches over to Ala's office, ready to set things straight. "Ala, are you overloading Shih-Han? She seems stressed to the max!" Suddenly, Ala feels attacked and misunderstood. He shifts from potential Persecutor to Victim. "What? I'm just following your directives, Barbara! We need this project done ASAP!" The triangle spins. Shih-Han is still the Victim, Barbara was playing Rescuer, but now she is the Persecutor, and Ala is flipping from Persecutor to Victim. Shih-Han overhears the commotion and feels guilty. She jumps in to defend Ala, assuming the Rescuer role. "It's not Ala's fault! I should have spoken up sooner." Barbara, feeling like her attempt to help has backfired, slides into the Victim role. "I was just trying to support the team..."

This corporate merry-go-round could spin forever, leaving everyone dizzy and the actual work untouched. So, how can they stop it?

- Shih-Han needs to own her challenges and communicate directly with Ala. The victim should take charge.
- Ala should create an environment where Shih-Han feels safe asking for help.
- Barbara could encourage open communication rather than acting as a go-between.

In the end, this scenario isn't about who's right or wrong. By recognizing these drama patterns, our corporate trio can skip the theatrics and focus on what really matters—getting that project done. The key is to take a step back and own your part in the drama. Instead of pointing fingers, focus on fixing the problem. In the office drama triangle example, instead of complaining, Shih-Han could have spoken directly to Ala about the workload. Ala could have explained what's going on without getting defensive. And Barbara? Well, she could have stayed out of it altogether unless asked for help.

Here is how an approach that bypasses the Drama Triangle might play out. Shih-Han takes the initiative to address the problem directly by explaining to Ala that she has been working on the project and is finding some aspects of it challenging. She expresses her wish to discuss this with him before it becomes a bigger issue. Then she elaborates that the data analysis is taking longer than she anticipated, and she is worried about meeting the deadline. Shih-Han also admits that she might be missing some key insights due to her inexperience with this type of project. Then she explains her specific issues. Now that Ala understands the problem, he will most likely extend the deadline. Shih-Han follows with an appreciative comment and a reflection that she was hesitant to admit she was struggling, but she sees now that it's better to address issues early.

The Drama Triangle model helps you spot trouble before it spirals. Whether you are dealing with office politics or family feuds, understanding these dynamics can help you turn potential dramas into productive conversations. Try to spot when you are playing one of these roles and consciously step out of the triangle through honest communication. Are you always the one complaining? Maybe you are stuck in Victim mode. Are you always rushing to save the day? You might be a chronic Rescuer. Once you recognize the Drama Triangle and the roles you play in it, you can start to change your behavior.

3.4   Conversations Around Salary, Raises, and Promotions

Salary negotiations present unique challenges for women. Research shows that both male and female evaluators often react negatively to women who negotiate for higher pay, whereas men do not face the same penalty for similar behavior (Bowles, 2014). As you read in Chap. 1, women have made substantial progress and are indeed asking for more; however, certain self-defeating behaviors remain prevalent. For instance, many women wait for recognition rather than self-advocate, underestimate that negotiation is both expected and appropriate, or fail to prepare thoroughly for these critical conversations.

With recent changes in legislation in some countries, salary negotiations will become a bit easier. In the United States, since 2019, a growing number of US states and cities (e.g., Colorado, California, Washington, Washington DC, New York City, and others) have passed pay transparency laws that require employers to disclose salary ranges for external job postings and internal promotion opportunities. The main objective of these pay transparency laws is to help address gender and racial pay inequality. A new EU Directive on pay transparency, approved by the European Parliament and the Council in 2023, will require employers to disclose salary ranges and prohibit asking about a candidate's pay history. The Directive is expected to become national law in member states by 2026.

As a woman entering salary negotiations, prepare well and approach the process with confidence, knowing that negotiating your salary can increase your starting pay significantly. For years to come, your starting salary will determine future raises and bonuses. This underscores the importance of actively engaging in salary discussions rather than accepting the first offer.

Begin by establishing your salary range and determining your "walk-away" rate, the minimum amount you are willing to accept. Next, identify your "ideal" rate (what's the best you could reasonably hope for) based on market research using resources like Glassdoor.com, Salary.com, and Payscale.com. Experts on negotiation emphasize the effectiveness of having clear reservation (walk-away point) and aspiration (dream outcome) prices in negotiations (Neale & Bazerman, 1991).

Range offers can lead to better outcomes than single-point offers because they convey both flexibility and politeness (as they signal openness to discussion) while also anchoring the negotiation at a desirable point (Ames & Mason, 2015). If your location doesn't require employers to post salary ranges when discussing salary, you might say, "Based on my research and experience, I was expecting a salary in the range of [lower end] to [higher end]. Is there room to discuss this further?" Explain that your flexibility within this range depends on factors such as benefits, bonuses, and growth opportunities. This demonstrates your consideration of the total compensation package, not just the base salary. It also allows room for negotiation while ensuring you don't price yourself out of consideration. Remember, it's okay to negotiate, and the people you are negotiating with want to hire a confident individual. If asked to provide a single number, you can ask the interviewer what they are thinking of compensating someone for that role. Having the other side name the price will help you avoid underbidding. If still asked for a single number, emphasize your value by saying, "Given my track record of [specific achievement] and my skills in [relevant areas], I believe I can bring significant value to this role. With this in mind, I'm hoping we can agree on a salary of [desired amount]."

When negotiating salary, resist the urge to fill the silence with nervous chatter. When we feel anxious or want to be liked, we tend to talk too much during these conversations: explaining, justifying, or even undermining our own position. Instead, state your case clearly and concisely, then pause. Let the other person respond. This silence might feel uncomfortable, but it's powerful. Listen carefully to their response without interrupting; you'll gain valuable information and show confidence in your position. In negotiations, sometimes the person who speaks less holds more power.

Should the initial offer fall short of your expectations, don't be afraid to make a counter offer. You might say, "I appreciate the offer. However, based on my research and the market rate for this position, I was expecting something closer to [your desired salary]. Can we explore ways to bridge this gap?" If a higher salary isn't feasible, consider negotiating for nonmonetary benefits. Some people prefer additional benefits, such as more paid time off, over a pay increase. Experts suggest looking for common ground by providing the opportunity to negotiate instead of pushing. Your prospective employer may not be able to increase your starting salary, but they might have more flexibility in other areas. Salary is just one element of the overall compensation package, so you can explore alternative areas for compensation. You could ask, "If we can't reach the salary I had in mind, I'm open to discussing other forms of compensation. For instance, would it be possible to include [your role, title, responsibilities, specific benefit, e.g., additional vacation days, flexible working hours, professional development budget]?" If you need time to consider an offer, it's perfectly acceptable to ask for more time to consider it.

Negotiation is a normal part of the hiring process. The Society for Human Resource Management in the United States reported in 2022 that the average cost-per-hire was $4683, and the average time to fill a position was 54 days (Society for Human Resource Management, 2022). This means that employers invest significantly in finding the right candidate and are often willing to negotiate to secure their top choice. By approaching salary discussions with research, confidence, and a willingness to explore various forms of compensation, you can increase your chances of securing a package that reflects your true value.

As you'll remember from the last chapter, when women ask for a raise or promotion, some downplay their achievements due to discomfort with self-promotion, rooted in societal expectations that women should be humble and avoid appearing boastful. This reluctance can result in their contributions going unnoticed, making it harder for managers to recognize their value. Another self-defeating behavior is approaching the conversation with hesitation, often appearing unsure, which can signal to employers that they are not fully convinced of their own worth. Women may also fail to prepare adequately, neglecting to research market rates or quantify their accomplishments, which weakens their case for a raise. As you read in Chap. 2, assuming that hard work alone will be noticed and rewarded, or avoiding the negotiation altogether because you believe you "shouldn't have to ask," can also sabotage efforts to secure promotions or pay increases. Framing the request around personal needs rather than professional contributions can further diminish the effectiveness of your pitch.

You won't get unless you ask. When you ask for a pay increase, try to frame the argument around the benefit for the company and your mutual interest with the employer. A template for asking for a raise or promotion includes the following steps: setting the context, highlighting your achievements, discussing your value to the company, clearly stating your request, providing market research when asking for a pay increase, showing willingness to negotiate, and concluding with gratitude and openness.

Set the context: Start by setting a positive and professional tone. Begin by thanking your manager for their time and expressing your appreciation for the opportunity to discuss your role. Highlight your commitment to the team and the company, emphasizing how much you enjoy your work and your dedication to delivering high-quality results. This approach sets a collaborative and constructive foundation for the conversation.

Highlight your achievements: Highlight your achievements to demonstrate your value. Share specific responsibilities or projects you've taken on over a defined time period, and connect them to measurable results or improvements. Provide concrete examples, such as increased sales, streamlined processes, or successful project outcomes, to clearly show the impact of your contributions. When you discuss your accomplishments, try to be concise and crisp, and avoid sounding defensive by providing a long list of accomplishments. Highlighting one or two accomplishments should suffice.

Discuss your value and future value addition: Emphasize how your unique skills and efforts align with the company's needs. Highlight specific abilities, experiences, or expertise that set you apart, and explain their relevance to current challenges or goals. Mention any additional training, certifications, or skills you've acquired to further enhance your contributions. Share your forward-looking plans, such as strategies for generating revenue, reducing costs, attracting talent, or entering new markets. Connect your role and responsibilities directly to the company's priorities, demonstrating your impact and potential for continued success.

State your request clearly: Clearly state your request. Explain that, given your contributions and the value you bring to the team, you'd like to discuss the possibility of a salary review or promotion. Express that you believe an adjustment in your compensation or job title would appropriately reflect your role and achievements.

Provide market research when asking for a pay increase: Support your case with market research. Explain that you've reviewed industry salary data and found that your current compensation is below the average for similar roles and levels of experience. Share specific data from credible sources, such as salary surveys or industry reports, to back up your findings. This approach demonstrates preparation and provides a solid foundation for your request.

Show willingness to negotiate: Demonstrate openness and collaboration. Acknowledge that salary or promotion decisions involve multiple factors, and express your willingness to discuss what would be a fair adjustment. Invite your manager to share their thoughts and explore how you can move forward together.

Conclude with gratitude and openness: Thank your manager for considering your request and for their support, and let them know you look forward to their feedback. Offer to provide any additional information they might need to assist in the decision-making process.

Asking for a promotion or pay raise is an opportunity to advocate for yourself and showcase your value to the organization. Regardless of the outcome, this process demonstrates your professionalism and commitment to growth, both of which are essential for your long-term success.

3.5 Managing a Difficult Relationship with Your Boss

Vignette 3.2: Nia

Nia is a high-performing marketing associate at a renowned fashion brand, a job she once considered her dream. She takes great pride in her work, pouring creativity into every campaign. Her boss, Pedro, can be quite demanding, often setting aggressive deadlines and expecting near-flawless execution. Determined to avoid conflict and "keep the peace," Nia rarely expresses concerns about her ever-growing workload. She silently shoulders extra assignments, staying late to meet Pedro's ever-increasing demands.

Initially, Nia tells herself she can handle the pressure. But as the months pass, the stress accumulates, leading to small mistakes and growing resentment toward Pedro. She desperately wants to protect her reputation, so, rather than speaking up about her struggles, she internalizes them, fearing that any admission of difficulty will make her look incompetent. From Pedro's perspective, Nia appears perfectly capable; after all, she never complains or sets boundaries.

Her unspoken frustration soon begins to affect her demeanor. She becomes withdrawn in team discussions, offers fewer ideas, and starts interpreting every new request from Pedro as a personal affront. What was once an enthusiastic partnership slowly sours into an atmosphere of tension and mistrust. Despite her talent and commitment, Nia's inability to voice her concerns drives a wedge between herself and Pedro, ultimately undermining both her performance and their working relationship.

Interpersonal dynamics, workplace biases, or mismatched expectations can cause the relationship with your boss to deteriorate. In some cases, the tension may stem from the boss's behavior, such as insecurity, micromanagement, or a lack of leadership skills. However, some self-defeating behaviors on the part of direct reports can also contribute to the deterioration.

Nia's case demonstrates the impact of her self-defeating behaviors. By not voicing her concerns or pushing back on workload demands, her boss, Pedro, remains unaware that she is overwhelmed, while deadlines and tasks continue to pile up. Over time, Nia's hidden resentment and the boss's belief that "all is well" drive a wedge between them. By not clarifying her limits, Nia inadvertently sets unrealistic expectations. When her performance eventually slips, Pedro perceives it as a sudden drop in commitment or capability, leading to frustration and eroding trust. While Nia worries that admitting her struggles will make her appear incompetent, her boss, left in the dark, interprets her stress-related mistakes or withdrawal as a lack of engagement, further straining their relationship. As Nia grows increasingly resentful yet remains silent, Pedro misconstrues the situation, causing mutual misunderstandings and further damaging their working relationship.

Remember that you are hired to create value, and you have to demonstrate it to your boss. Whitney Johnson, named a 2021 Top #10 Business Thinker by Thinkers50, offers some good advice (Johnson, 2014). Revisit the job description for the position you were hired to fulfill. Try not to focus solely on solving the problems that might seem interesting or important to you. You need to help your boss solve their problems as well. In that sense, it's essential to understand the job your boss was hired to do.

Let's say that every now and then your boss is hostile (even angry), defensive, or resistant to ideas that you share during team meetings. Does this mean that you have a negative relationship with your boss?

Not necessarily. Occasional stress or frustration can arise in any workplace. A single tense exchange with your boss does not mean you have a difficult relationship. If your boss occasionally snaps or becomes defensive once every few months, especially under high stress, it may be an isolated issue rather than a pattern. However, if you notice hostility or dismissiveness in most meetings or almost every time you propose something, it indicates a more entrenched problem. Watch out for frequent or constantly recurring negative patterns of behavior, intensity of emotional tone, and lack of positive interactions. In considering the emotional tone, ask yourself: "Is the boss merely short-tempered sometimes, or do they escalate to personal attacks or public criticism?" The more extreme the response, the more it signals a broken communication channel.

A difficult relationship often manifests in one-directional or consistently negative feedback. If all your interactions revolve around criticism or conflict, the relationship is likely suffering. Alternatively, if your boss avoids giving you guidance, withholds useful information, or shuts down your ideas without discussion, this might reflect deeper tension or a lack of trust.

Self-Reflection 3.1: Identifying the Source of a Difficult Relationship

To develop a strategy for improving your relationship, you must first figure out the source of your boss's negative reactions.

- Is your boss indecisive, and are they easily irritated when you bring up deadlines?
- Does your boss have an inflated ego that makes them defensive when you raise concerns?
- Does your boss frequently change their mind and then respond with hostility when you point it out in a meeting?
- Is your boss too hands-off, and do they get angry when you point out problems due to their laissez-faire management style?
- Is your boss perhaps just not smart enough, leading them to become annoyed when they cannot follow your logic in a discussion?

A negative relationship with your boss can make you feel undermined. You may find that your input is routinely dismissed in front of others, or your contributions are overlooked. If your boss excludes you from relevant conversations, fails to loop you into decisions, or shows little interest in collaborating on solutions, it can make you feel isolated, anxious, and stressed.

Self-Reflection 3.2: Managing a Difficult Relationship

1. Do you bring problems or solutions to your boss?
2. Is your boss insecure? If this is the case, it's not about you; the problem lies elsewhere. Your best strategy would be to strengthen your boss' ego by asking for their opinion, suggestions, and feedback, and by acknowledging their contribution to your success.
3. Could you be part of the problem? What is your internal reputation? Would your colleagues agree that you overpromise and underdeliver?
4. How do other people perceive your relationship with your boss? Would they say that the two of you are good friends and that you are one of their favorites? Would others describe your relationship with your boss as purely transactional, one where you invest effort only for personal gain? This perception could undermine your authenticity and professional reputation. How do you handle boundaries if you and your boss were peers before your boss got promoted?
5. Could your boss have concerns that they might be accused of favoritism?
6. Does your boss dislike you? If yes, you need to explore why. Consider the following hypotheses:

   • Do they have an issue with your integrity?
   • Do they mistrust your competence, which is evident in their microman-agement of you?
   • Is it about personality differences, which impact how you do things?

7. Try to understand what makes your boss tick and the differences in their perspectives.

   • Does your boss enjoy talking while you prefer solitude, causing them to perceive you as secretive?
   • Does your boss like details/data while you prefer the big picture, and do they get upset when you fail to provide backup for the ideas you share?
   • Does your boss enjoy competing while you prefer cooperation, and are they disappointed because you are not a "fighter"?
   • Is your boss a perfectionist, while you are more relaxed?
   • Is your boss easily angered and stressed, and do they interpret your resilience as not caring enough, especially during a crisis?

In all of these cases, it's worth having an honest conversation to discuss what drives those perceptions. To prepare, get some input from your peers about possible sources of those perceptions. The conversation with your boss could go like this:

"Thank you for meeting with me. I wanted to chat about something that's been on my mind. Is this a good time?" ... "I can't help feeling like things have been a bit off between us lately. I'm worried it might be because you're not too happy with the way we work together or with my performance. Am I way off base here?" ... "I want to address this directly and understand where I'm falling short. I want to fix this." ... "I see. Can you please provide specific examples? I'm committed to improving and want to understand exactly where I need to focus my efforts." ... "Thank you for being straight with me. I honestly didn't realize it was coming across that way, and I'm grateful for the specific feedback. I'd like to propose a plan to address your concerns. Would you be open to discussing some concrete steps I can take?" ... "Thanks, I really appreciate you being open about this. Anything else you think I should focus on?"

In this chapter, we explored how managing challenging conversations can empower women to navigate even the most daunting interactions with confidence. As you learn to deliver tough messages, offer constructive criticism, express dissent, manage workplace conflicts, negotiate fair compensation, and navigate demanding relationships with superiors, you simultaneously strengthen both your professional acumen and the bonds you share with colleagues.

However, managing difficult conversations is only half the battle. External forces, such as microaggressions, gaslighting, and other subtle yet harmful behaviors, can just as easily undermine your progress. Recognizing them for what they are is the first step in countering their impact. In the next chapter, we'll explore strategies to identify and deflect these external challenges so you can continue building a thriving, fulfilling career on your own terms.

References

Ames, D. R., & Mason, M. F. (2015). Tandem anchoring: Informational and politeness effects of range offers in social exchange. *Journal of Personality and Social Psychology, 108*(2), 254.

Bowles, H. R. (2014, June 19). Why women don't negotiate their job offers. *Harvard Business Review.* https://hbr.org/2014/06/why-women-dont-negotiate-their-job-offers

Conscious Leadership Group (2021, March 23). *The Drama Triangle.* [Video]. YouTube. https://www.youtube.com/watch?v=dQbxd3kJ78g

Gallo, A. (2014, December 5). The right way to bring a problem to your boss. *Harvard Business Review.* https://hbr.org/2014/12/the-right-way-to-bring-a-problem-to-your-boss

Johnson, W. (2014, December 15). Managing up without sucking up. *Harvard Business Review.* https://hbr.org/2014/12/managing-up-without-sucking-up

Karpman, S. (1968). Fairy tales and script drama analysis. *Transactional Analysis Bulletin, 7*(26), 39–43.

Neale, M. A., & Bazerman, M. H. (1991). *Cognition and rationality in negotiation.* Free Press.

Society for Human Resource Management. (2022). *SHRM benchmarking: Talent access report.* https://www.shrm.org/content/dam/en/shrm/research/benchmark ing/Talent%20Access%20Report-TOTAL.pdf

Weger Jr, H., Castle Bell, G., Minei, E. M., & Robinson, M. C. (2014). The relative effectiveness of active listening in initial interactions. *International Journal of Listening, 28*(1), 13–31.

4

Recognize and Deflect

Vignette 4.1: Aude

Aude is a dedicated mid-level manager at a fast-growing tech firm, known for her sharp analytical skills and collaborative spirit. Yet, despite her strong performance, she often struggles with subtle but persistent slights. In team meetings, for instance, her male colleagues frequently interrupt her mid-sentence or dismiss her suggestions, only to resurface the same ideas later as their own. It's frustrating and disheartening, especially when it happens in front of senior leadership.

When Aude musters the courage to talk to her manager about this behavior, he waves off her concerns with statements like, "Are you sure you're not overreacting?" or "Maybe you're just misreading their intentions." Each time, Aude is left questioning herself: *Am I really overreacting? Are my instincts off?*

Even worse, clients and executives from other departments assume she's someone's assistant and address her male subordinates for final decisions. Aude tries to remain professional, gently reasserting her position as team leader, but the constant need to prove she's in charge is exhausting, and it stings to see her expertise ignored because of sexist assumptions.

Despite her qualifications and impressive track record, Aude is regularly passed over for high-visibility projects. When she asks her manager for more challenging assignments, he brushes it off, saying, "I don't want to overwhelm you; I know you have a lot on your plate." In reality, Aude is eager to take on new responsibilities to showcase her capabilities. This well-intended yet patronizing response leaves her feeling sidelined.

Despite wanting to excel in the field she loves, Aude finds herself wondering how much longer she can endure an environment where her voice is so frequently drowned out.

© The Author(s), under exclusive license to Springer Nature Switzerland AG 2025
G. Toegel, *The Confidence Myth*,
https://doi.org/10.1007/978-3-031-97305-5_4

Aude's case highlights how microaggressions (e.g., interruptions, dismissals of her ideas, or appropriating them later), gaslighting (e.g., suggestions that she is overreacting, making her question her own perceptions), devaluation (e.g., assumptions that she is the assistant rather than the team leader), and benevolent sexism (e.g., infantilizing her and denying her opportunities for growth) can create a toxic work environment that undermines women's professional advancement. This chapter will examine the impact of these factors and discuss actionable steps women can take in such situations.

4.1   Microaggressions

Microaggressions are indignities that communicate hostile, derogatory, or negative discriminatory or insulting prejudices or stereotypes, which negatively affect individuals from marginalized groups—communities that experience exclusion, discrimination, or disadvantages due to systemic imbalances of power. These groups are often pushed to the margins of society, meaning they have limited access to resources, opportunities, and decision-making processes. Marginalization can occur based on characteristics such as race, ethnicity, gender, sexual orientation, disability, socioeconomic status, or religion. As a result, members of marginalized groups face barriers in areas such as education, employment, healthcare, housing, and political participation.

Sometimes, microaggressions can appear as compliments or neutral comments, but they still perpetuate underlying stereotypes or biases that can be harmful. For example, complimenting a Black woman's hairstyle might seem positive, but it can also perpetuate the idea that her natural hair is unusual or exotic, reinforcing systemic biases about beauty standards. Similarly, commenting on a child's appearance as "pretty" in a way that implies surprise based on their racial or ethnic background can subtly suggest that attractiveness is not expected of their group, which is another form of stereotyping. Microaggressions can be verbal or behavioral indignities that question or challenge a person's competence. For example, Aude's boss waves off her concerns, asking her if she is overreacting or misreading their intentions. Other examples of microaggressions include a team leader ignoring the contribution of a female team member, instead giving credit to others, or making demeaning and inappropriate comments on a person's appearance or emotional state, as well as other behaviors that make people feel minimized and othered. Sometimes, the lack of positive behaviors can be experienced as a microaggression. For example, a leader who smiles and establishes eye contact with some people in the room, but not with others, is microaggressing by withholding positive nonverbal behaviors from certain people in the room. Multitasking by checking messages while a team member from a marginalized group speaks can also be experienced as a microaggression, as it implies that what the speaker has to say is not valuable.

The term "microaggressions" was coined by psychiatrist Pierce (1974). Originally, it was used to describe the subtle insults directed at Black people by non-Black Americans—for example, by excluding them from conversations or activities. The concept was later expanded to encompass "brief, everyday exchanges that send denigrating messages to certain individuals because of their group membership" (p. xvii), based on race, gender, sexual orientation, disability, age, etc. (Sue, 2010).

Microaggressions can be broken down into three primary categories: microassaults, microinsults, and microinvalidations (Sue et al., 2007).

Microassaults are explicit derogations. For example, a male colleague might make a sexist joke in a meeting, saying, "Maybe we should let the men handle this; they'll be decisive," and then brush it off with a comment like, "I was just joking." This comment demeans the status of his female colleagues. While framed as humor, it is an intentional act meant to belittle and exclude. In some cases, comments like these might not be intended to be offensive; they might be the outcome of unconscious stereotypical beliefs about women and their place in society. Nonetheless, such language is at best inappropriate and at worst belittling. Language used in different ways to describe men and women also constitutes a microassault. For example, when a man works late, he is celebrated as "dedicated," but a woman might be labeled as "selfish" and questioned about her role as a wife and/or mother. If the woman is single with no children, she might be pitied as having "no life."

Microinsults are subtle communications or actions that demean a person's identity. For example, questioning a woman's ability to make decisions under pressure, implying that her gender makes her less capable; complimenting a woman of color on how articulate or well-spoken she is, suggesting it's atypical of people of her gender and race; telling a woman in a leadership position, "You're quite assertive for a woman"; or commenting that a woman got her job due to a diversity quota rather than her qualifications.

Microinvalidations are comments or actions that negate or ignore the experiences of members of a marginalized group, such as telling a woman she is overreacting when she points out sexism or stating that there is no longer a problem with inclusion and that she should not expect "special treatment."

Microaggressions are often unintentional. They tend to be an expression of internalized biases and prejudices that the person holds, which can be traced back to childhood. But their cumulative impact on the targets of microaggressions, in this case women, can be profound. For instance, one study found that women in STEM fields often face microinvalidations that question their competence based solely on their gender (Williams et al., 2016). This can lead to increased stress, anxiety, and a feeling of not belonging, which likely contributes to the high attrition rates of women in these fields. Overt forms of discrimination are easy to notice, but microaggressions are more ambiguous and subtle. They might seem small, but their impact, however, could be worse than overt discrimination.

Vignette 4.2: Kim

For example, Kim is a highly qualified software engineer whose male colleagues are often invited to informal meetings and after-work gatherings where important project discussions take place. However, Kim is consistently forgotten or not invited to these events. When she inquiries about it, she is told, "Oh, we didn't think you'd be interested," or "It was just a last-minute thing." Over time, Kim notices that she is missing out on crucial information and networking opportunities. When she applies for a promotion, she is told she lacks the necessary "team spirit" and "leadership qualities." Kim starts questioning whether she is truly underperforming or if she is a target of discrimination. She thinks, "Had I been told 'women aren't suited for leadership roles in our company,' it would have been easier to address through legal channels, because this would have been obvious discrimination." The uncertainty increases her anxiety and self-doubt. She begins to ruminate about possible reasons, which further amplifies her self-doubt and anxiety. She keeps suffering in silence, which significantly depletes her emotional resources (see King & Jones, 2016).

We can consider a person as a complex puzzle, where each piece represents a part of who they are—their race, gender, ethnicity, social class, sexuality, age, and many more characteristics unique to them. The concept of intersectionality looks at how these pieces fit together to influence a person's life and helps us understand how different aspects of a person's identity combine to shape their experiences in society. Kimberlé Crenshaw coined the term in 1989 (Crenshaw, 1989), but it has its roots in Black feminist thought and activism, with origins dating back to Sojourner Truth's 1851 "Ain't I a Woman" speech, which exemplified intersectional thinking by highlighting the unique experiences of Black women.

We all have a myriad of characteristics that make us who we are. These characteristics don't exist in isolation; rather, they interact with each other.

The combination of these identities creates distinct advantages or challenges for each person. Intersectionality examines how these combinations relate to social structures and systems of power. The intersectionality of race and gender means that women of color face a unique set of microaggressions. For example, a Black woman might face challenges that are different from those experienced by a white woman or a Black man. Her experiences are shaped by both her race and gender together, not just one or the other. A notable case is that of Serena Williams, winner of 23 Grand Slam titles and one of the greatest tennis players of all time. Williams has publicly discussed how she has been subjected to both racial and gender-based microaggressions throughout her tennis career, which have damaged her reputation as well as her mental health.

The concept of microaggressions has not been without controversy. Critics argue that the term can be used to label unintentional and benign interactions as aggressive, potentially stifling open communication. Additionally, some people question the subjective nature of what constitutes a microaggression, suggesting that reliance on individual perception could lead to misunderstandings or misuse of the term (Lilienfeld, 2017).

One problem is that men are less likely to notice microaggressions toward women. The Integrating Women Leaders Foundation (2022) conducted a state-of-allyship-in-action benchmark study, asking both men and women the following question: "Based on your own experience or what you have observed, how often do you believe these things (referring to different microaggressions) happen to women within your organization?"

Figure 4.1 illustrates the discrepancy between how women and men perceive the frequency of microaggressions. The most commonly observed or experienced microaggressions against women include being interrupted or spoken over; having their judgment questioned; not receiving credit for their contributions; being asked to handle office "housework"; being overlooked for promotions; having their emotional state scrutinized; and being dismissed as inexperienced. Men who participate in allyship communities—networks of individuals committed to actively supporting and advocating for underrepresented groups—are more likely to recognize these microaggressions. However, a significant gap still remains between the microaggressions women experience and what their male colleagues perceive.

The cumulative effect of microaggressions can lead to confidence issues. Targets of microaggressions may feel vulnerable, start doubting themselves, and lose trust in their competence, even when the transgression is inadvertently offensive. What matters is how the target of the microaggression perceives its impact.

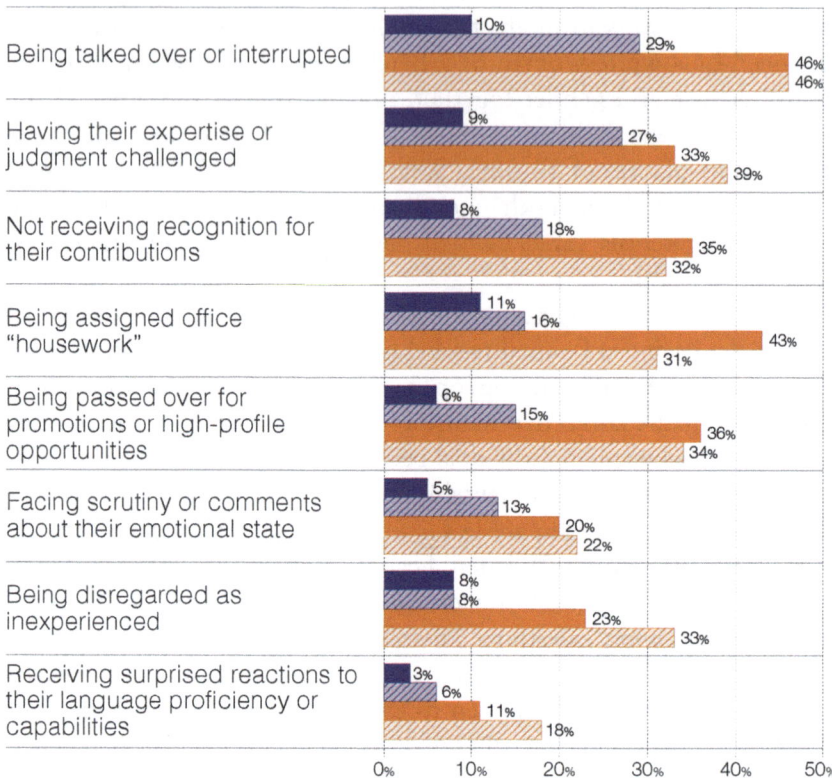

Fig. 4.1 Noticing microaggressions against women. This chart shows the percentage of respondents reporting "always" or "frequently" in response to the question: "Based on your own experience or what you have observed, how often do you believe these things (referring to different microaggressions) happen to women within your organization?". *Source* Adapted from "State of Allyship-in-Action Benchmark Report" by Integrating Women Leaders Foundation (2022). https://ywomen.Biz/wp-content /uploads/2023/10/IWL-SOAIA-Allyship-In-Action-Benchmark-Study-2022.Pdf

Microaggressions can inflict significant harm. They are often brushed off as "just a joke" or banter. Perpetrators even accuse targets of microaggressions of not being able to take a joke. These behaviors have a detrimental impact since they normalize microaggressions and ignore the cumulative effect microaggressions have when the targets are repeatedly made to feel inferior or are bound to gender role stereotypes.

How Should You Respond to Microaggressions?

There are three ways of addressing microaggressions (Washington et al., 2020): letting go, responding immediately, and responding later. Each approach has its pros and cons to consider before deciding which way to go.

Letting go: Historically, this has been the default response, particularly in a climate of silence and a culture of fear. This approach helps to avoid being consumed by negative emotions and reduces the stress associated with confronting microaggressions, especially when addressing them directly might lead to further conflict or retaliation. However, leaving microaggressions unaddressed comes at a high emotional cost because your feeling of self-worth is undermined.

Responding immediately: This approach offers certain benefits, as it sets clear boundaries. By calling out denigrating messages or behaviors as soon as they happen, this approach signals that you are not going to tolerate these kinds of transgressions. When your judgment is questioned or you are interrupted in a meeting, for example, reacting immediately is most effective, as failing to address these behaviors can contribute to a perception of incompetence. Even a small interjection such as "Ouch!" could draw attention to an unacceptable comment or action and initiate a meaningful conversation. It's helpful to be prepared with go-to phrases, for example: "I would like to understand why you are saying that … where does it come from?"; "What you just said/did makes me feel uncomfortable, because …"; "I heard you saying … is that what you meant to say?" Never underestimate the power of a good question to initiate a deep and impactful conversation.

Responding later: Responding later in a follow-up conversation is the third approach. The time lag might create additional problems if the perpetrator claims they don't remember what actually happened or blames the target of the microaggression for overreacting. However, this might be the best response when the immediate impact of the microaggression leads to a strong emotional reaction. Even if you do not report the microaggression in the moment, keep a record of the conversation, the people who were present, and any email or message exchanges. You might decide to report it at a later stage.

There is also the option of leaving the team, department, or organization altogether, but this should typically be considered a last resort. While leaving a toxic environment can be liberating, it is not without its challenges. Such a departure can be costly both professionally and personally, potentially disrupting your career trajectory and financial stability. Before taking this step, carefully consider alternative solutions, such as seeking allies or escalating concerns. However, if the situation becomes untenable and affects your mental health and well-being, leaving may indeed be the most appropriate course of action.

Manterruptions and How to Counter Them

Interruptions are some of the most frequently observed microaggressions against women. In fact, compared to men, women are twice as likely to be interrupted in a meeting (Heath & Wensil, 2019). "Manterrupting," a term coined by Jessica Bennett, a columnist for *Time*, refers to those cases where men interrupt women while they are trying to speak, often undermining their contributions. This is a power play that indicates the manterrupter believes he has a higher status than the woman who is speaking. This behavior is driven by an unconscious bias, which reflects to whom we attribute power, respect, and status.

When you experience manterruption, it's important to address it directly. Interrupt the interrupter by calmly stating that you have a few more points to make and would appreciate their waiting until you've finished. Following up with a private conversation can also be helpful; explain how being interrupted makes you feel and why it's important for everyone to have the opportunity to contribute without being cut off. This can open the door to a broader team discussion about setting clear guidelines for meetings, such as allocating speaking time for each participant.

As an ally, you play a critical role in fostering respectful communication and addressing gender bias in the workplace. Speaking up during meetings is one way to set boundaries and signal zero tolerance for interruptions or inappropriate comments. For instance, if someone interrupts Alma, you could say, "I would like to hear what Alma was about to say. Alma, could you please continue sharing your thoughts?" Similarly, simple but firm phrases like, "That wasn't very cool to say," can help call out inappropriate behavior and create a more inclusive environment.

This approach aligns with the "small wins" strategy, which suggests that small, measurable changes can lead to larger cultural shifts. Correll (2017) identifies four key mechanisms of gender bias against women: extra scrutiny, holding women to higher standards, shifting evaluation criteria, and the "double-bind." A "double-bind" occurs when an individual is faced with conflicting expectations, making it impossible to satisfy both demands. No matter what they do, they are likely to face criticism or negative consequences.

For example, a woman might be expected to be both assertive and nurturing at work, but if she leans too much into assertiveness, she is seen as aggressive, and if she focuses on nurturing, she is viewed as lacking authority. This creates a no-win situation where she can't fulfill both expectations simultaneously, leading to frustration and emotional distress.

Correll's change model emphasizes targeting organizational processes rather than individuals by empowering teams of managers to implement incremental improvements. Each small win creates momentum by inspiring new allies, building confidence in the change process, and highlighting the next milestone. By combining immediate actions, like speaking up, with systemic efforts to address bias, organizations can create lasting and meaningful change.

When You Are Called Out for Microaggressions

How do you react when you are called out for a microaggression (Knight, 2020)? Most likely, you will feel embarrassed, ashamed, and quite stressed. Your first impulse might be to become defensive and say, "I'm not a misogynist/racist," instead of feeling grateful for the feedback provided. Whatever you say needs to be sincere and not performative. In a one-on-one conversation, your response should make the other person feel heard. You should offer a sincere apology, which acknowledges the negative impact of your words or actions and signals that you want to change for the better. Your apology could have the following structure: "Thank you for sharing how my words/behaviors made you feel, and thank you for trusting that I can do better. I'm sorry that what I said/did was offensive. I was wrong, and I regret it. (There's no need to over-apologize; it's not about you!) I would appreciate a suggestion on how I could have said it differently."

When the microaggression is called out in a public setting, your response could have two steps. First, in the presence of others, you could say: "Thank you for sharing that piece of feedback. I'm not going to use that word/phrase in the future." You can then follow up with the person via email including a statement similar to one you would use in a one-on-one conversation.

Reaching out to the people who have pointed out your microaggression approximately four to six weeks later can be very meaningful. It shows you value their feedback, are actively working on changing your behavior, and intend to stay accountable in the future. This gesture makes them feel heard and gives them confidence that you will avoid repeating the same mistakes.

Ultimately, you should view their feedback as an integral part of your personal growth journey.

Because microaggressions often stem from or are exacerbated by imbalances in power or status, it's crucial for leaders to recognize how these dynamics shape workplace interactions. Understanding the difference between power and status can help managers create environments that foster respect and mitigate the risks of harmful behaviors. As you read in Chapter 1, power is linked to a formal position of authority, while status reflects the level of respect and admiration a person commands. Research suggests that when individuals have high power and high status, they are perceived as dominant and warm, which makes it easy for people to follow them (Fragale et al., 2011). But when individuals in power lack status, in other words, they are not respected and admired, they are perceived as cold. This finding helps explain why women who have power but who have not earned respect, and therefore lack status, might become victims of microaggressions and be labeled "bossy," for example. Leaders who play the power game and don't invest in earning respect and admiration risk focusing on the outcome without laying the necessary groundwork. In other words, they prioritize achieving authority and control without first building the foundation of trust and credibility that truly sustains leadership. In a way, status is a prerequisite for possessing power without negative social consequences. The best ways to earn status are to demonstrate competence and to be perceived as giving and generous (Grant, 2013).

4.2   Gaslighting

Gaslighting is a manipulative tactic that has a profound and harmful impact on women's confidence, mental health, and well-being. The term originated from the 1938 stage play "Gas Light" by British playwright and novelist Patrick Hamilton, and the subsequent 1944 film adaptation "Gaslight," in which a husband manipulates his wife and causes her to doubt her sanity. He lights the gas lamps on an unused upper floor, causing the rest of the lights in the house to dim. When his wife comments on it, he dismisses her, insisting she's imagining things.

Gaslighting is a form of emotional and psychological manipulation used by individuals to gain power and control over their victims. This is achieved through a series of tactics that make the person being gaslighted doubt their perceptions, memories, and overall sense of reality. Gaslighting often occurs in relationships with a power imbalance, where the gaslighter positions themselves as superior to the person being gaslighted, who cannot hold the perpetrator accountable. The manipulator exploits their position of authority or trust to undermine the victim's confidence and self-esteem and to exert control.

Women are disproportionately affected by gaslighting, as it frequently occurs in intimate relationships, workplace interactions, and societal contexts where gender inequalities persist. Gaslighting can perpetuate gender stereo-types and contribute to the silencing of women's voices, as it often dismisses their experiences, opinions, and concerns as irrational or oversensitive. Microaggressions are considered a form of gaslighting.

Gaslighting is subtle and gradual, which is what makes it so dangerous. Unlike bullying, gaslighting does not involve direct confrontation (Jones, 2023). It often begins with small lies, distortions, and denials, leading the victim to question their judgment. On the surface, the perpetrator appears concerned for the victim's well-being, thereby suggesting that the latter is incapable of making judgments on their own. The perpetrator seeks to sow seeds of doubt in the victim's mind and attack the foundation of their identity. Over time, this erodes the victim's self-esteem and fosters dependence on the gaslighter, who then gains an unhealthy level of control over the victim's emotions and actions.

The gaslighter may isolate their victim from friends and family, leaving them with no external validation. They sow seeds of doubt about their loved ones, subtly hinting that those individuals are not good for them, driving a wedge between the victim and their support system. For example: "They (e.g. friends, family members) don't really care about you like I do. You should distance yourself from them."

In the business world, gaslighting is a form of psychological manipulation where an individual or group causes someone to question their perceptions, memory, or judgment, often leading to confusion, self-doubt, and diminished confidence. For example, a manager might deny making a promise or agreement, leaving the employee unsure of their recollection. Unlike bullying, which is often overt and aggressive (e.g., yelling, intimidation, or public humiliation), gaslighting tends to be covert and insidious, relying on subtle tactics like denial, misdirection, or contradiction to undermine the victim's sense of reality. While both are harmful workplace behaviors, gaslighting is distinct in its focus on eroding the victim's trust in their own thoughts and perceptions rather than relying on direct aggression.

Gaslighters employ two main strategies to confuse and control (Stark, 2019): sidestepping and displacement. In *sidestepping,* the gaslighter may deny events and conversations, renege on promises, or tell blatant lies, making the target doubt their recollection. They might dismiss reports of harassment or discrimination, for example. When the victim expresses concern about the gaslighter's behavior, the latter often lashes out in response: "I never said that, you must be imagining things." Or they redirect conversations ("Aren't there more important things to focus on right now?"), making the target question the validity of their perceptions and concerns. Another sidestepping strategy employed by gaslighters is minimization. Some examples of minimization include downplaying the victim's feelings, trivializing women's experiences of sexism or misogyny as oversensitivity, belittling women's accomplishments, nitpicking aspects of the victim's work, and making sarcastic comments about her capabilities, leading to self-doubt. Similarly, gaslighters using this strategy might attribute women's success to factors other than their abilities, for example, luck or receiving "special treatment," etc.

The *displacement* strategy attributes a credibility deficit to the victim based on some perceived defect. For example, instead of addressing the issue at hand, the perpetrator might respond with a personal attack that questions the credibility of the woman speaking out against harassment: "As always, you're blowing this out of proportion. It was just a joke." They may also project their negative behavior onto the target, making her feel guilty. For instance, when caught in a lie, the gaslighter might accuse their target of being dishonest and untrustworthy.

Gaslighters may manipulate past events to make the victim question their memory or perception of reality. Consider the case of Loth, whose boss constantly denies or alters past conversations, making her doubt her own recollections. If Loth confronts him about an argument they had, he responds: "You must be imagining things. We never talked about that." This makes Loth uncertain about her memory, and she starts doubting her ability to remember things accurately. The manipulation gradually chips away at Loth's confidence in her ability to recall past events, leaving her more reliant on her boss's version of reality.

Gaslighters often project their own shortcomings onto their victims, making them believe that they are the ones at fault, as you will see from Rachel's experience.

Vignette 4.3: Rachel

Rachel, Head of Operations in Europe, is struggling to rein in one of the CEOs in her region who has a habit of overspending and accumulating debt. Whenever Rachel tries to discuss the problem, he shifts the blame onto her, saying, "If you were better at managing the operations, we wouldn't be in this mess." As the CEO repeatedly blames her for their financial troubles, Rachel begins to internalize this narrative. She may start to believe that she is, indeed, responsible for the region's financial problems, despite evidence to the contrary. This projection of blame reinforces the gaslighter's control over Rachel's self-perception and subsequent behavior. Rachel might begin to doubt her own decisions, overcompensating by working excessively to "fix" the perceived issue, or withdrawing from her colleagues out of shame and self-blame.

Gaslighting causes immense emotional distress; women subjected to this manipulation experience heightened anxiety, confusion, and depression. The constant feeling of being on edge, questioning one's judgment, and doubting one's own reality can lead to serious psychological problems.

Self-Reflection 4.1: Are You a Target of Gaslighting?
- Do you feel that your ideas and contributions are met with a pattern of dismissive or invalidating responses?
- Do you feel like you are constantly second-guessing yourself?
- Do you experience a sense of confusion or disorientation as a result of persistent remarks or repeated statements that challenge your perception of reality?
- Do you apologize excessively for your actions or feelings?
- Do you feel isolated and disconnected from friends and family because someone insists they are a negative influence on you?

Strategies for Countering Gaslighting

Once women have identified that they are experiencing gaslighting, it is essential for them to prioritize their own well-being and take steps to protect themselves. First of all, they need to remind themselves that they are not the source of the problem and trust their own instincts and perceptions. They need to be aware of the signs of manipulation, such as frequent denial of their experiences, emotions, or memories. Some other strategies include:

- Reassurance from a supportive community can help counteract the effects of gaslighting. Seek the opinions of trusted friends, family members, or colleagues, as they can provide an objective perspective and emotional support. Look for validation from external sources if necessary.
- Set clear boundaries and communicate them assertively. Refuse to accept manipulative behaviors and stand firm in your convictions. If at all possible, consider ending relationships or limiting contact with manipulative individuals. Recognize the time to retreat and be prepared to sever ties with the gaslighter if they persist in their manipulative behavior.
- Maintain a record of gaslighting incidents, including dates, times, and specific examples. This documentation can help you gain clarity and serve as evidence if you need to seek help from authorities or pursue legal intervention.
- Engage in self-care to promote emotional resilience. Unexpected wells of inner strength often lie in practices or perspectives you may overlook. For example, journaling can provide clarity and emotional release; supportive friendships can offer fresh perspectives during challenging times; and enjoyable activities can bring a sense of calm and focus during difficult moments.
- Seek professional help if needed. Consulting with a mental health professional can be immensely beneficial in navigating the complexities of gaslighting. Therapists can provide tools and coping strategies tailored to your specific situation.
- Educate others who might be going through a similar experience. Raising awareness about gaslighting is crucial to prevent its proliferation. Talk with friends, family, and peers about the signs of gaslighting, its impact on victims, and how to support those who may be experiencing it.

What Can Organizations Do?

Organizations have a responsibility to create a safe and supportive environment for their employees, including combating emotional abuse such as gaslighting. By implementing training programs, establishing anti-harassment policies, and providing support mechanisms, organizations can play a significant role in empowering women and fostering a culture of respect and empathy. A collective effort from leaders, employees, and the organization as a whole is crucial in creating a workplace where everyone feels valued, heard, and free from emotional abuse.

> **Self-Reflection 4.2: Countering Gaslighting as a Manager**
>
> - Does the work environment prioritize respect, inclusivity, and open commu-nication? What mechanisms currently exist within the organization to encourage employees to support and respect one another?
> - Are managers and supervisors trained to recognize the signs of gaslighting? Are they equipped to respond appropriately and supportively to employees facing such challenges?
> - How does the organization hold leaders and managers accountable for promoting a healthy and respectful workplace culture? Do leaders set an example of zero-tolerance for emotional abuse and microaggressions?
> - How does the organization encourage the formation of peer support net-works, where employees can share experiences and provide emotional sup-port to one another?
> - Are there confidential and safe reporting channels in the organization for employees to report instances of gaslighting or emotional abuse? Do employees feel assured that their concerns will be taken seriously and addressed promptly?
> - To what extent does the organization offer Employee Assistance Programs (EAPs) that provide counseling and support services for employees experien-cing emotional distress? EAPs can offer a safe space for employees to seek help and guidance.
> - What information and resources from external organizations are offered to support victims of gaslighting?
> - How often does the organization conduct regular assessments to gauge the effectiveness of implemented measures and gather feedback from employ-ees? How is this feedback used to make improvements and adapt strategies?

4.3   Myths Perpetuated by Gaslighting

Gaslighting perpetuates stereotypes about women, such as the notions that they lack vision, are overly emotional, or talk too much, by exploiting societal biases and reinforcing them through manipulation. For example, gaslighters may dismiss a woman's innovative ideas as impractical, subtly eroding her credibility as a visionary leader. Likewise, labeling legitimate concerns as "overreacting" exploits the cliché of women being excessively emotional, prompting them to doubt their own self-worth. Silencing women in conversations, while accusing them of "talking too much," not only invalidates their contributions but also reinforces the idea that their voices are unwelcome. Together, these tactics foster a cycle of self-doubt, causing women to lower their expectations of themselves and enabling gaslighters to maintain power in both professional and personal contexts.

Myth #1: "Women Are Not Visionary"

The myth that "women are not visionary" is one example of how gaslighting operates. It often involves belittling women's accomplishments or abilities, which can undermine their self-esteem. For example, Agnieszka had successfully completed a challenging project and received praise from all her peers and direct reports. However, her boss responded with the remark, "Your approach was not strategic, and you were lucky this time." His remark puzzled everyone. Over the following months, Agnieszka's boss continued to question her vision, causing her to doubt her skills and accomplishments despite a proven track record. This led Agnieszka to lose confidence and rely on her boss for validation. Agnieszka's boss continuously downplayed her achievements, and as a result, she became hesitant to take on new challenges, fearing she might fail or be perceived as not strategic enough. As her self-confidence decreased, she became more vulnerable to gaslighting.

What does empirical evidence suggest about women's visionary capabilities? Based on four decades of research and analysis of 27 million employee reports, Gallup concludes that female leaders outperform their male colleagues when it comes to employee engagement (Gallup, 2016). Another recent study reveals that women were perceived, particularly by their male managers, as more competent than their male colleagues in leadership capabilities that differentiate excellent leaders from average or poor ones (Zenger & Folkman, 2019). They were rated significantly higher than men on capabilities measured in thousands of 360-degree reviews. The two exceptions were "develops strategic perspective" and "technical or professional expertise."

The perception that women are not strategic or visionary is not new, and evidence suggests it has persisted over the past ten years. This persistence indicates that women continue to face challenges in being viewed as equals in terms of strategic competence. One important skill leaders need to master is articulating a compelling vision of the future. Herminia Ibarra and Otilia Obodaru analyzed the 360-degree feedback provided to executives based on the Global Executive Leadership Inventory developed at INSEAD (Ibarra & Obodaru, 2009). There was either no difference between women and men on every skill measured, or women outperformed male leaders, with one exception. Women scored lower on envisioning, which encompasses three skills: sensing opportunities and threats in the environment, setting strategic direction, and inspiring constituents. Women's self-evaluations did not contribute to the lower score, as they were higher than those of men on four of the

10 dimensions analyzed. The difference in the score for envisioning was due mainly to the lower ratings of women by their male peers, whereas female peers, male line managers, and male direct reports gave them higher ratings.

Contrary to the commonly held belief that women are not as strategic as men, research suggests otherwise (Ibarra & Obodaru, 2009). The researchers put forth three explanations. The first suggests that women are, in fact, as visionary as men, but because they have a more collaborative style, invite contributions from everyone, and label the output as the group's vision, they receive less credit for the result from their peers. The researchers' second explanation is that women lack the confidence to talk about a vision, an explanation that is not supported by solid data since it is a projection into the future. The third explanation is that women do not believe envisioning is critical to leadership and are skeptical about how it can help achieve results. Instead, they value a practical, down-to-earth, here-and-now approach.

The way women talk about strategic change may also play a role in how they are perceived. Organizational members gain status when they speak up, but there are different ways in which they can do it, for example, when talking about strategic change (Liang et al., 2012). One of the approaches is to discuss it *promotively* by putting a positive spin on the ideas or suggestions of how the work can be improved in the future. The other option is to do it *prohibitively* by expressing concerns about current practices or harmful behaviors or incidents that need to be stopped. A recent study examined how voice type (promotive versus prohibitive) and gender impacted status and subsequent leader emergence (McClean et al., 2018). The results suggest that speaking promotively, but not prohibitively, increases status and the likelihood that the individual will emerge as a leader. A positive framing about the future appears to be more appealing to peers than a focus on a problem that needs to be fixed. The benefits, however, were not equal for men and women; women were perceived by their peers as less leader-like than their male colleagues who spoke up promotively. One of the reasons could be that women's ideas often get lost in meetings (see Chap. 2), which makes the role of allyship even more important. Giving credit to the person who puts forward the promotive idea recognizes women's contributions and makes it more likely that people will remember who contributed the idea and ascribe status to her. In sum, when sharing ideas for change, speaking up promotively is the best strategy for women to gain status.

Asking thought-provoking questions can increase the perception of visionary capabilities. In the past, leaders often enjoyed a guru-like status and were highly respected for their ability to provide answers to questions from peers and direct reports. However, in today's world, we face a formidable competitor in artificial intelligence (AI), and it's unrealistic to expect that we'll be able to compete with AI in terms of finding answers in the near future. Nevertheless, the human brain possesses a unique advantage: its ability to meaningfully integrate multiple dimensions, including relationships, feelings, and intuition. This integration forms a solid foundation for asking insightful questions that consider numerous aspects of a situation. By leveraging this ability, women leaders can stimulate the thinking of others and contribute value in ways that AI currently cannot match. By asking thought-provoking questions, women leaders cultivate an image of being forward-thinking, strategic, and innovative—all of which are hallmarks of visionary capabilities.

Self-Reflection 4.3: Honing Visioning Skills

- To what extent do you consider visioning important?
- What is your strategy for improving your visioning skills?
- Who are your role models for strengthening your visioning skills?
- How do you use your network to develop your vision and test it?
- To what extent do you fear others might judge your vision because it doesn't have all the details, isn't articulated well enough, or might be perceived as superficial?
- What kind of language do you use when you share your vision: tentative and ambivalent, or firm and unambiguous?
- When you lead, do you explain how your vision fits into the strategy of your organization?
- How strategic are you when navigating your career to ensure you acquire the experience needed to be visionary?
  - Have you held P&L positions, been involved in cross-functional projects, or taken on assignments outside your immediate expertise?
  - To what extent do you focus on the big picture and how the different pieces come together?

- When you pitch an idea, do you rely on concrete language and use a promotive voice?
- To further develop your visioning skills, think carefully about your next career move:
  - Does it involve P&L responsibility?
  - How big is the team you are going to lead?
  - Does the role provide you with an opportunity to gain international experience? Will you be part of, or leading, a global team?

Take Action 4.1: Elevate the Conversation to the Strategic Level

How can you make the conversation more strategic and dispel the myth that women are not strategic? Chevallier et al. (2024) suggest a framework of questions grouped into five categories that you can apply to strategic decision-making:

1. Investigative questions: What's known? Analyze the issue in depth.
2. Speculative questions: What if? What else? Reframe the issue to see the broader context.
3. Productive questions: What now? Assess feasibility and resources to decide on a course of action.
4. Interpretive questions: So what? Redefine and delve deeper into the implications.
5. Subjective Questions: What's unsaid? Reveal the emotional aspects, such as unspoken reservations, frustrations, or hidden agendas, that can derail the process.

Myth #2: "Women Are Too Emotional"

You have probably witnessed the following gender-based emotional manipulation: A woman voices her concerns about gender disparities in the workplace, hoping to initiate positive changes. Instead of addressing the issues, her male superiors and colleagues respond by labeling her as "too emotional," "oversensitive," or "playing the victim card," effectively gaslighting her and discrediting her valid concerns.

Evolutionarily, emotions have proven valuable for our survival as a species. Emotions are adaptive because they help us navigate the world by guiding our actions: fear keeps us safe from danger, love strengthens our bonds with others, and joy motivates us to seek out experiences that enrich our lives. Despite this, some leaders claim that emotions, positive or negative, have no place in the workplace. However, this view overlooks the integral role emotions play in our daily lives. We rely on emotions when making decisions, solving problems, bonding with others, and navigating various aspects of our personal and professional lives. In practical terms, ignoring emotions doesn't make them disappear. Instead, acknowledging and understanding our emotions can lead to better self-awareness.

In 1998, Martin Seligman founded a new domain of psychology called "positive psychology" as a reaction to traditional psychology, which he felt focused too much on humans' disorders and weaknesses. The term positive psychology dates back to 1954, when Abraham Maslow published his book

Motivation and Personality with the final chapter titled "Toward a Positive Psychology."

Positive psychology studies the conditions and processes that contribute to subjective well-being, happiness, and flourishing. However, one of the critiques is that the movement makes people believe that negative internal thoughts or feelings should be avoided. For example, you often hear that optimism and confidence are key ingredients for success. While this can be inspiring, it can also lead people to assume they did not succeed because they were not optimistic or confident enough (Ciarrochi et al., 2016). Toxic positivity refers to people not fully acknowledging, processing, or managing the whole spectrum of human emotions, including anger and sadness (Lukin, 2019). A manager who tells their direct report, "Why don't you look at the bright side of life?" is an example of toxic positivity.

Being overly positive can lead to positive illusions and overlooking possible threats (Gruber et al., 2011). Not surprisingly, people who experience the highest levels of happiness are the most successful when it comes to close relationships, but people who experience slightly lower levels of happiness are the most successful with regard to income and education (Oishi et al., 2007). In addition, being overly optimistic or happy may lead to complacency or prevent people from benefiting from natural coping mechanisms that follow negative emotions.

Throughout centuries, societies and organizations have developed norms about how emotions should be expressed; often, the dominant view is that strong emotions should be suppressed. Indra Nooyi, former CEO of Pepsi, writes that when she was angry with people within and outside of the company because they wouldn't understand what she was trying to achieve, she would "go into the little bathroom attached to my office, look at myself in the mirror, and just let it all out. And when the moment had passed, I'd wipe my tears, reapply a little makeup, square my shoulders, and walk back out into the fray, ready, again, to be" (Nooyi, 2020).

A Blueprint for Processing Negative Emotions

Negative emotions can be useful because they signal that something is wrong, prompting self-reflection, boundary-setting, or action. If a person feels anxious about an upcoming presentation, they might start preparing well in advance, and the negative feelings will help them mobilize internal resources to achieve their goal and avoid failure. Following negative life events, such as the death of a close friend or relative, pessimists were found to be less likely than optimists to experience depression (Isaacowitz & Seligman, 2001). This may be because negative emotions help people mentally prepare for adverse outcomes.

In the context of gaslighting, however, negative emotions are unhelpful when they spiral into self-doubt, chronic anxiety, or shame. If left unprocessed, negative emotions can erode a person's confidence. Processing them helps targets of gaslighting reconnect with their sense of self-worth and rebuild confidence in their own thoughts and decisions, while resisting the psychological control of the gaslighter. When negative emotions are suppressed instead of processed, people may experience lower levels of well-being and physical symptoms, such as suppressed immunity, hypertension, chest pain, and many others. Researchers in the 1980s started noticing that when traumatic experiences were kept secret, as opposed to being spoken about, they were more likely to lead to health problems (Pennebaker & Sussman, 1988).

Acknowledging and labeling emotions are the first steps in processing them. Research suggests that identifying and naming emotions can help reduce their intensity and make them more manageable. This process, known as "affective labeling," engages the prefrontal cortex, the brain's cognition center, and reduces activity in the amygdala, the brain's emotional center, thereby diminishing emotional reactivity (Lieberman et al., 2007). When searching for the right label for an emotion, it's important to recognize that the first association might be inaccurate. For instance, what initially feels like sadness might actually be masking deeper feelings of disappointment or anger. It's also crucial to remember that all emotions have a propensity to intensify, sometimes very quickly.

Research has shown that people who talk or write about painful personal emotional events subsequently experience significant long-term improvements in mood and overall well-being. Sharing our emotions with others has several positive effects. It stimulates us to label and make sense of our emotions, which can be therapeutic in and of itself. Interestingly, there is an additional benefit (Collins & Miller, 1994): People who disclose more tend to be more liked by others. This creates a positive feedback loop, as we tend to disclose more to people we like and, in turn, like people to whom we have disclosed.

While talking about emotions can be beneficial, writing about painful events can further help in processing these experiences, analyzing underlying emotions, and labeling them correctly. The process of putting your thoughts on paper can be highly beneficial, regardless of whether you keep or discard the final product. The act of writing itself is what matters most. Research has found that writing by hand results in deeper processing, while typing on a laptop results in shallower processing (Mueller & Oppenheimer, 2014).

Writing about these experiences also encourages shifting perspectives, moving from using the pronouns "we, you, she, he, they" to more personal pronouns like "I, me, my" (Pennebaker & Chung, 2007). Owning your emotions in this way helps you become more aware of your feelings, which can then lead to insights into the root causes of your thoughts and behaviors. This self-awareness motivates you to manage your reactions more effectively rather than feeling overwhelmed or stuck in negative patterns.

Take Action 4.2: Journaling about Painful Events

Journaling can help you process negative experiences, analyze underlying emotions, and label them correctly (Pennebaker & Smyth, 2016). During this writing exercise, you'll likely engage in cognitive reappraisal, a powerful technique that involves changing how you think about a situation to alter its emotional impact. Cognitive reappraisal can help you gain a fresh perspective on the situation, identify potential positive aspects or learning opportunities, reduce the emotional charge associated with the event, and develop more balanced and realistic interpretations.

- Write it down: When you find yourself ruminating after a negative event, try writing down your feelings.
- Reframe the negative experience: Consider viewing the event in a more positive or neutral light to reduce the intensity of negative emotions and their lasting effects.
- Identify patterns: Notice any recurring themes or triggers that surface repeatedly. Reflect on what specifically activates these patterns, and explore strategies to address them.

This practice of writing and reappraising can help break the cycle of negative rumination, allowing you to process your emotions more effectively and move forward with greater emotional resilience. The goal is not to produce a polished piece of writing but rather to engage in a therapeutic process of emotional exploration and reframing.

Tom Drummond, an emeritus educator of children and adults, provides a publicly available vocabulary of emotions and feelings, which can help enhance your ability to enrich your personal emotional lexicon (https://tomdrummond.com/leading-and-caring-for-children/emotion-vocabulary/). This resource, developed for people working with children, serves as an excellent tool for expanding your understanding and expression of various emotional states. To further develop this skill, you can practice by articulating the emotions of those around you. This exercise not only sharpens your

Table 4.1 Emotion vocabulary

Happy	Confident	Positive	Angry	Sad	Afraid
Cheerful	Prepared	Optimistic	Annoyed	Depressed	Scared
Satisfied	Assured	Grateful	Frustrated	Upset	Anxious
Excited	Strong	Appreciative	Furious	Humiliated	Hesitant
Content	Courageous	Warm	Resentful	Rejected	Intimidated
Delighted	Determined	Gentle	Irritated	Disgusted	Suspicious
Enthusiastic	Motivated	Caring	Hostile	Miserable	Frightened
Charmed	Curious	Compassionate	Outraged	Gloomy	Worried
Proud	Interested	Engaged	Disappointed	Shy	Confused
Invigorated	Ambitious	Considerate	Bitter	Lonely	Horrified
Inspired	Dynamic	Empathetic	Hostile	Desperate	

emotional intelligence but is often perceived as helpful by others, as it helps them understand their own emotions. Accurately identifying and verbalizing the emotions you observe in others helps you demonstrate empathy and improve your interpersonal communication. Regularly engaging with emotion vocabulary and applying it in real-life situations can lead to more nuanced and effective communication in both personal and professional contexts. Table 4.1 provides an example of emotion vocabulary, including both positive and negative emotions.

Negative Emotions Can Contribute to Well-Being

Negative emotions play a vital role in human well-being by signaling that something in our environment or inner world requires attention. Among these, anger and crying are both powerful emotional expressions for women, shaped by how society teaches them to handle their feelings. From an early age, girls learn that showing tears is acceptable, while direct displays of anger are discouraged. Yet both anger and crying can offer meaningful ways to cope with negative emotions. Anger often signals that our boundaries have been crossed or that we're facing an injustice, prompting us to stand up for ourselves, while crying can provide emotional release and invite others' support. Despite the different social reactions these emotions elicit, each serves an important role in processing life's challenges.

Commonly perceived as a negative emotion, anger has long been associated with adverse outcomes such as aggression, violence, and relationship conflict. Anger, however, is not a monolithically negative emotion; it encompasses a range of potential positive effects that can contribute to personal growth, social change, and improved interpersonal dynamics. Scientific research has moved beyond the negative perception of anger and reveals that, when experienced and expressed appropriately, it can play a beneficial role in personal and social development. For example, anger can be a powerful motivational force, propelling individuals toward action in the face of injustice or wrongdoing. It can inspire people to engage in activism or support social movements aimed at bringing about change.

Contrary to the belief that anger harms negotiations, research indicates that the strategic expression of anger can lead to more favorable negotiation outcomes (Van Kleef et al., 2004). Expressed anger can signal strength and determination, leading opponents to reassess their positions and make concessions. However, this strategy must be used judiciously, as inappropriate expressions of anger can backfire.

Anger can act as an important signal that personal boundaries have been violated (Potegal & Stemmler, 2010). This emotional response can encourage individuals experiencing anger to assert themselves and communicate their needs more clearly, potentially leading to healthier relationships. By recognizing anger as a sign of unmet needs, individuals can address underlying issues and work toward resolving conflicts.

Interestingly, experiencing anger can sometimes improve analytical thinking. It can reduce cognitive biases by promoting a more analytical and less heuristic approach to problem-solving (Lerner & Tiedens, 2006). This means that, in certain contexts, anger can lead to more careful consideration of arguments and evidence.

The benefits of anger come from its constructive expression and management. Uncontrolled or misdirected anger can still lead to negative outcomes, highlighting the importance of emotional regulation skills. As our understanding of the multifaceted nature of anger deepens, so too does our ability to use this powerful emotion in positive and transformative ways.

Self-Reflection 4.4: Anger Management

The following strategies can help you process anger mindfully (see also Table 4.2):

1. Identify anger triggers: Think of situations that have triggered anger reactions in you. Briefly describe these incidents, focusing on the key elements that led to your emotional response.
2. Recognize patterns in your reaction: Look for commonalities in situations that provoke anger to identify triggers that lead to a similar emotional response. Look for underlying themes or common patterns. For example, you might notice that your anger is often triggered when someone appears to underestimate your capabilities or patronize you.
3. Develop response strategies: For each identified situation, consider two potential responses:

- Reframing or letting go: How can you reappraise the situation to reduce or release your anger? This might involve changing your perspective.
- Acting with confidence: What can you do to address the situation productively? This could include assertive communication, problem-solving, or seeking support from others.

Table 4.2 Anger triggers, reaction patterns, and response strategies

Anger trigger	Reaction patterns	Reframing/letting go	Acting with confidence
A colleague interrupts you during a meeting	Feeling disrespected	Understand that this interruption may not be personal	Politely assert yourself and address the interruption
Your manager disinvites you to an important meeting at the last minute	Feeling unimportant or ignored	Remind yourself that plans can change for various reasons	Communicate openly with your manager about how it affects you
A peer criticizes your choice of action	Feeling judged or unsupported	Understand that the critic may not understand your decision	Engage in a calm discussion to clarify your choice

Men's and Women's Expression of Emotion is Perceived Differently

When men and women express the same emotion, they are perceived differently. Brescoll and Uhlmann (2008) explored the link between gender, status, and emotion expression at work. The results suggest that men who expressed anger at work were seen as more competent and were given higher status compared to men who showed sadness. But for women, it was a different story. Both male and female evaluators assigned lower status to angry women. This bias held true no matter what position the woman held in the organization. Interestingly, people tended to explain women's anger as a reflection of their personality (e.g., "she's out of control"), while men's anger was seen as a reasonable reaction to external circumstances. The gender bias disappeared when people were explicitly told that a woman's anger was caused by external factors.

Some studies suggest that people are more likely to attribute expressions of anger to personal characteristics when the individual is a Black woman (Moto et al., 2022). This negative stereotype can lead to unfavorable performance evaluations and unfair assessments of leadership capability.

While women are punished for expressing emotion, men are rewarded with attention. Indra Nooyi observes this double standard in her book: "I had heard of and seen male CEOs yell, throw things, and use four-letter words with great gusto, apparently a sign of their passion and commitment. But I was well aware that showing any of these emotions myself would set me back with the people around me" (Nooyi, 2020).

Many men feel uncomfortable when women visibly express strong emotions. This discomfort can lead to problematic situations in the workplace. Male managers may fear being accused of insensitivity if they speak firmly to female employees. As a result, they might opt to play it safe by withholding feedback from women altogether. This approach, however, may deprive women of the constructive feedback necessary for personal development, which can stall their career progression.

Tears, in particular, can be challenging for male managers to handle. Women cry for various reasons, including frustration, stress, or feelings of helplessness. These emotional expressions are not necessarily signs of weakness but can be manifestations of complex feelings and situations. What is it that horrifies men when they see a woman in tears in their office? Scholars have found that, though the odor of tears is not consciously perceptible, their "smell" activates specific olfactory receptors in the human nose and reduces testosterone levels. An experiment at the Weizmann Institute of Science suggests that emotional tearing may also have a chemosignaling function (Gelstein et al., 2011). Sniffing tears from female donors who had experienced negative emotions induced sexual turnoff in male participants.

Emotional tears are a uniquely human experience. In the 1980s, psychologist William Fry explored how often people cry (from moist eyes to full-on sobbing). He came to the conclusion that, on average, women cry 5.3 times a month, while the number for men was 1.3 times a month (Collier, 2014). One of the explanations is that testosterone likely inhibits crying, while prolactin, which is produced in higher levels in women, may stimulate it. However, the difference may be triggered by cultural factors in addition to biological factors (Van Hemert et al., 2011). For example, people living in countries where more freedom of expression is accepted tend to cry more often. In affluent, more democratic countries that value relationships and nurturing behaviors (e.g., Sweden, Norway, the Netherlands), gender differences in the tendency to cry are greater, which means that cultural norms permit and do not penalize this kind of behavior.

Another study reports that, in all countries where data was collected, women tended to cry more frequently, for more reasons, and in more contexts compared to men (Fischer et al., 2013). Participants perceived men who cried for work-related reasons as experiencing more sadness and as being more emotional. They also penalized them by considering them less competent.

This gender difference in crying is linked to socialization. Boys are socialized not to cry from a young age, while girls are not expected to suppress crying. Managers need to consider crying as an expression of frustration and anger, similar to an angry facial expression or raising one's voice during a meeting.

People's assessment of crying in the workplace is more nuanced than simply rejecting the idea of women showing emotion. While shedding tears on the job isn't inherently problematic, it can harm your reputation if it happens in the wrong context (Elsbach & Bechky, 2018). Interestingly, men and women react in the same way when they witness a female coworker crying at work. When professional women become tearful, observers show nuanced reactions. Crying will not hurt the crier's reputation if coworkers think the woman crying is dealing with "difficult personal issues" or "a tough situation at work." In tough circumstances, such as the death of a close person or problems at home, such as a serious illness, observers perceive crying to be legitimate since it does not violate behavioral scripts. On other occasions, however, criers are perceived as weak (e.g., coming out from a performance appraisal); unprofessional (e.g., crying in a heated meeting); or manipulative (e.g., crying during a performance appraisal). Men are more likely to conclude that women are crying on purpose. To a large extent, the negative attributions are connected to disrupting the work of others. Therefore, women are advised to leave the public situation if they cannot control their crying. In conclusion, the perception of crying depends on the context.

Myth #3: "Women Talk too Much"

In 2021, the President of the Tokyo Olympic and Paralympic organizing committee, Yoshiro Mori, resigned amidst a furor over his comments that female board members talk too much. Meetings take "twice as long," he complained, when there are women participating. "If one raises her hand to speak then all the others feel they have to do the same. So it ends up with everybody talking" (Harding, 2021). Mori is only one in a long line of misguided proponents of this myth that women speak more than men. In fact, researchers have been disproving this myth since the 1970s. And yet the myth is so entrenched; it is embedded in sayings from many cultures around the globe (Homes, 1998). There's a German expression that translates as "One man, one word—one woman, one dictionary." The Japanese have a saying: "Where there are women and geese, there's noise."

The comment "You talk too much," directed at a woman, can be a form of gaslighting in certain contexts. For example, imagine a workplace scenario where Aicha is presenting her ideas during a team meeting. She's articulate, well-prepared, and contributes valuable insights to the discussion. However, her colleague, Phil, interrupts her and says, "You talk too much, Aicha. We don't have all day." This comment is a form of gaslighting because it dismisses Aicha's contributions by implying that they are excessive or unnecessary. It makes her doubt the value and appropriateness of her input and may cause her to second-guess herself in future meetings, potentially leading to self-censorship. If Phil's behavior persists, Aicha may become hesitant to share her ideas, fearing criticism or dismissal. This self-doubt and self-censorship are classic outcomes of gaslighting. The gaslighter, in this case, Phil, might defend his comment by deflecting: "I'm just trying to keep the meeting on track. You're being too sensitive." Or, "I didn't mean anything by it. You're overreacting."

When it comes to talking, it's difficult to say how much is "too much." Because of the subjective nature of perceptions, it's important to discuss the evidence and the bias. Empirical evidence suggests a more nuanced picture, one that is more in line with the idea that men are actually the ones who talk more. In the 1980s, a number of experiments concluded that women speak less than men in public settings (James & Drakich, 1993). Things have not changed dramatically. In 2017, a study commissioned by Bloomberg and carried out by Prattle analyzed 155,000 company conference calls held over the past 19 years and found that men spoke 92% of the time. Another study concludes that even when women have a seat at the table, men do 75% of the talking in the average business meeting (Karpowitz et al., 2012). This study further suggests that the talk-time deficit will continue until women make up a super-majority in a group. In 2015, the average male justice on the US Supreme Court interrupted his female colleagues 3.9 times more often than other male justices during oral arguments.

This pattern can be observed from kindergarten onward. Since there is no biological reason why one gender should talk more than the other, we look to socialization to explain the myth. Volubility, or the amount of talking we do, is associated with the status of the individual who is talking. Boys learn to assert their status early in life through verbal contributions in public settings. In private contexts, however, talking builds interpersonal connections, friendships, and intimate relationships, which is the primary interest of girls. And while men emphasize the informational aspect of talking, women tend to use its supportive function. The sociolinguist Janet Holmes provides a revealing quote by a 16-year-old girl that explains why girls might prefer a lower profile: "Sometimes I feel like saying that I disagree ..., but where would that get me? My teacher thinks I'm showing off and the boys jeer. But if I pretend I don't understand, it's very different. The teacher is sympathetic and the boys are helpful" (Holmes, 1998, p. 261). Of course, a lot has changed since this schoolgirl said this in the 1990s, but there is still more work to do in many contexts and cultures to overcome the bias against women being labeled as "talking too much" when they are just talking.

If it's a myth that women talk more than men, why do so many people perceive that women talk more than necessary? There are three major contributors to this misconception.

First, there are proportionally fewer women in leadership positions. For example, at the beginning of 2025, the percentage of women CEOs at Fortune 500 companies was 11.6% (7.5% of DAX and 9% of FTSE) (Hinchliffe, 2025). The small number of women in leadership roles increases their visibility, which can be explained by "tokenism," a concept coined by the US sociologist Rosabeth Moss Kanter. She considers tokenism a structural phenomenon that occurs in groups where one demographic group is significantly underrepresented. Kanter defines tokens as individuals who are treated as symbols of their minority group rather than as individuals, leading to heightened visibility, performance pressures, and social isolation (Kanter, 1977). Women often find themselves in this category, particularly in stereotypically male domains. People who are "tokens" are much more visible than others in the workplace, and whatever they do is strongly registered by the group. In other words, male colleagues will notice the one woman in the meeting and generalize her behavior to all women. If you then look at the distribution of roles, there are more men than women in positions of power chairing meetings. More often than not, women are asked questions (by these men) and asked to elaborate, placing them in the spotlight again.

Second, women's communication styles involve saying more, often to maintain interpersonal connections. As you read in Chap. 2, women tend to use more filler phrases ("sort of, well, you see") and more tag endings ("don't you think?"). This means women use more words, and why they do so brings us to the third point: Women's motivation to interact is different from men's.

Women's language is driven by a desire to engage the other party in a conversation. By contrast, men seek to inform and signal status. From a woman's perspective, the length of her speech makes sense given this goal, but men don't see it the same way. Scholar Dale Spender explains that how much women talk is not judged "on the grounds of whether they talk more than men, but of whether they talk more than silent women" (Holmes, 1998, p. 261).

People in power talk more and interrupt more. And yet, women in power do not. Why is this? Indeed, there is a strong positive relationship between volubility and power for men, but not for women (Brescoll, 2011). Ironically, women probably aren't talking enough. Women talk less than men, essentially because they fear a backlash if they talk as much as men, and they are right to do so. Women CEOs who talked longer were evaluated as significantly less competent and less suitable for leadership than a male CEO who talked an equal amount of time. This was based on a latent belief that women do not have the status to talk as much as men. Fascinatingly, even women penalize other women for talking more.

Self-Reflection 4.5: How Much Do You Talk?

1. Are you talking more than others, or is this perception influenced by gender stereotypes?
2. In what contexts are you being told you talk too much? Is it in meetings, social settings, or elsewhere?
3. Are your contributions being undervalued due to the "double bind," where women are criticized for both speaking up and staying silent?
4. Are you using language that might make your speech seem longer, such as fillers or tag endings? Some small tweaks, including speaking in shorter sentences, physically leaning in when you speak, maintaining eye contact, and using firmer language ("will" instead of "might" or "know" instead of "believe"), can help change perceptions.
5. Are you making yourself "small" in other ways, such as through body language or voice pitch, which might contradict your verbal contributions?
6. Do you feel the need to prove yourself by explicitly discussing your accomplishments, and could this be contributing to the perception that you talk too much?
7. Do you trust that people will listen to and act on your message, or do you feel the need to overexplain?
8. Have you discussed "no interruption rules" during meetings with your team?
9. How well do you perform your gatekeeper role when you chair meetings?
10. How do you prevent the loudest voice from dominating the conversation? Do you invite silent participants to share their views?

4.4   Role Incredulity, Untitling, and Uncredentialing as Forms of Devaluation

Devaluation significantly undermines women's confidence, eroding both their sense of self-worth and their professional authority. Three mechanisms drive this process: role incredulity, untitling, and uncredentialing. Role incredulity occurs when women are presumed to occupy subordinate or traditionally feminine positions, casting doubt on their leadership abilities or authority. Untitling involves denying or ignoring women's professional titles, thereby minimizing their expertise and achievements. Uncredentialing goes further by dismissing or downplaying women's qualifications, which undercuts their credibility and limits their opportunities for advancement.

Role Incredulity

Vignette 4.4: Marjan

Marjan, a seasoned software engineer with over a decade of experience, has recently joined a new tech startup as a senior developer. Her team is diverse, but she is the only woman in a senior technical role. During her first team meeting, Marjan introduced herself and briefly mentioned some of her key projects and areas of expertise. Later in the meeting, the team discussed a complex technical issue and proposed several solutions. When Marjan offered a solution based on her previous experience, one of her colleagues, Lukas, expressed surprise and said, "Oh, I didn't realize you had such a strong technical background. I thought you were part of the admin team helping us coordinate the project." Marjan felt a mix of surprise and frustration. She noticed a few nods of agreement from other team members, which added to her discomfort. It was clear that some of her colleagues had not listened to her initial introduction or had assumed that her role was nontechnical due to her gender.

Marjan addressed the situation calmly but firmly. She reiterated her role and qualifications, highlighting her technical contributions and leadership in previous roles. She also requested a few minutes after the meeting with Lukas and the team leader to clarify her responsibilities and how she would be contributing to the team going forward. After the meeting, the team leader apologized for the misunderstanding and ensured that Marjan's skills and role were clearly communicated in the team's internal newsletter. Lukas apologized for his assumption and committed to paying closer attention to his colleagues' introductions. Marjan also started a monthly technical showcase where team members could present their current projects and areas of expertise, which helped in breaking down assumptions and fostering a culture of respect and recognition for all team members' skills and contributions.

Researchers call what Marjan experienced "role incredulity," which involves assuming that women occupy gender-stereotypical or supportive roles, such as administrative assistants or nurses, rather than leadership positions, such as CEOs or doctors (Dzubinski, 2021). At first glance, this mistaken assumption may not seem harmful, but its effects on women can be significant. It can lead to diminished self-esteem and confidence, increased stress, and a sense of isolation in the workplace. Colleagues can manifest skepticism as surprise, overt questioning, or dismissive attitudes toward individuals who do not fit traditional or expected roles. Women often have to work harder to demonstrate and validate their actual positions, and their statements might not be taken as seriously as those from their male counterparts. Additionally, if women aren't recognized as leaders, they will likely not be considered for roles typically dominated by men.

Expressing skepticism or disbelief about another person's ability to fulfill the responsibilities of their position due to preconceived biases related to gender, age, race, or other personal characteristics can derail career paths. Career advancements and professional recognition have a broader impact, as they affect job satisfaction and growth opportunities. Role incredulity can also contribute to a toxic work environment, promoting a culture of disrespect and exclusion.

Women often struggle with how to introduce themselves as they try to establish credibility without coming across as bragging or arrogant. They need to signal competence in their introductions, but this is tricky since people tend to judge women more harshly than men when they don't come across as warm in social situations. Women in positions of authority tend to be judged disproportionately negatively if they are perceived to lack warmth (Chalmers, 2021). This means that when women introduce themselves at work, they need to signal both competence and warmth.

Untitling and Uncredentialing

Researchers Amy Diehl and Leanne Dzubinski have identified two other devaluing practices: untitling and uncredentialing (Diehl & Dzubinski, 2021). Untitling is the practice of deliberately omitting or disregarding a woman's professional or social titles in contexts where such titles are normally acknowledged. This practice can undermine their authority and credibility in professional environments. It often occurs in subtle ways, such as referring to women by their first names in professional settings where men would be addressed by their full titles and last names. One study has uncovered a subtle but significant gender bias in how we talk about professionals across various fields (Atir & Ferguson, 2018). Men are more likely than women to be referred to by their surname alone—a linguistic shortcut often associated with authority and prestige. For example, students reviewing professors online, political commentators on the radio, and participants discussing well-known figures like authors or athletes all showed this pattern. Even in controlled experiments, participants discussing a fictional male scientist were more likely to use his surname alone compared to an identical female scientist. Why does this matter? Further experiments revealed that referring to someone by their surname alone influences perceptions of their status and eminence. Participants judged researchers referred to by surname as more famous, accomplished, and deserving of awards and funding than those referred to by their full name. For example, scientists referred to by their last name only (e.g., Professor Adebayo) were viewed as 14% more deserving of a National Science Foundation career award (Atir & Ferguson, 2018). This seemingly small linguistic bias can have real-world consequences, subtly reinforcing gender disparities in how professionals are perceived and valued.

Uncredentialing occurs when a woman's professional qualifications or credentials are overlooked or minimized. This might include not using a woman's academic degrees (such as Dr or Professor) in contexts where her male counterparts' credentials are highlighted. It often manifests as questioning her competence or denying her the respect that her credentials merit.

In most cases, untitling and uncredentialing are unintentional; nevertheless, they have a negative impact, as they undermine the self-confidence of women who experience this type of disrespect. Both of these behaviors stem from deeply ingrained gender stereotypes and biases that underestimate women's capabilities and roles. These biases can be unconscious, reflecting societal norms that prioritize male authority and expertise. In professional settings, such behaviors may also stem from competitive dynamics or power plays, where diminishing a colleague's professional standing can be a strategy to undermine her influence or authority.

How prevalent are these practices? One study suggests that during Internal Medicine Grand Rounds—formal educational sessions designed to enhance the knowledge and clinical skills of healthcare professionals—women introduced speakers using their formal titles 96% of the time (Files et al., 2017). However, when the introductions were made by men, women were likely to be addressed by their professional titles only 49% of the time, compared to 72% for their male colleagues. Professional titles are especially crucial for highlighting the expertise of women who look younger, Black women, and women of color, who might not experience the assumptions that their same-aged white male colleagues enjoy. Compared to white women, Black women and women of color are even more likely to be targets of role incredulity.

The linguist Deborah Cameron examines patterns of language use that enact and normalize what she labels as "the gender respect gap" (Cameron, 2020). The term refers to a common form of everyday sexism that results in respect tokens, such as professional titles, being systematically withheld from women. This gendered disrespect, in the form of sexist linguistic practice, can be quite subtle. The unconscious assumption is that women are not entitled to the same level of respect that is routinely given to men of comparable status.

Titles are often associated with elitism, and some people dislike using them when addressing others. But when the disparity affects only women, and only women experience their formal titles being consistently neglected, the rationale of egalitarianism can be questioned. Normally, titles are awarded after accomplishing formal study or to signal a qualification, but in some cultures, they are used more broadly to signify respect or status. There are some other cultural differences. For example, people are less likely to use titles in the United Kingdom and the United States compared to Austria or Saudi Arabia.

In many contexts, titles are important since they signal expertise and professionalism. This is especially true when establishing legitimacy for women and members of minoritized groups, whose expertise is more likely to be devalued, even if they are highly qualified. In fields such as medicine or academia, credentials matter because they communicate expertise and therefore impact the trust we have in our doctors, lawyers, or educators. Perceptions of expertise influence women's promotions within organizations, their pay, their status as role models, and their roles as members of society.

More and more women around the world are earning professional titles (see Fig. 4.2). For example, in 2021, half of all doctors in OECD countries were women, compared to 29% in 1990. However, there are significant differences across countries. In Latvia and Estonia, more than 73% of the doctors are women, but that number drops to 25% or lower in Korea and Japan.

Similarly, more women are earning PhD degrees. In the United States, 85,370 men and 108,690 women earned a doctoral degree in the academic year of 2020/21. By 2031/32, these figures are expected to grow to about 88,110 and 141,500, respectively (Statista, 2025).

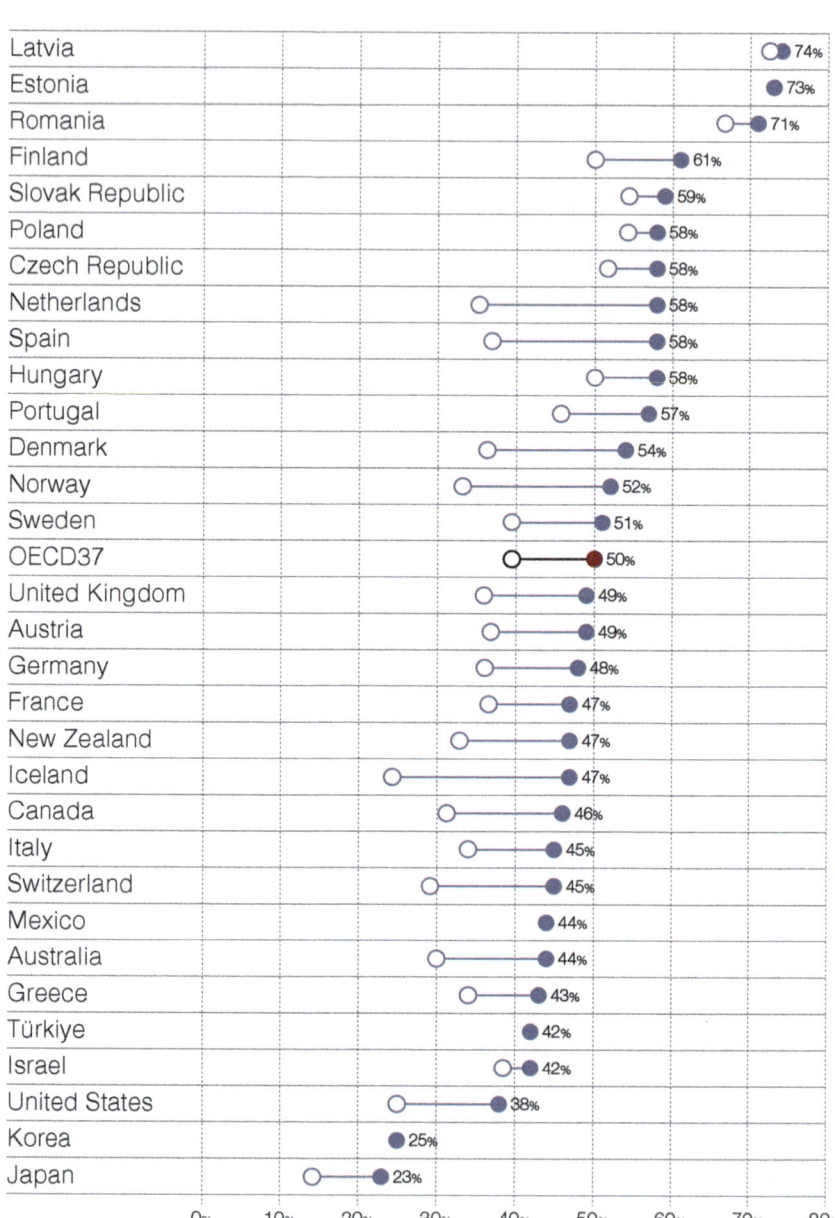

○ 2000   ● 2021

Latvia	74%
Estonia	73%
Romania	71%
Finland	61%
Slovak Republic	59%
Poland	58%
Czech Republic	58%
Netherlands	58%
Spain	58%
Hungary	58%
Portugal	57%
Denmark	54%
Norway	52%
Sweden	51%
OECD37	50%
United Kingdom	49%
Austria	49%
Germany	48%
France	47%
New Zealand	47%
Iceland	47%
Canada	46%
Italy	45%
Switzerland	45%
Mexico	44%
Australia	44%
Greece	43%
Türkiye	42%
Israel	42%
United States	38%
Korea	25%
Japan	23%

0% 10% 20% 30% 40% 50% 60% 70% 80%

Fig. 4.2 Women doctors in OECD countries. The number of women doctors differs significantly among OECD countries. *Source* Adapted from "Health at a Glance: OECD Indicators," by OECD (2023). https://doi.Org/10.1787/7a7afb35-en. Copyright 2023 by OECD Publishing

The omission of titles and credentials sends a subtle yet profound message that women's achievements and expertise are less valued than those of their male colleagues. When women's titles and credentials are consistently overlooked, downplayed, or ignored, they may start to doubt their own qualifications, despite their real skills and accomplishments. Women may feel that their hard work and sacrifices go unnoticed, and their motivation and engagement may be diminished, leading to feelings of underappreciation. Over time, untitling and uncredentialing chip away at women's confidence and may hinder their career progression. This internal conflict can lead women to hesitate in taking on new challenges or asserting themselves, perpetuating a cycle of self-doubt and perceived inadequacy.

In addition, observing male colleagues consistently being acknowledged by their titles, while women are not, reveals a systemic bias within their workplace. This perception of unequal treatment can promote feelings of alienation and undermine women's confidence in their ability to thrive within the organization, often resulting in heightened stress and potential burnout.

The cumulative effects of role incredulity, untitling, and uncredentialing are profound, perpetuating a harmful cycle where women's confidence is continuously eroded. As their confidence diminishes, women may become less inclined to advocate for themselves, pursue promotions, or seek leadership positions, further solidifying gender disparities in the workplace and perpetuating the very practices that undermine their confidence.

Vignette 4.5: Promotions in name only

The use of professional titles impacts the perception of expertise and gravitas of the individual in question. But what about promotions that are in name only, which offer a false sense of progress (Mallick, 2021)? This means that you have a title, but you can use it only when interacting with clients and not internally. It feels like being uncredentialed within the company. Some executives believe that upgrading your job title recognizes your hard work and shows appreciation. Others might use title-only promotions to keep employees from leaving, especially when turnover is high, or to save money when decision-makers do not want to give a raise. It's important to recognize these practices as fake promotions since they are not accompanied by an increased base salary or a bonus package. Such promotions may initially uplift a woman's morale, but the absence of genuine advancement in terms of responsibilities, authority, or compensation can result in frustration and disillusionment. This realization can leave women feeling stagnant and significantly impact their confidence, contributing to a sense of reaching a professional dead end.

Dealing with Role Incredulity, Untitling, and Uncredentialing

> ### Vignette 4.6: Leticia
>
> Dr. Leticia Gonzalez is a senior technology officer at an innovative renewable energy company. Despite her impressive credentials and years of experience in the energy sector, she frequently encounters role incredulity, especially in settings where her technical expertise is underestimated because of her gender. During a technical review meeting with potential investors, one investor, perhaps trying to be humorous or inadvertently revealing his bias, remarked, "It's so refreshing to see that you can keep up with the technical details, Leticia. I assume someone briefs you before these meetings?"
>
> With a composed smile, Leticia replies, "Actually, I prefer to do the briefings myself. It ensures I only have to hear the technical details once. Saves time, don't you think? Now, let's dive deeper into our photovoltaic integration process, which I designed."

Leticia reclaims her authority using friendly and inclusive humor. She makes a light-hearted but pointed remark, which is thoughtful and strategic. It helps her maintain professionalism as well as create positive workplace dynamics.

Role incredulity, which is what Leticia is experiencing, reinforces gender inequities in various spheres, from salaries to leadership opportunities, by systematically undermining women's contributions and abilities. Role incredulity not only undermines individuals who are directly affected, but it also reduces the overall productivity and harmony of the workplace. It can create an atmosphere of distrust, as colleagues who witness someone being undermined may feel uncomfortable or demoralized. Role incredulity can normalize microaggressions and bias, which may lead to higher turnover rates, difficulty attracting top talent, and reduced collaboration among team members.

Untitling and uncredentialing are subtle yet significant barriers that contribute to ongoing gender disparities in professional and social arenas. By understanding these phenomena, actively addressing them, and fostering environments that value and respect women's achievements and titles, we can make progress toward more equitable workplaces and societies. When women are empowered to assert their rightful titles and credentials, they play a pivotal role in dismantling these biases.

The practices of omitting titles, overlooking credentials, or expressing role incredulity are deeply embedded in organizational culture and society at large, but leaders, colleagues, and women themselves can take specific actions to address and mitigate them. These actions include establishing clear company policies regarding titling, fostering a supportive environment, acknowledging mistakes, and encouraging women by clearly stating their roles upfront.

Self-Reflection 4.6: Combating Role Incredulity, Untitling, and Uncredentialing

- In your organization, are people expected to introduce themselves with their titles in meetings or events where they may not know each other well? This might sound too rigid and formal, but it helps women build legitimacy and counteract role incredulity.
- To what extent does information about promotions and newly acquired job titles for senior leaders reach every part of the organization? Increasing the visibility of the promotions of women and members of minoritized groups counteracts role incredulity.
- When you act as an ally for your female colleagues, do you introduce them with their job titles and credentials? What do you do when the person chairing the meeting fails to include job titles and credentials in introductions?
- How do you set a standard for respect and equity in your team?
- How easy is it for you to call out untitling and uncredentialing?
- What do you do when your job title, qualifications, or credentials are dismissed or misidentified? Clear communication about your role, responsibilities, and accomplishments can help dispel doubts about competence.
- Are you concerned that you might be perceived as being "uptight," "needy," "insecure," or "entitled" if you ask people to use your formal titles (e.g., Dr., Professor, COO, etc.)?
- How do you use your network of supportive colleagues to counter baseless skepticism? Do you have allies who recognize and affirm your qualifications and reject attempts to undermine your professional standing?
- To what extent do you feel comfortable using humor to counter untitling or uncredentialing?
- What would be your approach if your organization uses the practice of promotions in name only?

4.5   Benevolent Sexism

Not too long ago, men wielded the power in the business world, as well as on the domestic front. Women were relegated to subservient, supportive roles, with their worth measured by their ability to nurture and care on the domestic front. In this world, women relied on the support of men for their very survival. This is the world that gave birth to benevolent sexism. Its roots are a tale as old as time.

Throughout history, traditional gender roles have placed women in a gilded cage, their wings clipped by the expectations of a patriarchal society. Men, on the other hand, have been viewed as knights in shining armor, the protectors and providers, the ones who hold the keys to the kingdom (see Glick & Fiske, 1996). Social psychologists Peter Glick and Susan Fiske coined the term "benevolent sexism," defining it as attitudes and behaviors grounded in stereotypes about women that may appear positive or protective, yet ultimately reinforce restrictive gender roles and perpetuate those same stereotypes by suggesting that women require special care, guidance, or support.

The Victorian era, with its tales of chivalry and the "cult of true womanhood," only served to reinforce these benevolent sexist attitudes. Women were seen as delicate flowers, pure and moral beings who needed to be cherished and protected by their male counterparts (Welter, 1966). This notion of women as fragile creatures in need of male guardianship has persisted through the ages, despite the many advancements women have made since the Victorian era.

As the tides of change swept through the twentieth century, women fought for their right to vote and to participate in professional and political life. But benevolent sexism adapted to shifting social norms. The "women are wonderful" effect, a term coined by Eagly and Mladinic (1994), describes how society began to view women positively, but only through the lens of stereotypically feminine traits such as kindness, caring, and cooperation. This seemingly rosy view of women, however, only served to reinforce traditional gender roles, limiting women's opportunities and potential and maintaining men's dominance.

Glick and Fiske (1996) revealed the two faces of sexism: hostile and benevolent sexism. They argued that benevolent sexism, with its sugarcoated words and patronizing attitudes, is a tool used to justify and maintain male dominance and keep women in their place. Hostile sexism, on the other hand, is a form of explicit and aggressive sexism characterized by negative stereotypes of women. It is rooted in the belief that women are inferior to men and should conform to traditional gender roles. It is often expressed through openly negative stereotypes, such as perceiving women as manipulative, incompetent, overly emotional, or unfit for leadership roles. Hostile sexism uses derogatory language and questions women's competence.

As a result of the work that organizations have done over the last 10–15 years, we may see less overt hostile sexism in the office, but in many cases, it has been replaced by subtle benevolent sexism, which tends to treat women as weak and sensitive individuals who need protection. On the surface, this view of women may seem positive; for example, women are considered kind and caring, while men are not. Benevolent sexism may be perceived as well-intentioned and appear harmless, but there is a cost attached, as it idealizes stereotypical gender role assumptions about men and women. For example, a professor of leadership was introduced to an executive audience with the comment, "She makes our team younger and more beautiful." Needless to say, this introduction trivializes her professional achievements by focusing on her appearance and age rather than her academic credentials, research contributions, or teaching awards. This sends a message to the audience that her value lies in superficial qualities rather than her intellectual and professional capabilities, which is particularly damaging in a setting where she should be recognized as an expert.

Benevolent sexism is still present in society; its roots are deeply entangled with cultural and religious beliefs that depict women as caregivers and men as providers and protectors (Mikołajczak & Pietrzak, 2014). Despite the progress made toward gender equity since the 1970s, these attitudes continue to shape expectations and limit opportunities for women. If a manager chooses not to assign a challenging project to a female employee on the assumption that it may be "too stressful" or interfere with her family responsibilities, they effectively confine her to a supportive role and limit her professional development.

Recent research has examined the gender gap in perceptions of unintentional gender bias (Armstrong & Ghaboos, 2019; see Fig. 4.3). The findings suggest that dealing with benevolent sexism is much more of a priority for men than for women. At first glance, these results may seem counterintuitive. One possible explanation is that women perceive benevolent sexism as a less urgent and lower-priority concern compared to more overt forms of bias. Additionally, the short-term "benefits" associated with benevolent sexism, such as offers of help or protection, may partially obscure its harmful long-term consequences. Since these interactions can feel socially rewarding in the moment, women themselves may not always recognize them as an issue requiring immediate confrontation. Another explanation could be that men have developed heightened sensitivity to benevolent sexism in the wake of the #MeToo movement.

Experimental studies in sports explored the impact of *underprovision of support,* which means an individual receives less support than they wanted, *adequate support,* where an individual receives as much support as wanted, and *overprovision,* where the individual receives more support than wanted, on self-confidence (Fu et al., 2021). The results confirmed that overprovision has a negative impact on both women and men since it is perceived as

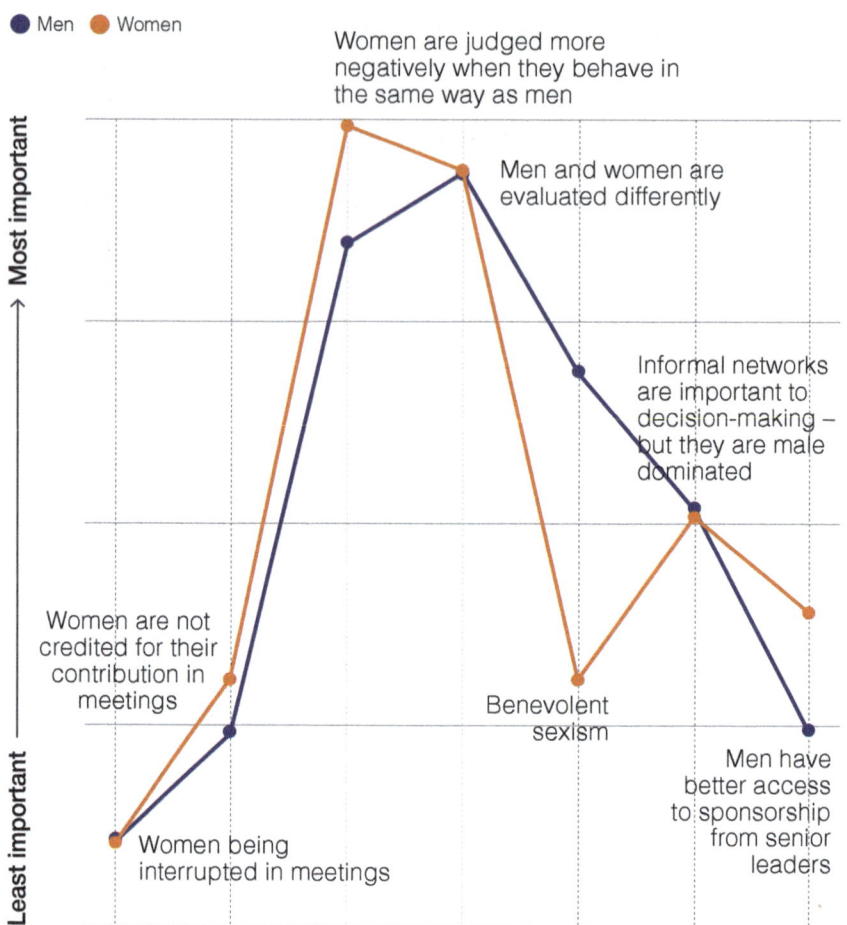

Fig. 4.3 Action priorities identified by women and men. Survey findings of 6942 participants (49% women, 51% men) from organizations across various sectors highlight the action priorities identified by women and men in addressing unintentional gender bias. While there is significant agreement between women and men on addressing many of the biases, a notable gap exists in how women and men prioritize addressing benevolent sexism. *Source* Adapted from Armstrong and Ghaboos (2019). Copyright 2019 by Murray Edwards College

a threat to self-esteem. By framing women's needs through a lens of assumed need for help, benevolent sexism parallels the negative effects of overprovision by eroding self-confidence and creating barriers to equal participation and recognition in professional or competitive environments.

Women seem to be slightly disadvantaged when it comes to being assigned challenging assignments—that is, tasks or projects that require individuals to step out of their comfort zones, engage in complex problem-solving, and develop new skills. In the 2016 "Women in the Workplace" report by Lean In and McKinsey, 62% of women, compared to 68% of their male colleagues, confirmed that they receive those challenging assignments (Yee et al., 2016).

Fears about hurting women's feelings, based on benevolent sexist views of their sensitivity, might prevent managers from providing women with honest and critical feedback, thus hindering their personal development. In the 2016 "Women in the Workplace" report, 66% of managers said they seldom hesitate to give difficult feedback to men and women, but only 36% of women confirmed that they receive difficult feedback "sometimes," "often," or "very often," compared to 46% of men. The top reason managers hesitate to deliver critical feedback is their concern about appearing mean or hurtful: 43% reported this hesitation when providing feedback to women, compared to 35% when providing it to men.

Another study (Correll & Simard, 2016) reports that women consistently receive less feedback related to specific outcomes, whether positive or negative. Since vague feedback correlates with lower performance ratings, the researchers argued that it can hold women back. How can a woman improve her job performance if she doesn't know exactly what needs to change? Researchers also found that when women received specific feedback, it focused primarily on their communication style rather than their business skills. Receiving low-quality feedback over a long period of time makes people unpromotable.

The Textio Research Report from June 2022 suggests that men receive feedback that focuses on the substance of their work, but women are 22% more likely to receive feedback related to their personality. For example, women are twice as likely to be described as "collaborative" and "nice"; seven times more likely to be described as "opinionated"; and 11 times more likely to be described as "abrasive." When men receive feedback on their personality, the word "confident" is three times more likely, and "ambitious" is almost four times more likely to be used than for women.

Benevolent sexism impacts women in many different ways. Women exposed to it are more likely to justify the status quo and are less willing to engage in collective action against inequality (Becker & Wright, 2011). There is a positive correlation between the acceptance of benevolent sexism and the acceptance of hostile sexism (Glick & Fiske, 1996). Facing hostile sexism on a weekly basis leads to increased anger, but encounters with benevolent sexism cause feelings of anxiety (Chawla & Gabriel, 2024). In that sense, it's important to raise awareness in a speaker about how their condescending undertone (e.g., "That's impressive, especially for a woman") contributes to a hostile work environment and perpetuates a sexist culture in the organization.

> **Self-Reflection 4.7: Addressing Sexism in Organizational Culture**
>
> As a manager:
>
> - Are you aware of making benevolent sexist comments?
> - Do the women on your team perceive you as an ally or as a "savior"? You might find it helpful to complete the Ambivalent Sexism Inventory (https://secure.understandingprejudice.org/asi/take) and get feedback from others on whether they have witnessed you making benevolent sexist comments.
> - How do you make sure you provide the women and men who report to you with equally challenging assignments?
> - Do you apply the same criteria when you provide feedback to the women and men who report to you?
> - Do you provide the women who report to you with useful feedback? How do you systematically link feedback to business outcomes? Is your feedback actionable?
> - Have you tried preparing feedback for two direct reports (a woman and a man) simultaneously? This practice might help you notice if you tend to apply different criteria to male and female direct reports.
> - Does your feedback focus on behaviors you have observed and not on personality traits (e.g., collaborative, nice, abrasive)?

Benevolent sexism, while superficially supportive, often boxes women into limited roles by highlighting their perceived fragility or nurturing qualities, thereby implying constraints on their competence or ambition. In contrast, adopting a "Not Yet" mindset reframes setbacks as stepping stones for development rather than indications of inherent inadequacy. Dr. Carol Dweck (see Chap. 1), renowned for her work on the growth mindset, illustrates this with a high school in Chicago that assigns students a grade of "Not Yet" instead of a failing mark for unfinished coursework (Dweck, 2014). This approach encourages a focus on progress rather than final judgments and can be applied to managerial feedback as well, framing evaluations as a continuous learning journey. By normalizing constructive critique as a catalyst for improvement, a "Not Yet" perspective creates a safe environment for honest, growth-oriented conversations.

4.6   The Queen Bee Phenomenon

In the bustling hive of corporate life, there is another phenomenon that buzzes with controversy and intrigue, the so-called "Queen Bee syndrome". Often depicted in popular media and discussions, the Queen Bee is typically portrayed as a woman who, having achieved seniority or significant success, becomes a gatekeeper actively keeping other women from advancing in their careers. But is this a fair characterization or a myth that simplifies complex workplace dynamics?

The Queen Bee phenomenon was first identified by psychologists Graham Staines, Carol Tavris, and Toby Jayaratne, who observed that women in positions of authority were, at times, likely to oppose the rise of other women within a male-dominated environment (Staines et al., 1974). This finding spawned numerous debates and further studies, leading to the question: What drives a Queen Bee? One of the most compelling explanations comes from considering the intense pressures these women face. In environments where women leaders are scarce, the few who rise often do so by adopting stereotypically masculine traits to fit in or by being exceptionally tough to prove that they belong. This pressure-cooker environment can lead to what some researchers suggest is a defensive response: If the positions at the top are limited, the incentive to pull the ladder up behind them can be strong.

Recent research offers a mixed view. A 2018 survey by the Workplace Bullying Institute highlighted that female bosses are more likely than their male counterparts to bully other women, indicating that Queen Bee behaviors do occur. On the other hand, there is no evidence to suggest that women are more vicious or untrustworthy in their working relationships with other women than men are in their interactions with other men (McNulty, 2018). This discrepancy in findings highlights the complexity of the issue. A growing body of literature critiques the Queen Bee label and advocates for replacing it with the term "self-group distancing" (da Rocha Grangeiro et al., 2024). This alternative framing reflects the idea that women may adopt Queen Bee behaviors as a strategic response to highly competitive, male-dominated environments, distancing themselves from other women to preserve their own status.

It's crucial to reframe the Queen Bee phenomenon not as a women's issue but as a broader organizational problem. Such behaviors are symptomatic of organizations that pit employees against each other, where resources are scarce and only a few can succeed. This is not a problem with women leaders; it's a systemic issue with how leadership is structured and rewarded. For organizations, it's essential to cultivate an inclusive culture that values diversity at every level of leadership. This includes providing training, creating policies that encourage female mentorship, ensuring equal opportunities for advancement, and recognizing diverse leadership styles.

To navigate a Queen Bee boss, your first priority is to maintain professionalism. Try to avoid engaging in personal conflicts to protect your reputation. Building alliances with colleagues who can provide support, mentorship, or advocacy can mitigate the impact of the Queen Bee's toxic behaviors. Try to understand the motivation of your Queen Bee boss. Often, it is rooted in insecurity, which drives a desire to maintain authority. Recognizing this can help you depersonalize her actions and respond more effectively. If appropriate, ask for a one-on-one meeting to address specific concerns. In that conversation, verbalize how certain behaviors affect your work without sounding accusatory. If mentorship within the organization is unavailable due to the Queen Bee dynamic, connect with external mentors who can provide unbiased advice and support. As a last resort, you can consider escalation to human resources or higher management.

The debate continues over whether the Queen Bee phenomenon is a significant barrier to women's advancement or a misunderstood aspect of broader workplace dynamics. Some argue that a focus on Queen Bees diverts attention from systemic issues like gender bias and discrimination, which are the real culprits behind inequities. The Queen Bee phenomenon presents a compelling narrative about leadership, gender, and power. Whether myth or reality, it highlights the complexities of female leadership in traditionally male-dominated sectors and prompts a broader discussion about how to create more equitable work environments.

Self-Reflection 4.8: Am I a Queen Bee?

- Feelings of superiority in one person can lead to feelings of inferiority in another. Has this ever happened to you?
- Do you think of your female colleagues as competitors or allies, and how does this influence your behavior?
- In what ways do you support or hinder the career progression of other women?
- How do you handle conflicts with peers who are women? What triggers these conflicts?
- You may be holding some biases against other women. What do you do to identify and challenge those biases?
- Do you find yourself adopting traditionally masculine leadership traits? If so, why?

> • What do you value more: fostering a collaborative environment or focusing more on individual success?
> • How do your experiences as a Queen Bee affect your overall job satisfaction and well-being?
> • What steps can you take to be more inclusive in your leadership approach, especially toward other women?
> • How can you contribute to breaking the cycle of Queen Bee behavior in your part of the organization?

The behaviors examined in this chapter—microaggressions, gaslighting, role incredulity, untitling and uncredentialing, benevolent sexism, and the Queen Bee syndrome—not only undermine women but also reinforce systemic inequities in professional and social spheres. These pervasive biases erode confidence, distort perceptions of competence, and create barriers to equity and inclusion. In the next chapter, we shift our focus inward, exploring authenticity and imposter syndrome to uncover how women can reclaim their sense of self in the face of these challenges. By addressing imposter thoughts and embracing authenticity, we can mitigate the psychological toll of external pressures and forge a path toward lasting resilience.

References

Armstrong, J., & Ghaboos, J. (2019). *Women collaborating with men: Everyday workplace inclusion.* Murray Edwards College, University of Cambridge. https://internationalwim.org/wp-content/uploads/2020/06/Everyday-Workplace-Inclusion_FINAL.pdf

Atir, S., & Ferguson, M. J. (2018). How gender determines the way we speak about professionals. *Proceedings of the National Academy of Sciences, 115*(28), 7278–7283.

Becker, J. C., & Wright, S. C. (2011). Yet another dark side of chivalry: Benevolent sexism undermines and hostile sexism motivates collective action for social change. *Journal of Personality and Social Psychology, 101*(1), 62.

Brescoll, V. L. (2011). Who takes the floor and why: Gender, power, and volubility in organizations. *Administrative Science Quarterly, 56*(4), 622–641.

Brescoll, V. L., & Uhlmann, E. L. (2008). Can an angry woman get ahead? Status conferral, gender, and expression of emotion in the workplace. *Psychological Science, 19*(3), 268–275.

Cameron, D. (2020). The gender respect gap. In C. R. Caldas-Coulthard (Ed.), *Innovations and challenges: Women, language and sexism* (pp. 19–33). Routledge.

Chalmers, J. K. (2021). *Perceptions of women in authority positions: The role of warmth and competence* [Master of Science by Research (MScRes) thesis]. University of Kent. https://doi.org/10.22024/UniKent/01.02.88012

Chawla, N., & Gabriel, A. S. (2024). From crude jokes to diminutive terms: Exploring experiences of hostile and benevolent sexism during job search. *Personnel Psychology, 77*(2), 747–787.

Chevallier, A., Dalsace, F., & Barsoux, J. -L. (2024). The art of asking smarter questions. *Harvard Business Review*.

Ciarrochi, J., Atkins, P. W., Hayes, L. L., Sahdra, B. K., & Parker, P. (2016). Contextual positive psychology: Policy recommendations for implementing positive psychology into schools. *Frontiers in Psychology, 7*, 1561. https://doi.org/10.3389/fpsyg.2016.01561

Collier, L. (2014). Why we cry: New research is opening eyes to the psychology of tears. *Monitor on Psychology, 45*(2), 47.

Collins, N. L., & Miller, L. C. (1994). Self-disclosure and liking: A meta-analytic review. *Psychological Bulletin, 116*(3), 457.

Correll, S., & Simard, C. (2016). Vague feedback is holding women back. *Harvard Business Review, 94*(1), 2–5.

Correll, S. J. (2017). SWS 2016 feminist lecture: Reducing gender biases in modern workplaces: A small wins approach to organizational change. *Gender and Society, 31*(6), 725–750.

Crenshaw, K. (1989). Demarginalizing the intersection of race and sex: A black feminist critique of antidiscrimination doctrine, feminist theory and antiracist politics. *University of Chicago Legal Forum, 1*, 139–167.

da Rocha Grangeiro, R., Gomes Neto, M. B., Silva, L. E. N., & Esnard, C. (2024). The triggers and consequences of the Queen Bee phenomenon: A systematic literature review and integrative framework. *Scandinavian Journal of Psychology, 65*(1), 86–97.

Diehl, A., & Dzubinski, L. (2021, January 22). We need to stop 'untitling' and 'uncredentialing' professional women. *Fast Company*. https://www.fastcompany.com/90596628/we-need-to-stop-untitling-and-uncredentialing-professional-women

Dweck, C. (2014, November). The power of believing that you can improve [video]. *TED Conferences*. https://www.lingq.com/en/learn-english-online/courses/183942/carol-dweck-the-power-of-believing-tha-490476/

Dzubinski, L. M. (2021, December 22). When people assume you're not in charge because you're a woman. *Harvard Business Review*. https://hbr.org/2021/12/when-people-assume-youre-not-in-charge-because-youre-a-woman

Eagly, A. H., & Mladinic, A. (1994). Are people prejudiced against women? Some answers from research on attitudes, gender stereotypes, and judgments of competence. *European Review of Social Psychology, 5*(1), 1–35.

Elsbach, K. D., & Bechky, B. A. (2018). How observers assess women who cry in professional work contexts. *Academy of Management Discoveries, 4*(2), 127–154.

Files, J. A., Mayer, A. P., Ko, M. G., Friedrich, P., Jenkins, M., Bryan, M. J., Vegunta, S., Wittich, C. M., Lyle, M. A., & Melikian, R. (2017). Speaker introductions at internal medicine grand rounds: Forms of address reveal gender bias. *Journal of Women's Health, 26*(5), 413–419.

Fischer, A. H., Eagly, A. H., & Oosterwijk, S. (2013). The meaning of tears: Which sex seems emotional depends on the social context. *European Journal of Social Psychology, 43*(6), 505–515.

Fragale, A. R., Overbeck, J. R., & Neale, M. A. (2011). Resources versus respect: Social judgments based on targets' power and status positions. *Journal of Experimental Social Psychology, 47*(4), 767–775.

Fu, D., Hase, A., Goolamallee, M., Godwin, G., & Freeman, P. (2021). The effects of support (in)adequacy on self-confidence and performance: Two experimental studies. *Sport, Exercise, and Performance Psychology, 10*(1), 15–26.

Gallup (2016). *The state of the American manager: Analytics and advice for lead.* https://www.gallup.com/services/182138/state-american-manager.aspx

Gelstein, S., Yeshurun, Y., Rozenkrantz, L., Shushan, S., Frumin, I., Roth, Y., & Sobel, N. (2011). Human tears contain a chemosignal. *Science, 331*(6014), 226–230.

Glick, P., & Fiske, S. T. (1996). The ambivalent sexism inventory: Differentiating hostile and benevolent sexism. *Journal of Personality and Social Psychology, 70*(3), 491–512.

Grant, A. (2013). *Give and take: A revolutionary approach to success.* Penguin.

Gruber, J., Mauss, I. B., & Tamir, M. (2011). A dark side of happiness? How, when, and why happiness is not always good. *Perspectives on Psychological Science, 6*(3), 222–233.

Harding, R. (2021, February 15). Tokyo Olympic boss's resignation fuels Japan gender equality debate. *Financial Times.* https://www.ft.com/content/0fb1b205-75a1-43b3-a056-d4996b580a74

Heath, K., & Wensil, B. F. (2019, September 6). To build an inclusive culture, start with inclusive meetings. *Harvard Business Review, 6.* https://hbr.org/2019/09/to-build-an-inclusive-culture-start-with-inclusive-meetings.

Hinchliffe, E. (2025, January, 8). The fortune 500 has two new female CEOs— Finally pushing that milestone over 11%. Fortune.com https://fortune.com/2025/01/08/the-fortune-500-has-two-new-female-ceos-finally-pushing-that-milestone-above-11/

Holmes, J. (1998). Women talk too much. In L. Bauer & P. Trudgill (Eds.), *Language myths* (257–263). Penguin Books.

Ibarra, H., & Obodaru, O. (2009). Women and the vision thing. *Harvard Business Review, 87*(1), 62–70.

Integrating Women Leaders Foundation (IWL). (2022). *State of allyship-in-action benchmark study.* https://ywomen.biz/wp-content/uploads/2023/10/IWL-SOAIA-Allyship-In-Action-Benchmark-Study-2022.pdf

Isaacowitz, D., & Seligman, M. (2001). Is pessimism a risk factor for depressive mood among community-dwelling older adults? *Behaviour Research and Therapy, 39*(3), 255–272.

James, D., & Drakich, J. (1993). Understanding gender differences in amount of talk: A critical review of research. In D. Tannen (Ed.), *Gender and conversational interaction* (281–312). Oxford University Press.

Jones, S. S. (2023). Gaslighting and dispelling: Experiences of non-governmental organization workers in navigating gendered corruption. *Human Relations, 76*(6), 901–925.

Kanter, R. M. (1977). *Men and women of the corporation.* Basic Books.

Karpowitz, C. F., Mendelberg, T., & Shaker, L. (2012). Gender inequality in deliberative participation. *American Political Science Review, 106*(3), 533–547.

King, E., & Jones, K. (2016). Why subtle bias is so often worse than blatant discrimination. *Harvard Business Review, 94*(7-8), 34–40.

Knight, R. (2020, July 24). You've been called out for a microaggression. What do you do. *Harvard Business Review.* https://hbr.org/2020/07/youve-been-called-out-for-a-microaggression-what-do-you-do.

Lerner, J. S., & Tiedens, L. Z. (2006). Portrait of the angry decision maker: How appraisal tendencies shape anger's influence on cognition. *Journal of Behavioral Decision Making, 19*(2), 115–137.

Liang, J., Farh, C. I., & Farh, J. -L. (2012). Psychological antecedents of promotive and prohibitive voice: A two-wave examination. *Academy of Management Journal, 55*(1), 71–92.

Lieberman, M. D., Eisenberger, N. I., Crockett, M. J., Tom, S. M., Pfeifer, J. H., & Way, B. M. (2007). Putting feelings into words. *Psychological Science, 18*(5), 421–428.

Lilienfeld, S. O. (2017). Microaggressions: Strong claims, inadequate evidence. *Perspectives on Psychological Science, 12*(1), 138–169.

Lukin, K. (2019). Toxic positivity: Don't always look on the bright side. *Psychology Today, 8*, August 1.

Mallick, M. (2021, November 18). So your boss offered you a meaningless promotion. *Harvard Business Review.* https://hbr.org/2021/11/so-your-boss-offered-you-a-meaningless-promotion

McClean, E. J., Martin, S. R., Emich, K. J., & Woodruff, C. T. (2018). The social consequences of voice: An examination of voice type and gender on status and subsequent leader emergence. *Academy of Management Journal, 61*(5), 1869–1891.

McNulty, A. W. (2018). Don't underestimate the power of women supporting each other at work. *Harvard Business Review* September 3.

Mikołajczak, M., & Pietrzak, J. (2014). Ambivalent sexism and religion: Connected through values. *Sex Roles, 70*, 387–399.

Motro, D., Evans, J. B., Ellis, A. P., & Benson III, L. (2022). Race and reactions to women's expressions of anger at work: Examining the effects of the "angry black woman" stereotype. *Journal of Applied Psychology, 107*(1), 142.

Mueller, P. A., & Oppenheimer, D. M. (2014). The pen is mightier than the keyboard: Advantages of longhand over laptop note taking. *Psychological Science, 25*(6), 1159–1168.

Nooyi, I. K. (2020). *My life in full: Work, family, and our future.* Hachette UK.

OECD (2023), Health at a Glance 2023: OECD indicators, *OECD Publishing, Paris.* https://doi.org/10.1787/7a7afb35-en

Oishi, S., Diener, E., & Lucas, R. E. (2007). The optimum level of well-being: Can people be too happy? *Perspectives on Psychological Science, 2*(4), 346–360.

Pennebaker, J. W., & Chung, C. K. (2007). Expressive writing, emotional upheavals, and health. *Foundations of Health Psychology,* 263–284.

Pennebaker, J. W., & Smyth, J. M. (2016). *Opening up by writing it down: How expressive writing improves health and eases emotional pain.* Guilford Publications.

Pennebaker, J. W., & Susman, J. R. (1988). Disclosure of traumas and psychosomatic processes. *Social Science and Medicine, 26*(3), 327–332.

Pierce, C. (1974). Psychiatric problems of the Black minority. In G. Caplan & S. Arieti (Eds.), *American Handbook of Psychiatry* (512–523). Basic Books.

Potegal, M., & Stemmler, G. (2010). Constructing a neurology of anger. In M. Portegal, G. Stemmler, & C. Spielberger (Eds.), *International handbook of anger: Constituent and concomitant biological, psychological, and social processes* (39–59). Springer.

Staines, G., Tavris, C., & Jayaratne, T. E. (1974). The Queen Bee syndrome. *Psychology Today, 7*(8), 55–60.

Stark, C. A. (2019). Gaslighting, misogyny, and psychological oppression. *The Monist, 102*(2), 221–235.

Statista. (2025). *Number of doctoral degrees earned in the United States from 1949/50 to 2031/32, by gender.* Retrieved April 2, 2025, from https://www.statista.com/statistics/185167/number-of-doctoral-degrees-by-gender-since-1950/

Sue, D. W. (2010). *Microaggressions and marginality: Manifestation, dynamics, and impact.* John Wiley & Sons.

Sue, D. W., Capodilupo, C. M., Torino, G. C., Bucceri, J. M., Holder, A., Nadal, K. L., & Esquilin, M. (2007). Racial microaggressions in everyday life: Implications for clinical practice. *American Psychologist, 62*(4), 271.

Textio. (n.d.). *Language bias in performance feedback.* Explore Textio. Retrieved April 2, 2025, from https://explore.textio.com/feedback-bias/language-bias-in-performance-feedback

Understanding Prejudice. (n.d.). *Ambivalent Sexism Inventory.* Retrieved April 2, 2025, from https://secure.understandingprejudice.org/asi/take

Van Hemert, D. A., et al. (2011). Culture and crying: Prevalences and gender differences. *Cross-Cultural Research, 45*(4), 399–431.

Van Kleef, G. A., De Dreu, C. K., & Manstead, A. S. (2004). The interpersonal effects of anger and happiness in negotiations. *Journal of Personality and Social Psychology, 86*(1), 57.

Washington, E. F., Birch, A. H., & Roberts, L. M. (2020, July 3). When and how to respond to microaggressions. *Harvard Business Review.* https://hbr.org/2020/07/when-and-how-to-respond-to-microaggressions

Welter, B. (1966). The cult of true womanhood: 1820–1860. *American Quarterly, 18*(2), 151–174.

Williams, J. C., Phillips, K. W., & Hall, E. V. (2016). Tools for change: Boosting the retention of women in the STEM pipeline. *Journal of Research in Gender Studies, 6*(1), 11.

Yee, L., Krivkovish, A., Kutcher, E., Epstein, B., Thomas, R., Finch, A., Cooper, M., & Konar, E. (2016). *Women in the workplace report.* McKinsey & Company and LeanIn.org. https://www.mckinsey.com/featured-insights/diversity-and-inclusion/women-in-the-workplace-archive#section-header-2016

Zenger, J., & Folkman, J. (2019). Women score higher than men in most leadership skills. *Harvard Business Review, 92*(10), 86–93.

5

Faking It, Authenticity, and Impostor Phenomenon

As you've read, external biases and systemic inequities can undermine confidence and distort perceptions of competence. However, the challenges women face are not only external but also internal, as feelings of self-doubt and the pressure to conform often complicate the pursuit of authenticity. In a world that constantly praises confidence, some of you may have tried "faking it until you make it" to seem self-assured when you are really unsure. But that approach raises a big question: Can you still feel authentic while putting on a brave face? Adding to this struggle is the ever-present nagging voice of impostor thoughts—the worry that we're not really good enough and might be "found out" at any moment. This chapter looks at how the desire to appear competent, the quest to be genuine, and the fear of being exposed collide. By exploring these ideas, you'll see how they shape our sense of who we are, affect our relationships with others, and guide our choices when we're under pressure to succeed.

First, this chapter looks at the advice to "fake it until you make it", a strategy often used by younger women to boost their confidence when feeling unsure of themselves. But does this strategy really work, and at what cost?

© The Author(s), under exclusive license to Springer Nature Switzerland AG 2025
G. Toegel, *The Confidence Myth*,
https://doi.org/10.1007/978-3-031-97305-5_5

5.1   Should We Really Fake It Until We Make It?

The phrase "fake it until you make it" has been a popular mantra in the business world for decades. It suggests that by imitating confidence and competence, we can eventually achieve genuine success. But where did this concept originate, and what does science have to say about its effectiveness?

The idea of "faking it until you make it" can be traced back to the self-help movement of the early twentieth century. In 1922, Alfred Adler, a prominent psychotherapist, introduced the notion of "acting as if," suggesting that by behaving as the person you aspire to become, you can create positive change in your life. This idea was later popularized by various self-help authors and motivational speakers. Over time, the concept has evolved and been applied to various contexts, including business, education, and personal development.

On the flipside, pretending to be someone you are not can be emotionally and mentally draining, potentially taking a toll on mental health and authenticity. In fact, dispositional authenticity is one of the strongest predictors of well-being (Wood et al., 2008). Dispositional authenticity refers to how true you are to yourself in your daily life. It means being aware of who you really are—your emotions, values, strengths, and flaws—and accepting yourself without judgment. It's about making choices and behaving in ways that align with your true beliefs and needs, rather than simply trying to meet others' expectations. It also involves being honest and genuine in your relationships, allowing others to see the real you. In essence, dispositional authenticity is about consistently living in a way that feels true to who you are at your core. Faking it can lead to stress and anxiety, as people may constantly worry about being exposed or not living up to the image they are projecting. It can damage relationships, reputations, and credibility if the truth is revealed or if people are unable to deliver on their promises or portray the image they desire.

In extreme cases, faking it can mean deception and dishonesty, which raises ethical concerns. It can involve presenting yourself in a way that is misleading or misrepresenting your abilities, which might have serious repercussions. Faking it can hinder personal development and prevent individuals from confronting their weaknesses or areas for improvement. This brings us to the case of Katina, who faces a critical dilemma.

> **Vignette 5.1: Katina**
>
> Katina, a senior manager at a manufacturing company, was having a tense meeting with her team. The project they were working on was behind schedule, and the client was growing increasingly impatient. Katina felt a mix of anxiety, frustration, and disappointment. She knew that the delay wasn't entirely her team's fault, but she also realized that they needed to step up and get the project back on track. As a leader, Katina faced a dilemma: How should she manage her emotions in this high-pressure situation to motivate her team effectively?

Option A: Katina should suppress her true feelings of frustration and anxiety. Instead, she should force herself to smile and maintain an upbeat tone throughout the meeting, even though she doesn't feel that way inside. She might say something like, "Everything is fine, we'll figure this out," while masking her inner concerns.

Option B: Katina should take a moment to reflect on her emotions before addressing her team. While she still feels frustrated and anxious, she should focus on reframing those feelings into determination and hope. By reminding herself of the team's past successes and their ability to overcome challenges, Katina can genuinely convey optimism. She might say, "I know this is tough, but I believe in our ability to turn things around. Let's focus on solutions together."

Option C: Katina should choose to be fully transparent with her team about how she is feeling while maintaining professionalism. She could say, "I'm frustrated about where we are right now because I know we're capable of better. I also feel anxious because the client is putting pressure on us. But I want you all to know that I'm here to support you, and I trust we can work through this together."

Throughout our professional lives, we often face dilemmas similar to Katina's. Should we fake it or be ourselves? Before discussing which path to take, it's worth reminding ourselves that leadership isn't just about giving orders and expecting followers to fall into line; it's a two-way relationship between leaders and the people who follow them. Leaders need the support and trust of their followers to represent shared values on behalf of the group.

For true collaboration, followers must recognize their leader as a legitimate authority figure, someone who can voice and uphold the group's values. If the leader lacks legitimacy, it becomes difficult to address disagreements about which values matter most or how to apply them. Even when a leader champions values that everyone agrees on, they still need to build enough connection with followers to achieve meaningful results. Katina's situation highlights how crucial it is for a leader to establish real legitimacy with their team in order to foster meaningful collaboration. Her team needs to feel that she truly understands their challenges and embodies their shared values, such as accountability and teamwork. Without that sense of alignment, it becomes harder to resolve disagreements about priorities or the best path forward. For instance, if Katina simply imposed decisions without first demonstrating trust and unity, her team might question her leadership, undermining collaboration. In contrast, by showing empathy for her team's struggles while staying aligned with shared goals, she can deepen their connection, a bond that will help address immediate challenges and motivate everyone to work together toward lasting results.

Simply stating their values, however clearly, isn't always enough for leaders to succeed, even if they hold a formal leadership title. For a leader to be successful, they must be perceived as authentic by their followers. As psychologist Alice Eagly (2005) reminds us, authenticity is all about relationships. A leader's values need to resonate with their followers in a way that makes them feel genuinely connected (Eagly, 2005).

Leadership and Gender

In many situations, leaders who are women face greater challenges than men in establishing legitimacy as representatives of the values that serve the group's interests. More broadly, leaders who belong to social groups that have traditionally been excluded from leadership roles may struggle to gain sufficient legitimacy to inspire their followers. Disagreements about values between leaders and followers can further erode perceptions of a leader's authenticity. For example, suppose Katina's team places a high value on openness and mutual accountability, prioritizing shared decision-making, owning mistakes, and learning together. As a woman in a leadership role, Katina may face greater scrutiny than a male counterpart in proving she upholds these values. If she makes decisions unilaterally without explaining her rationale or holds certain team members accountable while letting others off the hook, her actions could conflict with the team's expectations. Because women leaders often contend with biases that question their legitimacy, her team may be quicker to perceive such inconsistencies as evidence that she does not truly represent their shared values. This perception can erode trust and make it harder for Katina to inspire genuine collaboration.

Alice Eagly and Steven Karau use the role incongruity theory of prejudice (Eagly & Karau, 2002) to explain the prejudice that female leaders commonly encounter due to the perceived inconsistency between leadership roles and traditional female gender roles. The theory analyzes the mismatch between what people expect from leaders, which is typically associated with stereotypically masculine traits, and what people expect from women based on traditional gender roles. Society generally expects women to be warm, nurturing, caring, and emotionally attuned to others while not displaying the traits that are usually linked with men and leaders. These stereotypical masculine traits, or "agentic" qualities, include being assertive, ambitious, dominant, forceful, self-reliant, and confident in one's abilities. Agentic behaviors are those that demonstrate a sense of control over one's own actions and decisions or reflect belief in one's own power to impact outcomes; they include behaviors such as taking initiative or making choices.

When a woman steps into a leadership role, she often faces prejudice because people perceive a mismatch between what they expect from her as a leader and what they expect from her as a woman, based on ingrained gender stereotypes. Women leaders are caught between two conflicting sets of expectations: gender roles for women and leadership characteristics that align with stereotypical traits associated with men. Because the qualities associated with leadership align with stereotypically masculine characteristics, women leaders are often perceived as incongruent. As a result, many people frequently have negative reactions toward women in leadership roles, especially when they exhibit stereotypically masculine, authoritative behaviors. Table 5.1 illustrates how the same leadership qualities can be

Table 5.1 Gender-based perceptions of leadership behaviors

Male leaders	Female leaders
Passionate	Emotional
Demanding	Bossy
Assertive	Aggressive
Direct	Rude
Persistent	Pushy
Confident	Has an ego; arrogant
Ambitious	Power-hungry
Focused	Obsessive
Strategic	Manipulative
Charismatic	Flirtatious
Decisive	Impulsive
Strong convictions	Argumentative
Detail-oriented	Nitpicky
Vocal	Shrill
Results-driven	Ruthless

perceived and labeled differently based on gender, often reflecting societal biases and gender stereotypes.

A meta-analysis (Eagly et al., 1995) shows that leaders tend to be more effective when their roles align with their gender stereotypes. Women leaders often face challenges in male-dominated fields, while men may struggle in roles that are seen as more feminine, for example, a director of a childcare center. This is because it is harder for leaders to gain followers' support and to be identified as leaders when they are in an organizational context that is not typically associated with their gender.

For this reason, many women leaders feel that they need to be like men in order to succeed. Often, they try to adopt stereotypically masculine traits and tone down their feminine style. For example, they might smile less, suppress an inclination to be "warm and nice," or drop the pitch of their voice. Indeed, agentic male behaviors, such as projecting self-confidence, ambition, power, or control, are associated with effective leadership. But only doing what men do is not enough to establish legitimacy. When women are perceived only as agentic, they violate gender stereotypes, which prescribe feminine traits and behaviors, such as being helpful, friendly, caring, and gentle. As a result, women who emulate stereotypically male traits are perceived as inauthentic. In order to be successful, women need to be perceived not only as agentic but also as communal. For example, Indra Nooyi, former Chair and CEO of PepsiCo, is very agentic and projects confidence and control in negotiations. But, on the other hand, she is a very caring, warm, and supportive boss. Pairing stereotypically masculine behavior with communal, stereotypically feminine behavior can dispel perceptions of inauthenticity, along with all the negative consequences for female leaders.

The good news is that over the past 15 years, there has been a notable shift in how we define effective leadership. Gone are the days when a good leader was seen as someone who simply commanded authority and got results. Today, both male and female leaders are increasingly expected to demonstrate empathy, compassion, and emotional intelligence in their roles. Transformational leaders who prioritize building relationships and empowering others, traits often associated with feminine leadership styles, are respected and admired. While the tide is turning, we still have a way to go before these traditionally feminine qualities are fully integrated into our collective understanding of leadership.

Executive Presence

A recent survey (Hewlett, 2024) on executive presence finds that people's expectations of an ideal leader have shifted even further over the past decade, moving away from the archetype of a tall, wise-cracking man toward individuals who are authentic, inclusive, and respectful of others. This adds to a growing wealth of data suggesting that traditional myths about women and why they struggle to climb the leadership ladder are outdated and overblown.

Executive presence is the way you carry yourself. We all have a persona that we bring to our workplace. Put simply, executive presence is about your ability to inspire confidence in others by showing that you are competent, reliable, and capable of driving results. Three elements contribute to executive presence: gravitas, skillful communication, and appearance. Surveys of US executives conducted by economist and award-winning author Sylvia Ann Hewlett in 2012 and 2022 found that these three factors remain the main contributors to executive presence. However, in the 10 years between the two surveys, there have been some shifts in how important the survey respondents rated the components within each category to executive presence.

Hewlett's new research from 2022 shows that, while survey respondents rated confidence and decisiveness highly as contributors to gravitas, they considered elite credentials less important and placed greater value on inclusiveness and respect for others than in the earlier survey (see Fig. 5.1). In terms of communication traits, superior speaking skills and the ability to command a room, whether in person or virtual, still lead the list of desirable traits, but comfort with virtual conferencing, a "listen-to-learn" orientation, and authenticity have increased as desirable qualities. Projecting authenticity is also key to the appearance component of executive presence, as are dressing for the "new normal," maintaining an online image, and showing up in person.

As you can see from the results of Hewlett's surveys, authenticity has grown in importance and value. Authenticity can be defined as the quality or state of being genuine and aligned with one's true self. It involves being true to your own values, beliefs, and emotions, and behaving in a way that is consistent with your internal experiences and personal identity. Executives who lack authenticity are perceived as deceitful, pretentious, insincere, and false.

Some researchers consider the Greek word "authentikos," which means genuine and original, to be the origin of the contemporary term. Others explore a possible link to the Latin word for author, which leads to the

● New in 2022

Gravitas traits

	2012	2022	
Confidence	77%	76%	Confidence
Decisiveness	70%	71%	Decisiveness
Integrity	63%	68%	Inclusiveness
Emotional intelligence	59%	65%	Respect for others
Blue-chip pedigree	57%	61%	Vision
Vision	52%	60%	Integrity

Communication traits

	2012	2022	
Superior speaking skills	62%	66%	Superior speaking skills
Command of a room	52%	53%	Command of a room/Zoom
Forcefulness	48%	48%	"Listen to learn" orientation
Ability to read an audience	36%	42%	Ability to read an audience
Joking and bantering manner	34%	37%	Authenticity
Use of body language	23%	30%	Use of body language

Appearance traits

	2012	2022	
Polished look	36%	37%	Polished look
Physical attractiveness	18%	31%	Authenticity
"Next job" style of dress	13%	28%	Fitness/vigor
Tallness	10%	22%	"New normal" style of dress
Youthfulness/vigor	5%	20%	Curation of online image
Slimness	4%	14%	Willingness to show up in person

Fig. 5.1 The new rules of executive presence. Hewlett's new research reaffirms that gravitas, communication, and appearance remain the three main pillars of executive presence (Hewlett, 2024). However, certain traits within these pillars have evolved, with authenticity and inclusiveness emerging as important qualities for executives. *Source* Adapted from Hewlett (2024). Copyright 2024 by Harvard Business Review

interpretation of "be your self-author." Saying "I'm authentic" would sound absurd, since authenticity is something we typically let others recognize in us rather than declare ourselves.

There is growing research evidence that supports the positive impact of authenticity on well-being, work engagement, performance outcomes, image, and career outcomes. Additionally, authentic leadership increases the well-being of leaders themselves. As Weiss et al. (2018) point out, when leaders express emotions that genuinely mirror their inner thoughts and feelings, they experience their role as more natural and less draining. Conversely, when leaders have to mask or suppress their real emotions, the extra effort depletes mental resources. This additional strain decreases leaders' mental well-being by increasing stress and diminishing their engagement at work. The extent of this negative impact depends on how much leaders interact with their followers. Authentic leaders tend to experience less depletion as they are more engaged with their team members, and because those interactions help replenish their personal resources, reduce their stress, and boost their work engagement. In Katina's situation, by choosing to express her genuine emotions constructively (Option C), she not only builds trust and connection with her team, but she also fosters a collaborative environment that genuinely energizes everyone. This approach helps her lead with sincerity while preserving her own emotional well-being.

5.2   Authenticity

Humanistic psychologists, such as Abraham Maslow and Carl Rogers, have argued that people are motivated to fulfill a need to become their best selves: to express their full range of abilities and live a life that reflects their deepest values—a state Maslow called self-actualization (Maslow, 1968; Rogers, 1961). Centuries before the humanistic psychologists, classical Greek philosophers (e.g., Aristotle, *Nicomachean Ethics*) believed that living authentically is at the heart of what it means to flourish as a human being. In modern counseling psychology, being true to yourself is linked to positive emotions and general well-being. When we can openly express who we truly are, it feels good and supports our mental health. On the other hand, when this need is thwarted—if we feel compelled to hide or change who we are—we often experience frustration and negative emotions.

Authentic behavior meets three core psychological needs: autonomy, competence, and relatedness (Deci & Ryan, 2000). When these three needs are satisfied, people tend to thrive, feel more engaged, and experience better overall well-being.

- Autonomy: Because authentic behavior is guided by our own values and desires, it reinforces the feeling that we are in control of our own choices.
- Competence: By acting in accordance with our genuine selves, we naturally draw upon our skills and strengths, which helps us feel capable and competent.
- Relatedness: Authenticity fosters open and honest interactions, which allow us to connect more deeply with others.

In addition to meeting these psychological needs, being authentic boosts self-esteem because it roots our sense of self-worth in who we really are, rather than reflecting external standards or what other people think of us (Kernis & Goldman, 2006). This stable, genuine self-esteem helps us avoid constantly seeking approval or hiding mistakes and promotes healthier day-to-day functioning.

Authenticity is strongly linked to positive inner experiences. When we act in ways that match our true selves, we can more effectively tap into our personal energy, strengths, and resources (Ilies et al., 2005). We're also more likely to take responsibility for our choices, which can boost our motivation to invest effort in what we do. In turn, being true to ourselves generates positive emotions such as joy, satisfaction, and hope, which contribute to greater well-being and engagement (Luthans & Avolio, 2003).

People who come across as authentic leaders, often receive positive reactions from those around them (Gardner et al., 2005). For example, followers of authentic leaders typically report higher job satisfaction, greater loyalty, better work performance, a stronger commitment to the organization, and a lower inclination to leave. Scholars explain these benefits by pointing to mechanisms like follower identification (followers see a piece of themselves in the leader), trust (the leader is seen as genuine and reliable), and positive social exchanges that foster a sense of mutual support.

Psychologist Carl Rogers (1961) believed that children are naturally authentic, freely expressing their true feelings and desires. But as children grow up, they begin facing what he called "conditions of worth," unspoken rules from family, friends, and society about how they should think, feel, or act to be accepted. Over time, repeatedly molding ourselves to these outside expectations can alienate us from our genuine selves, creating a gap between who we really are and who we feel forced to be. Rogers believed that this inner conflict reduces our well-being and fulfillment. He emphasized the importance of rediscovering and embracing our true selves.

Characterizing Authenticity

Authenticity is characterized by self-awareness, self-acceptance, and the ability to express oneself honestly and transparently in various contexts and relationships (Wood et al., 2008).

Let's look at self-awareness first. Self-awareness is about taking a good, hard look at yourself and figuring out what makes you tick. What are your values, your goals, your strengths, and your weaknesses? Authentic leaders have a solid grasp of who they are and what they stand for. Having a strong inner compass guides their decisions and behaviors; these decisions and behaviors are based on their own values and principles, not on what everyone else thinks they should do. Authentic leaders have a solid sense of right and wrong, and they stick to it. They don't let their egos get in the way of making accurate self-reflections. They are fair and objective when evaluating themselves and others and are willing to take a step back to see things from different perspectives.

Feedback is a powerful tool for increasing self-awareness. If the feedback you receive at work is vague or ambiguous, don't try to guess what it implies or let it affect your meta-perceptions. Instead, ask the person providing you with feedback to give you examples that illustrate the impact of the behaviors in question, elaborate on their frequency, and the context in which you are more likely to behave this way.

To assess your self-awareness and identify incorrect meta-perceptions, consider the questions in the self-reflection below.

Self-Reflection 5.1: How Self-Aware Are You?

Think about your answers to each of the following questions. Then, ask 5–8 people you trust to answer these questions with you in mind and provide honest feedback. Your trusted critics' answers can help increase your self-awareness. Having formal or improvised meetings with this circle of "loving critics" can help you adjust your meta-perceptions (Eurich, 2018).

1. How well do you understand what triggers your emotions?
2. How often do you take time to reflect on your thoughts, actions, and decisions?
3. When you have negative thoughts, do you explore the root cause or react impulsively?
4. How do you leverage your strengths in your personal and professional life?

---

5. What are your areas for growth, and how are you actively working to improve them?
6. How do others perceive you, and does this align with how you see yourself?
7. Do you notice how your words or actions affect the people around you?
8. To what extent do your daily decisions reflect your values?
9. Are you living a life aligned with your goals and priorities, or are you being influenced by external pressures?
10. How well do you use constructive feedback as an opportunity for growth?

The second element of authenticity, self-acceptance, indicates that you are generally comfortable with yourself and accept both your positive qualities and imperfections. Self-acceptance doesn't mean you never want to improve; rather, it means that you don't dwell on self-doubt or try to pretend to be someone you're not.

The ability to express yourself honestly and transparently is the final element of authenticity. This means being your true self with the people around you—no fake smiles or hiding your true feelings. Authenticity means that your inner self (e.g., thoughts, feelings, identities, and values) is in sync with your outward behavior.

Authenticity is about being true to yourself rather than conforming to societal expectations or adopting a false persona. Authentic individuals are seen as sincere, transparent, and trustworthy because their actions and words reflect their true thoughts and feelings. However, it does not necessarily mean clinging to an unchanging self; authenticity can also involve expanding or revising your self-concept as you learn and grow (Rogers, 1961).

Experienced Authenticity and Externally Perceived Authenticity

Vignette 5.2: Ulla

Ulla is a project manager at a tech company. She has always been passionate about sustainable development and renewable energy. She was recently assigned to lead a new project focused on developing energy-efficient software solutions. As Ulla genuinely cares about sustainability, she feels that this project is meaningful and reflects her values. Because Ulla feels authentic in her role, she attributes her engagement and positive actions to internal motivations rather than external factors such as company pressure or rewards. This internal attribution increases Ulla's commitment to the project. She feels a personal responsibility and a strong desire to see the project succeed. Her sense of ownership and dedication is heightened because she believes in the importance of the work on a personal level. As a result of this increased commitment, Ulla is more likely to invest significant energy and effort in the project. She collaborates with her team to brainstorm innovative solutions, allowing them to experience firsthand her enthusiasm and strong sense of responsibility. Her enthusiasm is infectious, inspiring those around her. Ulla's motivation and dedication are evident in her actions, as she drives the project forward with energy and focus. Ulla is experiencing authenticity because this project aligns perfectly with her personal values and interests. She thinks to herself, "I'm dedicated to this project because it reflects who I am."

Experienced authenticity and externally perceived authenticity are two distinct perspectives of authenticity (Cha et al., 2019). These perspectives provide different insights into authenticity and its impact on individuals and their relationships. As you will see, Ulla experiences both types of authenticity.

Experienced authenticity refers to a person's subjective experience of being authentic. It reflects the individual's perception of the alignment between their internal sense of self and their outward behavior. This sense of authenticity creates alignment between a person's true self and their work and enhances motivation, engagement, productivity, and overall job satisfaction. Ulla is committed to her new project as she feels it aligns with her values around sustainable development and renewable energy, and in this way, she is experiencing authenticity. Her experienced authenticity makes her more trustworthy and inspirational to her team members. Experienced authenticity can be influenced by self-deception or biases, as individuals may believe they are authentic even if their behavior does not align with their true self. In a way, feeling "real" may contribute to feeling ideal (Lenton et al., 2013). *Externally perceived authenticity* refers to how an individual's authenticity is judged by others, such as colleagues, direct reports, managers, or friends. It is shaped by others' impressions of the person's behavior, words, and expressions. This perspective assumes that observers can accurately assess whether the individual is acting in a way that aligns with their true self. Externally perceived authenticity is often associated with perceptions of sincerity, transparency, and trustworthiness. Ulla is likely perceived as authentic by her team, as her passion and enthusiasm for the work motivate them and drive the project forward.

These two perspectives on authenticity may not always align, as individuals may perceive themselves as authentic while others may perceive them differently. We all have multiple thoughts; some thoughts resonate with who we believe ourselves to be, and we perceive them as belonging to us, but others feel more distant from who we think we are (Hitlin, 2003). This process is influenced by values, which are embedded in culture. Authenticity looks different depending on the cultural context. For example, in high-context cultures (e.g., parts of East Asia and India), where people are aware of the unspoken elements of communication, such as facial expressions, body language, and what is not explicitly said, being authentic may involve communicating indirectly to preserve harmony and avoid embarrassing others. Explicit and direct communication might be viewed as inconsiderate or disrespectful, even if it's a candid statement of how you feel. On the other hand, in low-context cultures (e.g., Germany, the Netherlands, Scandinavia), where people tend to expect and appreciate explicit and direct communication, indirect communication can be interpreted as being dishonest or evasive, and thus inauthentic.

In many Western (individualistic) cultures, such as the United States and Northern European countries, authenticity is often associated with "speaking your mind" and standing by your personal values, even if it creates conflict. In contrast, in Eastern (collectivistic) cultures, such as Japan or China, authenticity is more closely tied to maintaining harmony and fulfilling social roles. A person might feel "true to themselves" when they act in accordance with group expectations and show respect for social norms. Not voicing personal preferences to uphold group cohesion may not be seen as inauthentic but rather as honoring the cultural values of loyalty or respect. Approaching cultural interactions with humility and acknowledging that authenticity is perceived differently across cultures helps avoid misunderstandings. To find common ground, try to identify shared values or goals that transcend cultural differences. This allows you to connect authentically while respecting diverse perspectives.

While authenticity offers numerous benefits, such as fostering trust, improving relationships, and enhancing well-being, it is not without its challenges. These potential costs warrant consideration. For example, expressing your true self can sometimes create tension or conflict with social norms, cultural expectations, or professional environments, especially in cultures with different expectations for communication. This tension can potentially lead to exclusion or disapproval (Lenton et al., 2013). Complete transparency in every context may be counterproductive (Goffman, 1949).

For example, in highly political or hierarchical environments, being fully authentic might not always be safe if it jeopardizes professional relationships or job security.

Authenticity and Emotions

Emotions are central to the experience of authenticity. One of the challenges leaders face is expressing their emotions. Imagine there has been a significant setback in a crucial project, causing frustration and disappointment among your team members. Similar to Katina, as a leader, you have a few options for how to respond emotionally. You can either fake it (surface acting), try to genuinely feel the emotions you're supposed to show (deep acting), or just display your true emotions (genuine emotions). Think back to Katina's situation and your recommendation to her. Let's examine these three emotional response options in the context of the project scenario:

Surface Acting: If you suggested that Katina put on a brave face, suppress her true feelings, and force herself to smile (Option A), she would be faking it and performing surface acting. She might say something like, "Everything is fine, we'll figure this out. This is just a minor setback. We'll bounce back stronger!" despite feeling quite discouraged herself. Most likely, her team will notice the mismatch between her words, body language, and her true feelings that unintentionally leak out.

Deep Acting: If you advised Katina to go with Option B, she would reframe her own feelings by reminding herself of mastering challenging situations in the past, and she would feel genuinely positive and optimistic about dealing with the setback. She might tell herself, "This is a valuable learning experience that will make us stronger in the long run." By the time she addresses her team, she will have managed to change her feelings to be more positive, and then she can authentically express optimism. This approach would enable Katina to align her internal emotions with the positive outlook she wants to project. The success of this approach relies on her capacity to reframe negative thoughts.

Genuine Emotions: If you recommended Option C, Katina would openly express her true feelings about the setback to her team and might say, "I'm not going to lie, I'm really disappointed and frustrated about this setback. I know many of you probably feel the same way." She could follow up with a more constructive message, but the key is that she is not hiding or altering her initial emotional reaction. This could be a powerful communication to the team, as its authenticity can further strengthen her leadership position.

Each of these approaches has its potential benefits and/or drawbacks. Surface acting might maintain a positive atmosphere but could feel inauthentic. Deep acting could be more convincing and feel more authentic but requires more emotional effort. Displaying genuine emotions could build trust through honesty but might risk demoralizing the team if it's not balanced with a constructive outlook. The choice between these options often depends on the leader's emotional intelligence, the team's culture, and the specific circumstances of the situation.

Your emotional display can have a significant impact on both you and your followers. Depending on how sincere and appropriate your followers believe your emotional display to be, they will form either positive or negative impressions of you. This, in turn, affects how much they trust you. The more authentic your followers perceive you to be, the more favorable their impressions will be, and the more they will trust you. On the flip side, as a leader, you will also feel more or less authentic based on your emotional display, which can affect your overall well-being. Faking emotions can take a toll on your mental health.

Contrary to what you might expect, feeling authentic doesn't necessarily mean you rarely feel inauthentic, and vice versa. These experiences don't strongly oppose each other. In fact, most of the time, people find themselves in a neutral state, feeling neither particularly authentic nor inauthentic. The moments of strong authenticity or inauthenticity are temporary and often triggered by specific situations. While people generally desire to feel authentic and want to avoid feeling inauthentic, wanting these experiences doesn't mean they can control them (Lenton et al., 2013). This is especially true for feelings of inauthenticity, which seem to be influenced more by external factors beyond an individual's control.

This suggests that, although we may strive for authenticity, our environment and circumstances play a significant role in shaping these experiences. In essence, rather than being fixed, our sense of authenticity fluctuates based on social context, cultural norms, relationships, emotional states, and external expectations. This understanding challenges the notion that we are either always true to ourselves or not, highlighting the complex and dynamic nature of human experiences and self-perception.

Self-Reflection 5.2: Emotional Display

1. Are there certain emotions you find easier or harder to display? What might be influencing this?
2. Are there certain situations where you feel inauthentic when displaying certain emotions? If so, in what situations and why?
3. How do others typically respond to your emotional expressions? Do they feel understood or confused by them?
4. Do you adjust your emotional displays based on whom you are interacting with? How does this affect your relationships?
5. Have you ever regretted how you displayed (or didn't display) an emotion in a specific situation? What could you have done differently?
6. Do you feel pressured to conform to cultural or societal norms in how you display emotion?
7. Are you able to regulate your emotions effectively without suppressing them?
8. How can you become more mindful of the connection between your internal feelings and their external expression?

Some scholars question whether authenticity is always beneficial or achievable. For instance, existentialist views might argue there is no permanent "true self," but rather an ongoing process of becoming (Sartre, 1943/1956). Others suggest that aiming for authenticity can become another form of self-imposed pressure, ironically leading to feelings of inauthenticity if one can't live up to idealized conceptions of "the real me."

Advantages and Disadvantages of Faking It

Recent scientific research has shed light on the potential benefits and drawbacks of faking it. For example, in a widely cited study (Carney et al., 2010), participants who adopted "high-power" poses, such as expansive, open postures, reported feeling more confident and powerful after using such poses. High- and low-power body postures are nonverbal expressions of dominance and submission, respectively, and are characterized by the amount of space a person occupies and their openness or contractiveness. High-power postures are expansive and open positions that take up more space, such as standing with legs wide apart and hands on hips: the "superhero pose." These postures are associated with confidence, assertiveness, and feelings of control. Low-power postures are closed and contractive positions that make the body appear smaller, such as crossing arms and legs while standing. Such poses are linked to feelings of powerlessness, submission, or insecurity.

This self-fulfilling prophecy can help individuals overcome initial self-doubt and anxiety when facing new challenges. By projecting confidence, women in business may be more likely to take risks, assert themselves, and seize opportunities for growth.

Still, you have to be mindful of the potential drawbacks of faking it. As a leader, you have to establish relationships with your direct reports; otherwise, they won't follow you. Our trust in people is based on three factors: ability, integrity, and benevolence (Mayer et al., 1995). Ability is all about whether you've got the skills, knowledge, and resources to get the job done. Integrity is about being honest, fair, and consistent in your words and actions. Finally, benevolence is about genuinely caring for others and having their best interests at heart. When leaders demonstrate that they have ability, integrity, and benevolence, people are more likely to put their faith in them. People are pretty good at identifying fake confidence or attempts to conceal aspects of yourself. The moment they feel there's something amiss with any of the three factors, they will lose trust, and people will be reluctant to follow you, no matter how much effort you put into managing the impression you're trying to make. Even four-year-old children have a pretty good sense of people's authenticity and can distinguish between a person who is overestimating their abilities and one who deserves to be confident. They prefer to learn from the justifiably confident person and judge them to be more intelligent than someone who appears overly confident (Birch et al., 2020).

In almost every single program I run for women executives, a participant will ask the question, "Should I fake it until I make it?" Before delving into the answer, let's establish some fundamental principles about authenticity.

First, authenticity doesn't mean verbalizing every thought that crosses your mind. It does not require complete transparency at all times either. There are instances when you may choose not to proactively express your thoughts unless explicitly asked.

Second, authenticity is not an excuse for poor behavior. Being impolite, sarcastic, or hurtful to others and then labeling those actions as "being authentic" is not acceptable. Often, we engage in negative conduct when we are feeling frustrated or angry. Before justifying emotional outbursts as authenticity, take a moment to pause and reflect: Who am I truly angry with in this situation? Is it my direct report for not meeting expectations, or is it actually myself for delegating the task but then failing to provide adequate coaching and support? The answer to this question can help guide a more appropriate response:

1. If your anger is directed at a direct report because your expectations and standards were clearly communicated on multiple occasions, an authentic yet respectful way to express your emotions could be: "I'm feeling disappointed and frustrated. We have explicitly discussed the expected output in our last three meetings. Is there additional context I'm missing that would explain why the deliverables do not meet the expectations?"

2. If you are upset with yourself because you realize you should have provided more guidance, a genuine response may be: "I'm realizing I let you down by not creating enough opportunities for you to ask questions and get the support you needed. I'm disappointed in myself for that oversight. Going forward, please reach out if you need more direction. I'm committed to being more available."

The key is to be authentic in a way that is constructive and respectful. True authenticity is not just about unfiltered emotional responses, but the courage to engage in thoughtful introspection and communication, even when it's uncomfortable.

Self-Reflection 5.3: How Authentic Are You?

- Do you feel comfortable expressing your true thoughts and feelings, even when they might not be well-received?
- Are there situations where you feel like you're wearing a "mask" or pretending to be someone you're not? Why might that be the case?
- How often do you say or do things just to please others, even if it doesn't feel true to who you are?
- Are you honest in your interactions with others, or do you sometimes hide parts of yourself out of fear of judgment or rejection?
- When making decisions, do you prioritize what feels right for you over what others might expect or want from you?
- Do your words and actions consistently reflect your inner beliefs and emotions, or do they sometimes contradict each other?
- Are there areas of your life that feel misaligned with your true self?

The decision to adopt a "fake it until you make it" approach is a personal one, but it comes with significant risks. This strategy can be time-consuming, and by the time you've "made it," you may have inadvertently alienated your followers. The people you manage may perceive you as insincere, leading to a lack of trust and a reluctance to follow your lead. Remember that followers have the discretion to decide whom they will follow, and we typically follow individuals we trust.

The Cognitive Route

Instead of faking it, you can achieve similar results by using the cognitive route, which is based on the major premises of cognitive behavior therapy. The cognitive route suggests that it's not what happens to you, but rather how you respond to the event that influences your trajectory in life. Psychologist Albert Ellis explains this concept through the ABC model of Adversity (Ellis, 1957), where an adverse event activates a response. In the ABC model:

A—is the **A**ctivating event (usually perceived as an adverse event).
B—stands for the **B**eliefs about the event.
C—stands for **C**onsequences (emotional and behavioral responses).

The activating event refers to any situation that a person experiences. This could be an external event, such as receiving criticism from a boss, or an internal experience, for example, remembering a past failure. Note that the activating event is objective—it's what has actually happened, without interpretation.

Beliefs represent the individual's thoughts, interpretations, or attitudes about the activating event. These can be rational or irrational, conscious or unconscious. Ellis emphasizes the role of irrational beliefs in causing emotional distress. In his view, these often include (Epstein, 2001) imperatives such as "must," "should," or "ought," generalizations ("I must *always* perform perfectly and succeed in *everything*"; "They *all* are against me"), or catastrophizing ("If I fail, it will be a complete disaster"). These beliefs are often related to three core needs: the need for achievement and to be perceived as competent; the need for belonging, to be liked, appreciated, and included by others; and the need to be considered a good person.

Consequences are the emotional and behavioral outcomes that result from the interaction between the activating event and the individual's beliefs. These can include emotions such as anxiety, depression, and anger, and behaviors such as avoidance, aggression, and withdrawal.

To illustrate the ABC model, consider the example of Candela, who had an important presentation that didn't go according to plan. She was unable to answer the client's questions, revealing her lack of preparation. Her manager had to step in, and a member of the management committee expressed clear disapproval. Candela left the meeting feeling humiliated and distraught.

Candela's story can continue along two different scenarios:

Scenario 1: Candela's colleagues invite her to join them for lunch, but she declines, claiming she isn't hungry. The thought of facing her colleagues' questions about her dismal presentation was unbearable. Candela thought, "Everyone now thinks I'm stupid and incompetent. This is the end of my career. Forget about a promotion, I'm likely to lose my job . . ." Two days later, her boss asks her to prepare a presentation for another client the following week. Panicked, Candela makes up an excuse to avoid it. Her colleagues are puzzled by her refusals to join them for lunch or coffee, and eventually, they stop inviting her. As the days pass, Candela becomes increasingly withdrawn. Over time, her boss begins to perceive her as shirking responsibilities and not contributing enough to the team. He starts to question whether he should keep her on the team.

Scenario 2: After the presentation, Candela requests a short debrief with her boss. She expresses her remorse, saying, "I'm terribly sorry for letting down our team and the entire organization. It was not my best performance, and I admit I was not well-prepared for this presentation. I apologize for that. When can I have an opportunity to make things right and prove that I am capable of representing this organization?"

Let's apply the ABC model to these scenarios (see Fig. 5.2). In the first scenario, the adverse event activates the belief, "I'm not good at presentations; I should avoid them. Everyone is convinced I'm stupid, and this is the end of my career." The story Candela tells herself is self-destructive. She overgeneralizes by believing "everyone" thinks she is incompetent and catastrophizes by

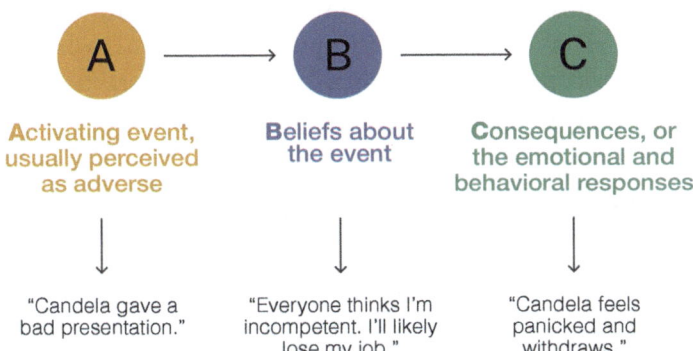

Fig. 5.2 The ABC model. According to Albert Ellis' ABC model, it's not the activating event, in this case the adverse event, that leads to negative consequences, but rather the dysfunctional beliefs that lead to those outcomes

thinking, "This is the end of my career at this company." This narrative leads to specific consequences: she starts avoiding her peers and becomes reluctant to take on any presentations, which are essential parts of her job.

In Scenario 2, Candela reflects and apologizes. The story she tells herself shifts to, "This wasn't my best performance because I wasn't well-prepared." As a consequence, she begins seeking a new opportunity to demonstrate her capabilities. By reframing her experience, Candela avoids the pitfall of developing counterproductive beliefs and sidesteps the self-destructive narrative that could lead to negative consequences.

How is this model relevant to our discussion of "fake it until you make it"? While "fake it until you make it" may seem like a quick fix, the cognitive route offers a more sustainable and authentic path to building confidence and resilience in the face of adversity.

5.3   The Impostor Phenomenon

Having established the importance of authenticity as a guiding principle in modern professional life, we now turn to a less visible issue that may undermine this pursuit: impostor phenomenon. Despite outward markers of success, some accomplished women secretly wrestle with the fear that they are merely "pretending" and are one misstep away from being exposed.

This phenomenon, known in the popular press as "impostor syndrome," underscores the striking gap between public achievement and private self-doubt, revealing how deeply cultural expectations and internalized beliefs can erode even the most hard-earned sense of achievement. In the following section, we will look at the roots of impostorism, discuss why it can persist even in the most competent individuals, and explore practical strategies for developing genuine confidence in tandem with professional authenticity.

Origins of the Impostor Phenomenon

In 1978, psychologists Pauline Rose Clance and Suzanne Imes wrote an influential article titled "The Impostor Phenomenon in High Achieving Women: Dynamics and Therapeutic Intervention" (Clance & Ames, 1978). Clance and Imes identified a psychological phenomenon characterized by persistent self-doubt and feelings of fraudulence despite evident success. The authors chose the term "impostor phenomenon" to describe the internal experience of feeling like a fraud, which they observed in high-achieving women. This phenomenon can be linked to concepts such as faking it, inauthenticity, or fakeness, as these women often feel they are pretending to be competent while fearing exposure as unworthy of their achievements. Women who experience the impostor phenomenon feel that they are not as smart as others think they are and believe they have tricked others into overestimating their abilities at work. They feel like frauds despite earning academic degrees, honors, and awards; achieving high standardized test scores; and attaining professional recognition, high status, rank, and salary. They rationalize that they have been admitted to university by mistake, sheer luck, or a grading fluke, and constantly worry that their cover will drop to reveal their incompetence. As a result, they feel anxious, depressed, and frustrated about being unable to meet self-imposed standards of achievement. In fact, people with impostor thoughts are often quite successful in their jobs, and individuals with self-doubts are frequently high-achievers.

Clance and Imes suggest that the impostor phenomenon occurs in men as well, but less frequently and with less intensity. The reason for this is that women tend to attribute success to external causes, such as luck or the easiness of the task, while men attribute their success to internal causes, for example, their knowledge or ability. The opposite is also true: when men are not successful, they tend to attribute it to external factors, such as bad luck or task difficulty, while women tend to attribute their failures to internal causes, such as a lack of ability. Even after repeated successes, women continue to discount their own abilities. If a person is consistently self-deprecating, after a certain point, they may start believing it.

People are not born with impostor thoughts. It starts with the family, for example, growing up in an environment where success is overly emphasized or where praise is inconsistent or tied to achievement. Instances of failure or criticism in childhood, especially during formative years, can leave lasting impressions that contribute to self-doubt. Clance and Imes' original article analyzes early family history and family dynamics as the origin of this dysfunctional cycle. Two distinct family patterns lie at the heart of the impostor phenomenon (Jamison, 2023). According to the first, "impostors" grew up having been told, directly or indirectly, that they are the "sensitive" ones in the family, while a sibling was labeled "the smart one." The young girl tries to disprove the family myth, but when her accomplishments receive no recognition at home, she begins to doubt any validation of her achievements. She might start thinking that her family is right and explain her success as the result of her social skills and attention to her teachers' expectations. According to Clance and Imes, these beliefs eventually lead to the impostor phenomenon.

Paradoxically, overachievement early in life and a history of being labeled "gifted" or exceptionally talented can lead to unrealistic expectations and subsequent feelings of fraudulence. This is the second pattern, where people were celebrated as "superior in every way" (intelligence, appearance, talents) as young children and considered perfect. They were made to believe they could achieve anything with ease. This dynamic creates unrealistic expectations that inevitably don't hold up to real-world experiences. These people soon start to question their parents' perceptions of them, followed by doubting their competence.

Both patterns create a profound disconnect between the messages these people receive from their parents and the messages they receive from other people around them. This disconnect manifests as a constant internal struggle. Women who were labeled as "sensitive" wonder, "Are my parents right about my inadequacy, or is the world correct in seeing me as successful?" Those who were lauded as superior wonder, "Were my parents right about my perfection, and is the world wrong in pointing out my flaws?" This inconsistency produces feelings of cognitive dissonance—the mental discomfort you feel when your actions, beliefs, or values conflict with each other. To reduce the discomfort of inconsistent ideas, the person concludes that they are an impostor.

Many people struggling with impostor feelings believe that being "perfect" will offset their self-doubt and resolve the disconnect between how they see themselves and how others see them (cognitive dissonance). Unfortunately, perfectionism often puts even more pressure on them, magnifying their fear of failure and reinforcing the belief that they are not truly competent, thus worsening feelings of inadequacy.

Perfectionism

Personality traits such as perfectionism or a tendency toward anxiety can predispose people to impostor thoughts. Perfectionism involves setting excessively high and unrealistic expectations for performance, both for oneself and others. While perfectionism may appear to be a pathway to success, research has uncovered significant drawbacks of perfectionism that can exacerbate impostor thoughts.

Psychologist Barry Schwartz and his colleagues conducted a series of studies (2002) suggesting that people who strive to maximize their outcomes, called maximizers, tend to experience higher levels of regret and even depression. Maximizers, or perfectionists, set exceedingly high standards for themselves and often engage in exhaustive searches to find the best possible outcomes in various situations.

Perfectionism has significant drawbacks. Maximizers, for example, are more likely to compare themselves to others, leading to feelings of dissatisfaction and regret, even if their actual outcomes are objectively better. Schwartz and his colleagues found that this tendency for social comparison and the perpetual pursuit of the best option was eroding maximizers' happiness, optimism, and satisfaction with life. In contrast, people who adopted a satisficing strategy, which involves settling for the "good enough," reported higher levels of happiness, optimism, and self-esteem.

One key reason for this difference is that maximizers often anticipate regret over missed opportunities and experience regret over their chosen options, thinking other alternatives might have been better in some respects. This constant second-guessing diminishes their overall satisfaction and well-being. Furthermore, the process of constantly seeking the best option can be exhausting and lead to higher search costs, which can further reduce satisfaction.

Perfectionism can also lead to anticipatory anxiety or *future tripping*. It's completely normal to feel a bit nervous about the unknown, and we have all experienced this type of anxiety at one point or another. But future tripping is much more than typical nervousness; it's a nagging worry that creeps into your mind, making you feel worked up over what might happen, even though the event hasn't occurred yet. For example, let's say you have a presentation coming up. Instead of feeling excited to talk about the topic, you find yourself obsessing over every little detail: "What if I say something stupid? What if they don't like me? What if I spill my coffee all over myself?" Future tripping often blows things way out of proportion. For some people, future tripping can become overwhelming and start to impact their daily life.

Perfectionism can further fuel future-tripping. By setting extremely high standards for yourself and feeling intense pressure not to fail, your mind goes into overdrive, magnifying worries about everything that *could* go wrong. Your brain is trying to protect you by preparing for possible threats, but sometimes it goes overboard, similar to an alarm system that is too sensitive. Instead of just giving you a gentle warning, it floods your mind with thoughts such as "What if this goes badly?" or "I won't be able to handle it," which only leads to more stress.

For women who may feel societal pressures to be perfect in their professional roles, aiming for perfection can be counterproductive. Instead of striving for an unattainable ideal, shifting the goal from "perfect" to "good enough" is the first step. Adopting a more balanced approach that recognizes and accepts good outcomes can lead to greater overall well-being and career satisfaction. By letting go of the need to maximize in every single situation and embracing a satisficing approach, women can reduce their stress and increase their confidence and well-being in the workplace for both the short and long term.

Self-Reflection 5.4: Are You a Perfectionist?

- Do people say that you set unrealistically high standards for yourself? How do you feel when you don't meet those standards?
- Do you tend to procrastinate if you believe you can't complete a task perfectly?
- Would you consider yourself a maximizer? If yes, how does this impact your personal and professional life?
- Do you frequently seek approval or validation from others to feel confident about your work or decisions?
- What are your thoughts on delegating tasks? Do you believe others won't do them as well as you would?
- Would you say your definition of success is narrow, while your definition of failure is broad?
- Does the idea of doing something "good enough" rather than perfectly make you uncomfortable?
- How do you react to imperfections in others? Do you often feel disappointed or critical of their work?
- Do you find yourself "future-tripping" by worrying excessively about potential outcomes or mistakes, and how does this affect your present actions?
- What fears or anxieties drive your need for perfection, and how do they affect your well-being and relationships?

To avoid being exposed, people with impostor thoughts often develop elaborate coping mechanisms. They might fake illness to avoid challenges or hide their efforts to maintain an illusion of effortless success. These behaviors feed into a vicious cycle: anticipating failure, working frantically to prevent it, experiencing brief relief when successful, only to quickly return to the conviction that failure is imminent. Perhaps most treacherously, repeated successes often fail to break this cycle. The very efforts made to avoid being discovered as a fraud end up reinforcing their belief in their own inadequacy. It's a self-fulfilling prophecy that can feel impossible to escape.

Impostorism exists on a spectrum, varying in intensity and in how it manifests for different people. On one end, individuals may feel mild, occasional self-doubt when tackling new challenges, which can be short-lived and even motivating. On the other end, people experience persistent impostor feelings across many areas of life, leading to chronic anxiety, overwork, or avoidance of opportunities due to a fear of failure.

Impostor feelings can also fluctuate based on external factors, such as social support or feedback. People in exclusionary environments may experience heightened self-doubt compared to those in more inclusive settings. Underrepresented groups, in particular, can be disproportionately affected, as systemic inequities amplify feelings of inadequacy.

For some, strategies like reframing negative self-talk or learning to accept praise can help. Others may need deeper psychological support to address ingrained self-doubt and perfectionism.

The prevalence of impostor phenomenon can vary widely as well, depending on how it is measured and who is measuring it. A 2019 review of literature on impostorism reports numbers ranging anywhere from 9 to 82% (Bravata et al., 2020). The research on whether this phenomenon is more common among women or people from marginalized racial backgrounds is not as clearcut as you might think. Tewfik et al. (2025) conclude that, when it comes to gender, the findings depend on who is being studied. For instance, when researchers study students and those in postgraduate training, they find differences between men and women in about half of the studies (see Fig. 5.3). But here's where it gets interesting: When researchers turn their attention to working professionals, gender differences in impostor phenomenon don't show up nearly as often. In fact, less than a third of the studies conducted with professionals found any significant gender gap in impostor phenomenon. This variation highlights an important point: Factors such as age, experience, or environment can play a big role in whether people experience impostor thoughts and how those thoughts manifest.

We all have moments when we feel like impostors, most of which are transient. They usually occur during times of professional vulnerability, such as career transitions. Ironically, quick advancement or recognition can sometimes trigger impostor experiences, as individuals may feel they haven't "earned" their success. Sometimes, we inadvertently fuel these thoughts by failing to realize that it's the context that leads to impostorism. Assuming new roles or levels of responsibility often increases self-doubt, particularly when there are no role models to boost self-esteem.

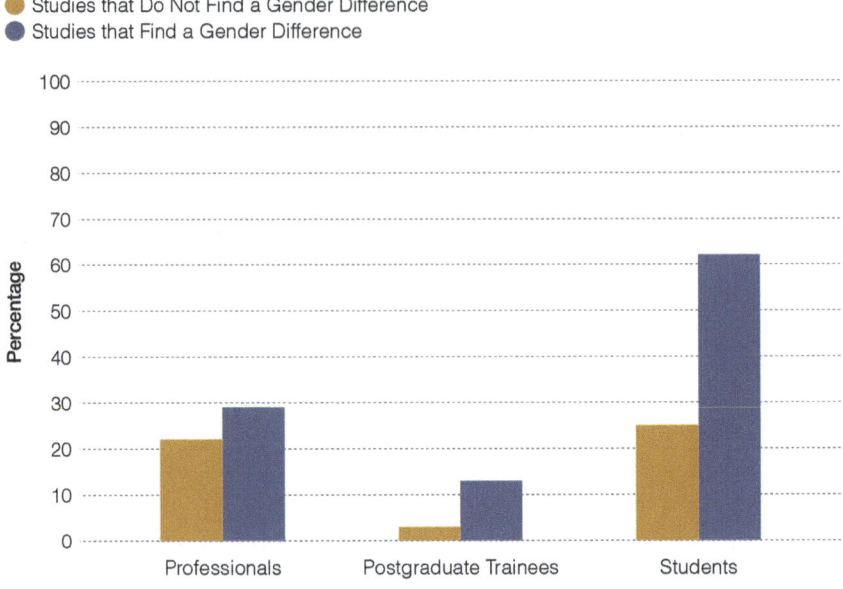

● Studies that Do Not Find a Gender Difference
● Studies that Find a Gender Difference

Fig. 5.3 Studies exploring gender differences in impostor thoughts. A meta-analysis found that studies conducted with professionals were less likely to identify a gender gap in impostorism compared to those conducted with postgraduate trainees and students. The gender differences observed in some studies may be influenced by the type of sample used—for example, students, trainees, or professionals. *Source* Adapted from Tewfik et al. (2025). Copyright 2025 by Academy of Management Journal

Impostor Phenomenon or Impostor Syndrome?

Clance and Imes's work laid the foundation for understanding the complex issues surrounding the impostor phenomenon. Over time, the concept gained traction in academic circles, with numerous studies expanding upon it. The term "impostor syndrome" began to gain popularity (see Fig. 5.4), especially in nonacademic circles, and the popular media started replacing the term "phenomenon" with the term "syndrome."

Tewfik et al. (2025) point out that, initially, the concept was conceived primarily as a cognitive phenomenon, which focused on the belief that other people overestimate a person's abilities compared to how the person perceives themself. However, in the 2010s, the concept was expanded to include emotions, which resulted in a blurring of boundaries between impostor phenomenon and related but distinct concepts, such as feelings of not belonging or fear of being

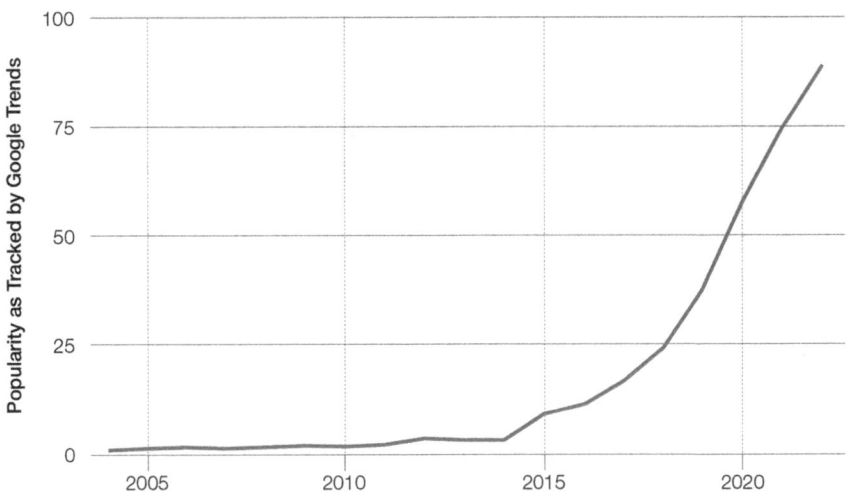

Fig. 5.4 Interest in impostor syndrome,2004–2022. Interest in impostor syndrome increased steadily in the twenty-first century. *Source* Adapted from Tewfik et al. (2025). Copyright 2025 by Academy of Management Journal

exposed. This shift from cognitive to affective language (e.g., feelings of intellectual phoniness) may explain the adoption of the label "impostor syndrome."

The term "syndrome," used in medicine and clinical psychology, implies a set of symptoms that occur together and are indicative of a physical or psychological disorder. Despite the popular use of "syndrome," it's crucial to note that impostor syndrome is not a clinical diagnosis or a mental disorder recognized in the Diagnostic and Statistical Manual of Mental Disorders (DSM), a professional reference for psychological disorders published by the American Psychiatric Association, or the International Classification of Diseases (ICD), the professional reference used in countries outside of the United States. The term "syndrome" may have gained popularity as a result of self-help literature, social media, and an increased awareness of mental health issues. It may also align with how people perceive their impostor feelings. However, the word "syndrome" pathologizes their experience. According to Clance and Imes, the term "impostor syndrome" is incorrect and misleading. They think of it as an experience rather than a pathology. In fact, everyone, even the most successful person, has moments of self-doubt and insecurity. These feelings are as much a part of the human experience as confidence and decisiveness.

While the core concept of the impostor phenomenon remains the same, our understanding of it has evolved. Initially, it was primarily associated with women, but research has shown that it affects individuals of all genders and backgrounds. Additionally, research has uncovered the role of societal and cultural factors in its development and perpetuation, moving the focus beyond individual psychology. Today, the impostor phenomenon is not considered a clinical diagnosis, but rather a common experience that can affect individuals at any stage of their career or personal development.

How can we differentiate between normal self-doubts and impostor phenomenon? Table 5.2 summarizes some of the research findings.

Impostor phenomenon has been criticized, and there have been calls to drop it altogether. Some researchers question the claim that it's impostor syndrome that makes women doubt their success. For example, systemic stereotypes and biases related to gender and race can fuel feelings of otherness and not fitting in (Tulshyan & Burey, 2021). More and more, the "fixing the woman" narrative has been replaced

Table 5.2 Normal self-doubts and impostor phenomenon

Aspect	Normal self-doubt	Impostor phenomenon
Persistence and intensity	Temporary and situation-specific	Persistent, pervasive, and intense
Response to success	Often alleviated by achievements	Successes discounted or attributed to luck
Impact on behaviour	May cause hesitation but doesn't prevent action	Can lead to self-sabotage or avoiding opportunities
Generalization	Limited to specific areas or situations	Tends to generalize across various life aspects
Relationship to failure	Seen as a learning opportunity	Seen as confirmation of inadequacy
Self-perception versus reality	Generally, aligns with objective reality	Significant discrepancy with objective achievements
Coping mechanisms	Addressable through self-reflection and feedback	May require more intensive interventions
Effect on self-esteem	Temporary impact	Chronic undermining of self-worth
Reaction to praise	Able to internalize and appreciate praise	Difficulty accepting compliments
Comparison to others	Realistic comparisons to peers	Tendency to idealize others' abilities
Anticipation of tasks	Nervousness, but willingness to try	Intense anxiety, fear of being "found out"
Duration	Often resolves with experience	Can persist despite years of experience

by a demand to fix the system. Being a member of a minoritized group in a particular profession and being aware of the social expectations around membership in that group can contribute to feelings of not belonging and incompetence.

However, some researchers argue that dismissing the concept of impostorism would deprive us of valuable insights, and they recommend studying it further by accounting for the unique experiences of individuals with intersecting identities. One example would be to introduce the notion of the racialized impostor phenomenon, defined as "persistent beliefs or actions of intellectual or professional self-doubt among racially minoritized people due to experiences, systems, or principles of racial oppression and inequity" (Cokley, 2024, p. 6). This approach acknowledges that people from minoritized groups can experience the impostor phenomenon as a result of the prejudice and/or discrimination they face due to their race or ethnicity, as well as their gender.

While much of the existing research has focused on the negative aspects of the impostor phenomenon and assumes it is harmful, more recent studies have found hidden upsides. Tewfik's research (2022) highlights some interpersonal benefits; for example, people who more frequently have impostor thoughts are perceived as more interpersonally effective compared to their nonimpostor peers. People with impostor thoughts perceive a threat to their self-worth since self-worth is based on being perceived as competent. This threat leads to a need to restore their self-esteem. These individuals often exhibit a defensive response that involves an other-focused orientation, which means paying more attention to others and being interested and focused on them. The switch to the other-focused approach is a way to experience success in the interpersonal domain as a substitute for the competence domain, which also boosts feelings of self-worth. The other-focused orientation involves asking more questions, providing others with verbal or non-verbal assurances, and demonstrating active listening.

Tewfik's study points out a need to reframe our thinking about impostorism. We have to shift away from the pathologized concept of "impostor syndrome," which is perceived as uniformly detrimental and as something to "fix." Going back to the more nuanced concept of "impostor phenomenon" and considering impostor thoughts as a continuum of experiences, some of which have upsides, will enable reframing the experience of feeling like an impostor. This cognitive reappraisal will reduce the negative emotional response to the impostor thoughts. Needless to say, there will still be cases where some people will need therapy to overcome severe impostor thoughts.

Self-Reflection 5.5: Reframing Impostor Thoughts

- Where would you place yourself on a 7-point scale, where 1 represents a lack of confidence (self-doubt) and 7 signifies overconfidence (hubris)?
- Are there people in your organization who consider it a "confidence desert"? What are the reasons for that?
- Do you keep a journal of your successful experiences to refer to when you have impostor thoughts?
- How much do you second-guess yourself?
- Have you ever felt that you have tricked people into thinking you are competent when you actually believe you aren't? For example, do you think that you got a promotion by fooling decision-makers into believing you are smarter than you actually are?
- Do you struggle to delegate tasks? Research suggests that managers with impostor thoughts tend to delegate to direct reports who themselves have self-doubts (Bechtoldt, 2015).

Overcoming Impostor Thoughts

The tendency to "medicalize" impostor syndrome places an unfair burden on women, pushing them to seek individual solutions for problems rooted in discrimination and power imbalances. Recognizing that impostor feelings often arise from systemic inequities rather than personal failings helps shift the focus from self-blame to tackling the structural barriers that fuel these doubts. This reframing not only eases the pressure on individuals but also underscores the need for widespread organizational changes. Too often, "power games" take the form of exclusionary practices or biased performance assessments. By addressing deeper issues, like unequal access to leadership roles or gendered assumptions about competence, organizations can reduce the triggers that give rise to impostor thoughts.

The Gestalt Method

As we understand more about the impostor phenomenon, the strategies for addressing it have further evolved. Clance and Imes suggest that when struggling with impostor thoughts, the key is to recognize feelings of doubt and inadequacy for what they are—not facts, but maladaptive thoughts that we have the power to overcome. We often encounter parts of ourselves that we'd rather hide away. But what if embracing these very aspects could be the key to overcoming our deepest insecurities? This is the essence of the Gestalt method, a psychological approach that has proven particularly effective in combating impostor thoughts (Perls et al., 1951). At its core, the Gestalt method emphasizes the human experience as a whole rather than merely the sum of its parts: sensations, thoughts, feelings, behaviors, and so on. Rather than trying to suppress the parts you deem unworthy, the Gestalt approach encourages you to accept all parts of yourself—the good, the bad, and everything in between (Yontef, 1993).

One of the most intriguing aspects of the Gestalt approach is its recognition of the self as multifaceted. We are not static beings with a single, fixed identity. Instead, we are a collection of various selves, each playing a unique role in our lives. This understanding can be incredibly liberating, especially for people grappling with impostor thoughts, who feel compelled to present only their "best" self to the world. By facing these maladaptive beliefs head-on and seeing them for what they are—distorted perceptions rather than reality—you can begin to loosen their grip on your psyche (Sakulku & Alexander, 2011). The Gestalt method encourages you to accept and integrate all aspects of yourself, including your fears and insecurities, rather than trying to present a carefully curated version of who you think you should be. In essence, the journey to overcoming impostor self-doubts is not about becoming someone else or achieving some idealized version of yourself. It's about embracing who you are in your entirety, acknowledging your complexities and contradictions, and recognizing that your perceived flaws are just as much a part of you as your strengths. This process of self-acceptance is central to authenticity, as it allows you to live and act in alignment with your true self rather than conforming to external expectations or hiding parts of who you are.

Reaching for a Connection

In cases where chronic feelings of inadequacy and self-doubt affect multiple areas of life and coexist with high levels of anxiety and depression, Clance and Imes recommend a combination of therapeutic interventions. In their view, the key to healing lies in connecting with others. Group therapy, particularly with other women experiencing similar feelings, can be transformative. Bringing together women who share similar feelings of self-doubt can be incredibly powerful (Clance & Imes, 1978). Group settings, whether formal therapy or a more casual gathering, provide unique opportunities for connection and understanding. When one participant finds the courage to open up about her inner struggles, it often creates a ripple effect. Others feel encouraged to share their own experiences, realizing they are not alone in their feelings. As women observe and listen to each other, they often recognize the unrealistic nature of self-doubts more clearly in others than they can in themselves. This shared vulnerability can be both surprising and deeply comforting. Group interactions offer a valuable outside perspective. This external view can help women challenge their own internal narratives.

The Empty-Chair Technique

Another powerful Gestalt technique is the empty-chair technique. In this approach, the client sits facing an empty chair and imagines it is occupied by a significant person, a part of themselves (such as an inner critic), or a symbolic concept (e.g., fear or grief). The client engages in a dialog with the imagined presence, openly expressing their thoughts and emotions. Then, the client switches seats, stepping into the role of the other person or aspect they are addressing.

During the session, the therapist would ask the person with impostor thoughts to mentally revisit all the individuals they believe they have deceived and explain how they think they have tricked them (Jamison, 2023). Then, the person is asked to switch chairs, take the perspective of the person they were addressing, and voice that person's potential responses. These imagined replies might include statements like: "Your charisma didn't influence my decision to give you the highest grade. While I do like you, I graded you based on your exceptional work." Or perhaps: "I'm frustrated that you think I'm so easily fooled. Do you really believe I can't recognize genuine competence?" Another possible response could be: "It bothers me that you're dismissing both me and my professional judgment." The empty-chair exercise helps people confront their assumptions and reveals how unreasonable their beliefs about fooling others are when voicing those beliefs out loud.

The empty-chair exercise serves a dual purpose. First, it uncovers the often-unconscious belief that underpins the impostor phenomenon—the idea that you have somehow tricked everyone around you. Second, it gently challenges this belief by highlighting its inherent absurdity. The notion that we have fooled all these intelligent, accomplished individuals implies a belief that we alone are real, and everyone else is easily deceived.

Individuals with impostor thoughts are encouraged to start keeping track of the positive comments they receive on a daily basis from people around them and note how they tend to dismiss or downplay positive feedback.

Once they become more aware of their habit of rejecting praise, they are asked to change their behavior and do the opposite. Instead of brushing off positive comments, they are instructed to really listen to them, internalize the positive words, and fully appreciate and benefit from the encouragement. The purpose of keeping track of positive comments is to shift from a pattern of denial to one of acceptance and to learn to embrace and draw strength from the recognition of one's skills and accomplishments.

Take Action 5.1: A Step-by-Step Guide to the Empty-Chair Technique

- Set the stage

  Find a quiet, private spot where you feel safe and comfortable. Place two chairs facing each other. Sit in one, leaving the other empty. Take a moment to settle in—breathe, center yourself, and prepare for an open dialog.
- Decide who or what occupies the empty chair

  It could be a specific person (a boss, a family member), a part of yourself (your inner critic), or a concept ("ambition" or "authenticity"). Trust your instincts when choosing; pick whatever feels most relevant or emotionally charged right now.
- Begin the conversation

  Speak directly to the person, inner part, or concept as if they're truly there. Share your thoughts, feelings, questions, and boundaries, anything you've been holding back or need to express.
- Switch perspectives

  Move to the other chair and imagine yourself as the person or concept you were just addressing. Speak out loud, responding from this new perspective. Don't worry if it feels a bit awkward at first; try to step into their point of view as fully as you can. Continue switching chairs, letting the dialog unfold. Be open to hearing new insights, addressing unresolved emotions, or experiencing a shift in how you see the situation.
- Reflect and integrate

  When you finish, take a few moments to reflect on what came up. Notice any changes in how you feel or think, and carry any newfound understanding or empathy with you into your daily life.

This exercise can stir up strong emotions. It's perfectly fine to pause, take a breath, or even come back to it later. If it becomes overwhelming, consider talking with a trusted friend, mentor, or mental health professional for additional support.

Self-Distancing

Some of you might struggle with impostor feelings at some point—those nagging doubts that make you question your own abilities. In these moments, self-distancing can be a powerful tool to help break the cycle of negative thoughts. Rather than getting stuck in unhelpful rumination, self-distancing encourages you to step back and observe yourself as an outsider looking in. According to Kross and Ayduk (2017), this shift in perspective can turn maladaptive self-immersion into adaptive self-reflection, often leading to more insightful thinking and wiser decision-making. When you move away from merely recounting your worries and start reconstruing them, seeing them in a new light, you are better able to inoculate yourself against distress. Let's look at an example of how this technique can be put into practice.

Vignette 5.3: Nora

Nora is a seasoned cybersecurity expert with years of experience and a range of certifications attesting to her skills. Yet, like many professionals in her field, she works under immense pressure, facing high expectations, rapidly evolving technology, and intense competition, all of which can heighten feelings of inadequacy. Driven by empathy and a strong sense of responsibility, Nora strives not only to protect systems but also the people who depend on them. These admirable qualities, however, on top of her perfectionism, can make her prone to self-doubt. Despite her many accomplishments, she still wrestles with impostor thoughts, worrying that she may not live up to the demands of leading a team. Nora has been offered a promotion, but she is considering turning down the opportunity due to her fear of failure.

Follow along as Nora is guided in a three-step self-distancing exercise.

Step 1: Instead of thinking, "I'm not good enough for this role," Nora is encouraged to talk about herself in the third person: "Nora is worried about taking on this new role." This simple shift to self-distancing can help her examine her self-doubts more objectively. Now, Nora imagines observing herself in a meeting where she is leading the team. From this perspective, she might notice strengths that she typically overlooks, such as her clear communication style or her ability to break down complex problems. By observing herself from an outside perspective, Nora can more clearly see her strengths and capabilities, which might otherwise be obscured by her self-doubt. Self-distancing can reduce the intensity of negative emotions associated with self-doubt, allowing for more rational thinking.

Step 2: Nora is asked to imagine herself five years from now. What would future Nora say about this opportunity? She might realize that future Nora would regret not having taken this chance for growth. Alternatively, Nora can imagine her best friend in this situation. What advice would she give? She might find that she would encourage her friend to take the opportunity, highlighting her friend's skills and potential. We are often kinder to others than to ourselves. By imagining giving advice to a friend in the same situation, Nora can access more self-compassionate thoughts. She can also see the bigger picture of her career trajectory rather than focusing solely on her immediate fears.

Step 3: Nora writes down her self-doubts on a piece of paper, then sets it aside and physically steps back from her self-doubts. This physical act can help create emotional distance from the doubts.

The goal of the self-distancing technique is to help Nora realize that her doubts are not reflective of her actual abilities. She needs to see that, while the leadership role is new to her, she has consistently succeeded when taking on new challenges in the past. Self-distancing might give her the confidence to accept the promotion and approach it as an opportunity for growth rather than as a threat. It's about transforming Nora's internal dialog from one of self-doubt to one of realistic self-assessment and a growth mindset, enabling her to tackle new challenges with greater confidence.

How we choose to respond to impostor feelings makes a difference. The goal of all these techniques is not to eliminate self-doubt or uncertainty altogether, but to embrace these feelings as part of your story, allowing them to coexist with your confidence and achievements. In doing so, you might just find that you are more capable and more authentic than you ever realized.

Take Action 5.2: Visual and Linguistic Self-Distancing

Subtle shifts in the language we use to refer to the self can impact how we think, feel, and behave. The new perspective might help us see things differently, similar to looking at a familiar painting from a new angle.

- Recall a negative experience that has caused self-doubt.
- Picture yourself back in that situation.
- Close your eyes and change your perspective to that of a "fly on the wall." From this new vantage point, watch as the scene unfolds.
- As you observe, let the event play out again in your mind. But this time, do not let yourself get caught up in it. Watch it happen to yourself from a distance. Take in everything you can see from this perspective. What details stand out that you might have missed before? Let the scene continue to unfold, watching yourself navigate through the experience.
- Explore your feelings from that experience, but instead of using "I," use your name or "you" when describing what happened. For example, you would ask yourself, "Why did [your name] feel this way? What might have caused [your name]'s feelings?"

Adapted from Kross and Ayduk (2017).

In this chapter, we explored the delicate balance between being true to ourselves and managing how others perceive us. Authenticity is a powerful tool for building trust and credibility, yet it can also leave us vulnerable. Impostor thoughts can be especially debilitating, but by recognizing that they are common and manageable, we can begin to dismantle their hold over us.

It's crucial to remember that embracing authenticity is not about achieving perfection; rather, it's about cultivating self-awareness and resilience. This foundation will serve you well as you move on to the next chapter, where we'll discuss how to thrive at different life stages. By staying grounded in your authenticity, you can better resist adverse forces and maintain your integrity, no matter what challenges arise.

References

Bechtoldt, M. N. (2015). Wanted: Self-doubting employees—Managers scoring positively on impostorism favor insecure employees in task delegation. *Personality and Individual Differences, 86*, 482–486.

Birch, S. A., Severson, R. L., & Baimel, A. (2020). Children's understanding of when a person's confidence and hesitancy is a cue to their credibility. *PloS One, 15*(1), e0227026.

Bravata, D. M., Watts, S. A., Keefer, A. L., Madhusudhan, D. K., Taylor, K. T., Clark, D. M., Nelson, R. S., Cokley, K. O., & Hagg, H. K. (2020). Prevalence, predictors, and treatment of impostor syndrome: A systematic review. *Journal of General Internal Medicine, 35*, 1252–1275.

Carney, D. R., Cuddy, A. J., & Yap, A. J. (2010). Power posing: Brief nonverbal displays affect neuroendocrine levels and risk tolerance. *Psychological Science, 21*(10), 1363–1368.

Cha, S. E., Hewlin, P. F., Roberts, L. M., Buckman, B. R., Leroy, H., Steckler, E. L., Ostermeier, K., & Cooper, D. (2019). Being your true self at work: Integrating the fragmented research on authenticity in organizations. *Academy of Management Annals, 13*(2), 633–671.

Clance, P. R., & Imes, S. A. (1978). The imposter phenomenon in high achieving women: Dynamics and therapeutic intervention. *Psychotherapy: Theory, Research & Practice, 15*(3), 241.

Cokley, K. (2024). It's time to reconceptualize what "imposter syndrome" means for people of color. *Harvard Business Review.* https://hbr.org/2024/03/its-time-to-reconceptualize-what-imposter-syndrome-means-for-people-of-color

Deci, E. L., & Ryan, R. M. (2000). The "what" and "why" of goal pursuits: Human needs and the self-determination of behavior. *Psychological Inquiry, 11*(4), 227–268.

Eagly, A. H. (2005). Achieving relational authenticity in leadership: Does gender matter? *The Leadership Quarterly, 16*(3), 459–474.

Eagly, A. H., & Karau, S. J. (2002). Role congruity theory of prejudice toward female leaders. *Psychological Review, 109*(3), 573.

Eagly, A. H., Karau, S. J., & Makhijani, M. G. (1995). Gender and the effectiveness of leaders: A meta-analysis. *Psychological Bulletin, 117*(1), 125.

Ellis, A. (1957). Rational psychotherapy and individual psychology. *Journal of Individual Psychology, 13*(1), 38–44.

Epstein, R. (2001). The prince of reason: An interview with Albert Ellis. *Psychology Today, 34*(1), 66–76.

Eurich, T. (2018). What self-awareness really is (and how to cultivate it). *Harvard Business Review, 4*(4), 1–9.

Gardner, W. L., Avolio, B. J., Luthans, F., May, D. R., & Walumbwa, F. (2005). "Can you see the real me?" A self-based model of authentic leader and follower development. *The Leadership Quarterly, 16*(3), 343–372.

Goffman, E. (1949). Presentation of self in everyday life. *American Journal of Sociology, 55*(1), 6–7.

Hewlett, S. A. (2024). The new rules of executive presence. *Harvard Business Review,* 134–139

Hitlin, S. (2003). Values as the core of personal identity: Drawing links between two theories of self. *Social Psychology Quarterly, 66*(2), 118–137.

Ilies, R., Morgeson, F. P., & Nahrgang, J. D. (2005). Authentic leadership and eudaemonic well-being: Understanding leader-follower outcomes. *The Leadership Quarterly, 16*(3), 373–394.

Jamison, L. (2023, February 13). No fooling anyone. *The dubious rise of imposter syndrome.* The New Yorker.

Kernis, M. H., & Goldman, B. M. (2006). A multicomponent conceptualization of authenticity: Theory and research. *Advances in Experimental Social Psychology, 38,* 283–357.

Kross, E., & Ayduk, O. (2017). Self-distancing: Theory, research, and current directions In J. M. Olson (Ed.), *Advances in experimental social psychology* (Vol. 55, pp. 81–136). Academic Press.

Lenton, A. P., Bruder, M., Slabu, L., & Sedikides, C. (2013). How does "being real" feel? The experience of state authenticity. *Journal of Personality, 81*(3), 276–289.

Luthans, F., & Avolio, B. J. (2003). Authentic leadership: A positiv developmental approach. In K. S. Cameron, J. E. Dutton, & R. E. Quinn (Eds.), *Positive organizational scholarship: Foundations of a new discipline* 241–258. San Francisco, CA: Berrett-Koehler.

Maslow, A. H. (1968). *Toward a psychology of being.* Van Nostrand Reinhold.

Mayer, R. C., Davis, J. H., & Schoorman, F. D. (1995). An integrative model of organizational trust. *Academy of Management Review, 20*(3), 709–734.

Perls, F. S., Hefferline, R. E., & Goodman, P. (1951). *Gestalt therapy: Excitement and growth in the human personality.* Dell.

Rogers, C. R. (1959). A theory of therapy, personality and interpersonal relationships as developed in the client-centered framework. In S. Koch (Ed.), *Psychology: A Study of a science* (Vol. 3, pp. 181–256). McGraw-Hill Formulations of the person and the social context.

Rogers, C. R. (1961). *On becoming a person: A therapist's view of psychotherapy.* Houghton Mifflin.

Rowe, C. J., & Broadie, S. (2002). *Nicomachean ethics.* Oxford University Press.

Sakulku, J., & Alexander, J. (2011). The imposter syndrome. *International Journal of Behavioral Science, 6*(1), 75–97.

Sartre, J.-P. (1956). *Being and nothingness* (H. E. Barnes, Trans.). Philosophical Library, 257 (Original work published 1943).

Schwartz, B., Ward, A., Monterosso, J., Lyubomirsky, S., White, K., & Lehman, D. R. (2002). Maximizing versus satisficing: Happiness is a matter of choice. *Journal of Personality and Social Psychology, 83*(5), 1178.

Tewfik, B. A. (2022). The impostor phenomenon revisited: Examining the relationship between workplace impostor thoughts and interpersonal effectiveness at work. *Academy of Management Journal, 65*(3), 988–1018.

Tewfik, B. A., Yip, J. A., & Martin, S. R. (2025). Workplace impostor thoughts, impostor feelings, and impostorism: An integrative, multidisciplinary review of research on the impostor phenomenon. *Academy of Management Annals, 19*(1), 38–73.

Tulshyan, R., & Burey, J.-A. (2021). Stop telling women they have imposter syndrome. *Harvard Business Review, 11*, 1–7.

Weiss, M., Razinskas, S., Backmann, J., & Hoegl, M. (2018). Authentic leadership and leaders' mental well-being: An experience sampling study. *The Leadership Quarterly, 29*(2), 309–321.

Wood, A. M., Linley, P. A., Maltby, J., Baliousis, M., & Joseph, S. (2008). The authentic personality: A theoretical and empirical conceptualization and the development of the Authenticity Scale. *Journal of Counseling Psychology, 55*(3), 385.

Yontef, G. M. (1993). Awareness, dialogue and process: Essays on Gestalt therapy. *The Gestalt Journal Press.*

6

Thriving at Every Life Stage

6.1 Motherhood: Navigating Work-Life Balance

Vignette 6.1: Anne-Marie Slaughter

Anne-Marie Slaughter, former director of policy planning for the US State Department during the Obama administration, wrote an essay for *The Atlantic* describing her experience balancing a high-level government job with family life (Slaughter, 2012). Slaughter worked in Washington, DC, during the week and returned to Princeton, New Jersey, on weekends to be with her family. Her job required long hours and a demanding schedule, including commuting to Washington, DC, very early on Monday mornings and returning home late on Fridays. Despite having a supportive husband and understanding bosses, she struggled to be both the parent and professional she wanted to be. Initially believing that she had landed her dream job, Slaughter eventually left her position and returned to academia due to the challenges of maintaining a work-life balance. Her son's difficult adolescence influenced her decision to leave her government position. Slaughter ultimately concluded that "having it all" was not possible in many types of jobs, at least not for an extended period of time. This experience led her to reconsider her belief that women could have it all, regardless of their profession.

In an organizational environment that defines the ideal employee as someone who is prepared to sacrifice personal life, having it all is impossible, especially for women. But in the twenty-first century, many leaders are questioning the assumption that having work-life balance and a successful career necessarily contradict each other. Citigroup CEO Jane Fraser puts it this way: "You cannot have it all at the same time. You can have it all, spread

© The Author(s), under exclusive license to Springer Nature Switzerland AG 2025
G. Toegel, *The Confidence Myth*,
https://doi.org/10.1007/978-3-031-97305-5_6

over decades. I think of my life in different chunks. When the kids were little, I needed to be around more, but it's different now" (Harlow, 2014).

In 1999, Jessica DeGroot launched the nonprofit ThirdPath Institute with a mission to "assist individuals, families, and leaders in finding new ways to redesign work and life to create time for family, community, and other life priorities." The institute organizes regular calls, meetings, and hosts a biennial Pioneering Leaders summit to discuss strategies to achieve balance. This is just one example of how the movement aims to create positive role models and provide evidence that executives can be effective while also focusing on their personal lives, even if it's not always easy. Reshma Saujani, founder of the US nonprofit organization Girls Who Code, states: "Having it all was always a euphemism for doing it all" (Ottesen, 2022).

Motherhood and Confidence

Motherhood is a transformative experience that can profoundly impact a woman's life in many ways, including her confidence. The common perception is that becoming a mother boosts self-esteem and confidence, but the reality is far more complicated, with research indicating both positive and negative effects. Some studies report that women experience a decline in self-esteem. Manon Van Scheppingen and her colleagues report that, for many women, self-esteem dips during pregnancy, picks up again until the baby is about six months old, and then gradually fades over the following years, not returning to pre-pregnancy levels until approximately three years after giving birth (Van Scheppingen et al., 2018). The researchers found that this pattern was consistent across first-, second-, third-, and fourth-time mothers, suggesting it may be a typical change associated with motherhood. This prolonged dip in self-esteem highlights the profound and lasting impact of motherhood on women's self-perception. Researchers also found that the transition to motherhood can challenge a woman's sense of competence, particularly for first-time mothers. Mothers who feel more capable in their parenting roles tend to have higher self-esteem and better mental well-being (Hutchinson & Cassidy, 2022).

Motherhood brings significant changes to a woman's body, which can affect her confidence as well. The physical changes that come with pregnancy and childbirth, for example, can impact body image and self-esteem. A meta-analysis (Silveira et al., 2015) revealed that many women experience body dissatisfaction during the postpartum period, which can lead to decreased confidence. Hutchinson and Cassidy (2022) reported that mothers with higher body dissatisfaction showed significantly lower well-being, self-esteem, and perceived parenting competence.

Initially, motherhood can negatively affect a woman's confidence due to physical changes, new responsibilities, and shifts in identity, but it also has the potential to enhance self-esteem through personal growth and a stronger sense of self and purpose (Mercer, 2004). Some women report feeling empowered by their ability to give birth and care for a child.

One study reveals a notable contrast when first-time mothers return to work after maternity leave, between their confidence in their professional abilities and their maternal confidence (Ladge et al., 2018). Maternal confidence is a mother's belief in her ability to care for her child, her comfort level with motherhood, and the self-esteem associated with her maternal role. Participants in this study reported that resuming their work responsibilities was relatively easy, likely due to returning to familiar roles in their previous organizations. However, the transition period was marked by intense self-scrutiny regarding their new parenting roles. The majority of the women in this study expressed concerns about meeting their child's needs while working and struggled with feelings of guilt or inadequacy as mothers, despite feeling competent in their professional roles. Some of the women viewed work as a welcome respite from the challenges and self-doubt about being a good mother. About half of the interviewees reported feelings of pride in their ability to balance work and motherhood. However, many of them felt pressure to present an overly positive image of motherhood and struggled to honestly express the difficulties they faced.

Supporting mothers through various stages of parenthood, providing resources for managing work-life balance, and promoting body positivity can contribute to boosting mothers' self-confidence. By understanding the complex nature of this relationship, organizations can better support women as they navigate the transformative journey of motherhood.

Motherhood: Choices and Regrets

Not all women choose to become mothers, and those who don't should feel comfortable with that choice without feeling pressured by society. For those who do opt in, motherhood can be an intense, life-changing journey that deserves understanding and support, both at work and at home. Many new mothers, whether they are biological or adoptive, partnered or single, face challenges such as adjusting to a new baby, returning to work, and managing a career, though each group may experience these hurdles in different ways.

Regardless of whether women choose to return to work or stay home, the decision is not an easy one. Research reveals that women can experience two distinct types of regrets around their choices about motherhood and work: stay-at-home regrets and return-to-work regrets. The results of a longitudinal study (Wiese & Stertz, 2023) confirm that women who had higher levels of self-reported organizational commitment during their pregnancy were more likely to later develop stronger regrets about their decision to stay at home with their new baby. However, their organizational commitment did not seem to protect them from experiencing regrets about returning to work after their maternity leave. When women did feel regret about going back to their jobs, this tended to lead to a decrease in how much they valued their connection to the organization, their willingness to contribute, and how inspired and proud they felt as part of it. The transition back to work can be an emotionally charged time for new mothers. If they regret their decision to return, it can negatively impact their engagement and commitment at work.

What are the net effects of mothers returning to work? Earlier studies suggested that children fare worse on several dimensions if their mothers return to work in the first year of their lives (Belsky & Eggebeen, 1991; Waldfogel et al., 2002). However, more recent findings suggest that there are no negative emotional effects on babies and toddlers whose mothers work, as long as they are cared for by a warm and responsive caregiver.

In 2010, the National Institute of Child Health and Human Development in the United States published a study that questioned some of the earlier conclusions (Brooks-Gunn et al., 2010). They observed 1,364 children born in 1991 from 10 geographic locations. The first phase of the study followed the children up to age 3, and the second phase followed them up to age 7, tracking their development to gain a comprehensive view. This research found that, on average, a mother's decision to work during her child's first year of life doesn't have a significant impact, positive or negative, on the child's cognitive, social, and emotional development. In other words, while there may be some potential downsides to maternal employment during that critical first year, these are often counterbalanced by potential upsides, such as increased income, higher maternal satisfaction, and a greater likelihood that children will receive high-quality childcare. For the average child, the advantages and disadvantages seem to cancel each other out. The researchers suggest that full-time maternal employment in the first year is tied to lower cognitive scores for non-Hispanic white children (but not African-American children) at ages 3, 4½, and first grade. Part-time work in the first year is linked to better outcomes than full-time work, and employment in the second and third years shows no significant effect.

Full-time maternal employment in the first year had no effect on the attachment style. The key influences are the quality of parenting and the nature of children's childcare experiences, which play a more significant role in shaping developmental results.

These findings suggest that maternal employment is not inherently good or bad. It's the broader context surrounding the employment decision that determines the impact on the child. A mother working long hours in a stressful job, with little support at home and low-quality childcare, is in a very different situation than a mother, like Slaughter, who has resources, flexibility, and family support to help her balance her career with parenting. This nuance suggests that we can't make sweeping generalizations about working mothers. What matters most is ensuring that all children, regardless of their family circumstances, have their core needs for love, stability, stimulation, and quality care met.

A recent study (Lombardi, 2023) examined whether the relationship between mothers working in the first year of their child's life and the child's school readiness has changed over time. The researchers analyzed data from two large longitudinal studies of children born in the United States in 1991 and 2001. When looking at the links between early maternal employment patterns and children's reading/language skills and math skills at age 4 and when they started school, the researchers noticed some interesting shifts. Returning to full-time work by the time their children were 9 months old went from being negatively correlated with their reading/language skills in 1991 to having positive correlations in 2001. It appears that modern supports, such as flexible schedules, remote or hybrid work options, and high-quality childcare programs that may not have been as widespread in the early 1990s, benefit both mothers and children. Returning to full-time work in the first 9 months, however, was linked to higher levels of conduct problems at school entry in both time periods. This correlation doesn't mean working causes behavior problems, but it's a reminder for parents to be proactive and maintain open lines of communication with their child's caregivers or teachers about their social and emotional well-being.

Seeking support and being patient with themselves as they regain their professional footing after the arrival of a new child can help working mothers face common challenges as they try to balance the demands of their job with the significant life changes brought on by parenthood. Dymfke Kuijpers, a senior partner at McKinsey's Singapore office, shared her personal experience of returning to work after having her first child (Clark, 2021). When she returned to work, she felt completely lost and incompetent; she even considered quitting her job. Luckily, Kuijpers was given some advice that she now passes on to other new mothers: Don't make any major decisions in the first nine months after having a baby. The transition back to work happens more quickly than you might expect.

Mothers and fathers do not have fundamentally different priorities, especially regarding work and family balance (Tinsley & Ely, 2018). The desires and challenges regarding work/family balance are similar for both women and men, but their experiences at work after becoming parents differ significantly. The perceived differences in priorities are more a result of societal expectations and stereotypes about working mothers than inherent gender differences. Research, including a study of Harvard Business School graduates, shows that both men and women prioritize family over work (Ely et al., 2014). The gender differences in career achievements are not explained by career decisions made to accommodate family responsibilities. The main problem lies in how mothers and fathers are treated at work when they start a family. Women are seen as needing support, but men are expected to "man up" and not show stress or fatigue. Men who seek accommodations for family responsibilities may receive reluctant, temporary support, leading some to quietly reduce hours or travel, or limit family time and focus more on work to maintain their career trajectory. Mothers, on the other hand, are often expected to scale back at work; they may be moved to less demanding roles or given lower-status clients. This situation is not inevitable and can be changed.

Working parents, like Anne-Marie Slaughter, want to be perceived as meeting societal and family expectations as professionals and as parents. Being perceived as competent in both of those domains can be challenging and unrealistic. Research suggests that the fear of being judged as incompetent in one of those roles can trigger impression management work to adjust one's work-life image to meet the expectations of others (Ladge & Little, 2019). The pressure of potential judgment from coworkers, managers, family, and friends can create a sense of anxiety for working parents. In organizational culture, there's an outdated stereotype that the ideal employee prioritizes work over family, while the perfect parent is always present for their children's activities and home life. This contradiction between the two roles can motivate working parents to carefully curate their image in order to avoid being judged as incompetent in either domain. They may feel compelled to adjust their work-family balance to align with others' expectations, rather than doing what feels right for their unique circumstances. The fear of being labeled a "bad" employee or "bad" parent can weigh heavily on working mothers in particular. They feel that they are constantly walking a tightrope, trying to achieve the right balance to satisfy the different demands in their lives. This dynamic exposes the deep-seated societal biases and double standards that working mothers face. They are often trapped in a false dichotomy of being either the "ideal worker" or the "good mother," fueling assumptions that they are less committed, capable, or reliable because of their caregiving responsibilities. Women are expected to work as if they have no family obligations while managing their homes as though they have no careers. Meanwhile, men who take on caregiving roles tend to be celebrated, while women in similar situations are criticized for perceived lapses in their professional performance. The desire to be viewed as a dedicated professional while also fulfilling the role of a devoted caregiver can create immense internal pressure and stress. Empowering parents to define success on their own terms, without the burden of external judgment, could go a long way in alleviating this challenging dynamic. However, while redefining success can help alleviate societal pressures, the structural realities of modern work environments also play a critical role in shaping outcomes for working parents.

Recent research reveals that remote or virtual work arrangements can be a double-edged sword for women's career success (Villamor et al., 2023). On one hand, being able to work remotely can give women greater control over their work-life boundaries, potentially enhancing their work-family balance and overall well-being. If you work from home, you can be there when your children are home from school or take a break to nurse your baby, for example. On the other hand, it can also create new challenges that undermine career advancement and rewards.

Villamor et al. (2023) identified three key tensions that explain this complex dynamic. The first tension is between women's increased control over their boundaries (no need to travel to work or relocate) and the blurring of boundaries between work and family life. Virtual work gives women more flexibility, but it can blur the lines between their professional and personal responsibilities, creating new stresses, particularly for mothers. The second tension involves enhanced and reduced job opportunities. Remote work increases flexibility in when women can work and opens up new avenues for career growth, for example, opportunities for roles at companies located in different cities or even countries, but it can also lead to social isolation and exclusion from important opportunities for visibility and networking. The third tension is between social integration and exclusion. Working virtually can promote women's social integration through better connections with colleagues across diverse teams and geographic locations, but it can also make women feel disconnected from the organization and excluded from in-house company events and office chatter, which often provide useful information.

This research underscores the often contradictory effects that virtual and flexible work arrangements can have on women's career trajectories.

Breadwinners and Caregivers

Research has documented persistent patterns of the fatherhood advantage and the motherhood penalty. Men tend to experience professional benefits after becoming fathers, while mothers often face workplace discrimination and disadvantages (Yu & Hara, 2021). The fatherhood advantage is driven by a cultural bias against mothers in the workplace and societal perceptions that fathers, as breadwinners, are more stable, responsible, and committed workers, while women, as caregivers, are more dedicated to their families and, as a result, less dedicated to their work. Another study found that mothers were rated as less competent and less committed to their jobs than women without children, even when their qualifications were the same (Heilman & Okimoto, 2008). In addition, because there is a consistent stereotype of fathers as breadwinners, there is an unspoken belief that they deserve larger raises and bonuses, more promotions, and other benefits. Mothers, on the other hand, are held to harsher performance standards. For example, mothers might be penalized for not being constantly available or responding quickly, even if their actual work output is high.

A meta-analysis (Cukrowska-Torzewska & Matysiak, 2020) found an average motherhood wage gap of around 3.6–3.8% compared to women without children. There is an interesting and nuanced aspect of how parenthood affects earnings across different income levels and genders. For most women, having children typically depresses their earning potential, but career women earners in the top 10% do not lose income. In fact, they may even get a pay boost when they become moms, similar to the "fatherhood bonus" (Budig, 2014). You might think that top-earning moms are more highly rewarded because they have spouses who stay home with the kids, but this boost is not about having a stay-at-home spouse. The research shows that even when their spouses work full-time, these high-earning women are still more likely to get the motherhood pay boost. The more highly compensated women are, the less of a hit they take to their paychecks when they become mothers. Unfortunately, this perpetuates income inequality and hurts those who need their income the most. In general, for women and men earning high incomes, becoming parents doesn't hurt their wallets, and it might even help. But for women at lower levels who are earning less, motherhood often comes with a financial penalty. All of these findings are a stark reminder of how parenthood can affect careers and earnings based on gender, types of jobs, job titles, career trajectories, and income levels.

How Can Organizations Support Working Mothers' Careers?

Organizations need to recognize that people's career paths are dynamic and fluid, with individuals having different needs at various career stages. The Kaleidoscope Career Model (Mainiero et al., 2018) is a useful tool when designing flexible career paths that take into account changing priorities and life circumstances. This model views a career as a journey with three basic needs: authenticity, having a good work-life balance, and feeling challenged in your work. These needs are always present, but each one takes on a different level of importance over the lifespan. The model suggests that during significant career changes, such as when deciding whether to take a break from work or jump back in after becoming a parent, one of these three needs becomes more important than the others. For example, a new mother might want to focus on work-life balance, prompting her to consider taking a career break.

The importance of authenticity, balance, and challenge varies across career stages, but also by gender (see Fig. 6.1). The most significant gender difference occurs in mid-career, where women are more likely to follow a "beta kaleidoscope" pattern, prioritizing balance between work and family. Not surprisingly, this stage often coincides with increased family responsibilities. Both women and men show an increased focus on authenticity as they approach retirement. However, women exhibit a more pronounced increase in authenticity in late career stages. The desire for feeling challenged remains consistently important for both women and men throughout their careers.

Nowadays, more and more, we recognize that careers are not always linear. Organizations can help employees through return-to-work initiatives, which started more than 20 years ago with pioneering companies such as UBS, Goldman Sachs, and Sara Lee. Carol Fishman Cohen, CEO of iRelaunch, provides a detailed description of these programs that have become quite established (Cohen, 2021). The goal of these initiatives is to enable mid-career professionals to reenter the workforce after a career break for reasons such as parental leave, caring for elderly parents or family members, personal health issues, pursuing further education, taking a sabbatical, or a voluntary career break. Returning to work after a career break involves multiple challenges that differ from a typical job search. After time away from the

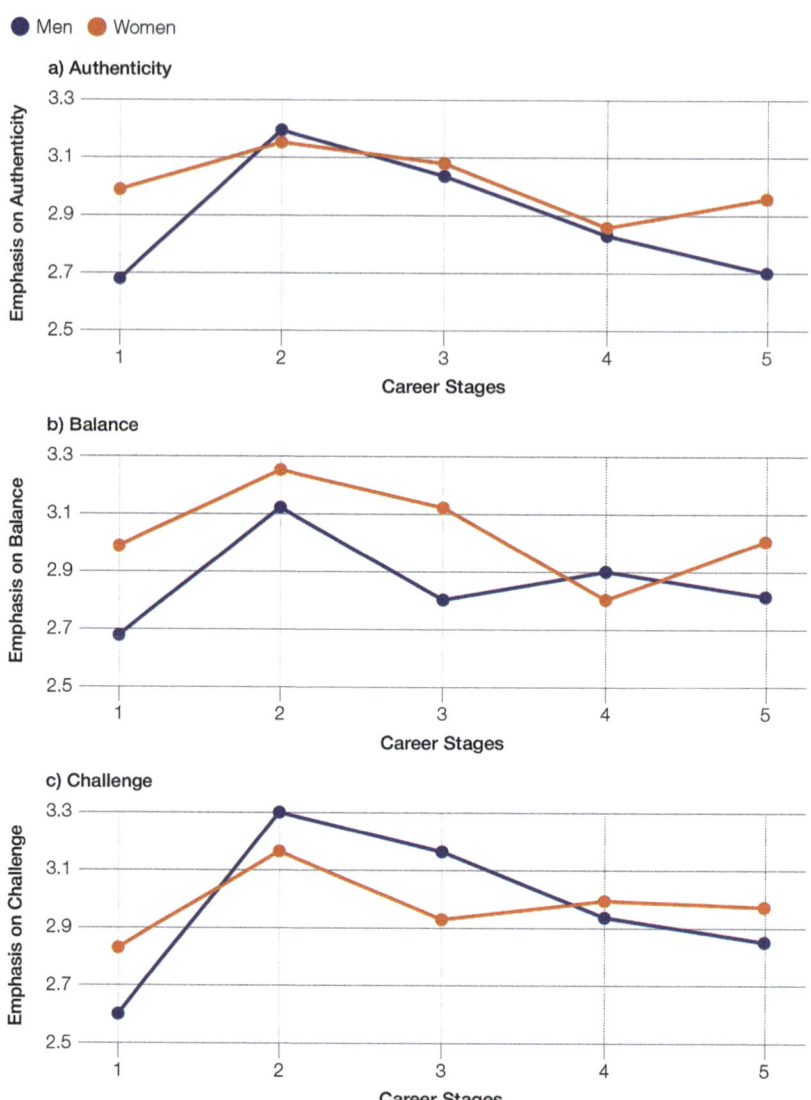

Fig. 6.1 The kaleidoscope career model parameters by career stage and gender (a) Authenticity follows a similar trajectory for both genders early on, with notable differences in later career stages. For women, authenticity gains importance as they approach the later phases of their careers, while for men, it gradually declines during this time. (b) As women progress into midcareer, achieving balance between work and personal life becomes increasingly important, whereas for men, it tends to hold less significance. (c) For both women and men, the importance of challenge diminishes over time as they advance through their careers. Career stages: (1) Early career; (2) early midcareer; (3) midcareer; (4) late midcareer; (5) late career. *Source* "The Kaleidoscope Career Model revisited: How midcareer men and women diverge on authenticity, balance, and challenge," Mainiero & Gibson (2018) (https://doi.org/10.1177/0894845317698223). Copyright 2017 by the Curators of the University of Missouri

professional world, relaunchers may need to regain confidence in their abilities. Professional connections may have weakened during the career break, requiring effort to re-establish and expand networking circles. Returnees often need to reevaluate their career goals and preferences, potentially leading to a career shift. To help with these objectives, return-to-work programs offer different career-building activities such as one-on-one coaching, mentoring, on-line courses, activities with the entire cohort of participants, and speeches by successful alumni.

Return-to-work initiatives are proving to be a goldmine for companies seeking well-educated, mature, experienced, and diverse talent as they tap into a rich pool of professionals who have taken career breaks but are eager to re-enter the workforce. These initiatives offer employers numerous significant benefits. Returning professionals bring a wealth of experience and soft skills that entry-level hires often lack. These professionals are adept at working in teams, managing diverse personalities, and thriving under pressure—skills honed through years of previous work experience. Moreover, they are quick to adapt and learn, and they are able to efficiently update their skills through various accessible and cost-effective means, such as online courses or additional degrees. For companies committed to improving gender diversity, these initiatives are particularly valuable, as they tap into a talent pool predominantly composed of women returning to the workforce after taking time off to raise their children. By embracing return-to-work programs, organizations can expand their workforce with seasoned professionals who combine past experience with freshly updated skills, creating a powerful blend of expertise and energy.

In many cases, women face unexpected hurdles in their careers when they take time off and then return to work. In fact, the longer they are away from work, the slimmer their chances of reentering with a promotion or pay raise, and they are more likely to be laid off or demoted. Research has found that when parents take longer leaves, their colleagues and bosses might unconsciously view them as less committed to their jobs and careers (Hideg et al., 2018). The good news is that there are ways to counter this perception. The study discovered that staying connected to work during their leave (through "keep-in-touch programs," including joining a team conference call once a month, participating in professional development opportunities, receiving updates on some projects, or having a colleague regularly provide updates from work) can make a big difference. These little touchpoints remind everyone that the new parent is engaged and ambitious. Long maternity leaves, like the ones enjoyed by women in Nordic countries, are fantastic for families, but organizations need to make sure they don't accidentally harm women's careers, for example, by fraying professional networks or limiting opportunities for career advancement. Companies can help by offering programs that keep new mothers connected, *if they want to be.*

Fathers can help as well. The more fathers make use of legislated parental leave, the more likely taking a longer leave to care for new babies will become normalized. And when mothers return to work, extra support and recognition can go a long way. Support can include, for example, offering flexible workday schedules or remote work options, allowing regular breaks for breastfeeding or pumping, providing lactation rooms with amenities like refrigerators and comfortable seating to support breastfeeding, offering childcare vouchers, on-site childcare facilities, or partnering with childcare services, returnship programs for individuals transitioning back to work after a career break, pairing returning mothers with mentors, and celebrating a mother's return to work to help validate her professional identity and contributions. Ultimately, the goal is to create an environment where women can take the time they need with their new babies without backsliding in their careers, because no one should have to choose between being a great parent and having a fulfilling career.

More and more critical voices suggest that the phrase "work-family conflict" oversimplifies the problem, identifying the real culprit of not being able to find a healthy work-life balance as the culture of long working hours driven by corporations' desire to "oversell and overdeliver" (Ely & Padavic, 2020). This culture of overwork affects men and women alike. What really "holds women back at work is not some unique challenge of balancing the demands of work and family, but rather a general problem of overwork that prevails in contemporary corporate culture" (Ely & Padavic, 2020, p. 67).

Organizations can experiment with unconventional career arrangements. Thinking outside the box can lead to solutions that accommodate the needs of working mothers while also benefiting employers. For example, Cynthia Cunningham and Shelley Murray pioneered a unique job-sharing arrangement at Fleet Bank and effectively functioned as one person in an executive role (Cunningham & Murray, 2005). They creatively managed to share one desk, computer, and phone line, demonstrating how two people can achieve a seamless integration and work as one cohesive unit. This arrangement allowed both women to maintain their career trajectories while balancing family life, demonstrating that part-time work doesn't have to mean career stagnation. They took the creative step of marketing themselves as one person and maintaining a single résumé while seeking future opportunities as a pair, reinforcing their commitment to the job-sharing concept. The arrangement was a win-win solution that benefited both the company, which got two minds for one position, and Cunningham and Murray, who achieved work-life balance without sacrificing their career ambitions. Their inspiring story presents job sharing as a viable option alongside other flexible work arrangements, encouraging creative thinking about how work is structured, potentially paving the way for more innovative work arrangements in the future.

In many cultures, societal expectations still impose distinct roles on mothers and fathers. Women, for example, are expected to take on primary caregiving responsibilities, which can lead to career interruptions, reduced working hours, or slower career progression. They may face stereotypes suggesting they are less committed to their jobs after having children. Men, on the other hand, are often expected to maintain or even increase their focus on work to fulfill the role of "provider." This can limit their opportunities to engage fully in caregiving or take advantage of parental leave policies without stigma. These differing expectations contribute to unequal experiences in the workplace, perpetuating gender disparities in pay, promotions, and leadership opportunities. However, this situation is not inevitable, as the current dynamics are rooted in cultural traditions and institutional structures rather than biological imperatives. Therefore, they can be changed through deliberate actions at multiple levels.

Governments and organizations around the world, for example, have started implementing policies that promote equality, such as paid parental leave for both mothers and fathers, flexible work arrangements that accommodate caregiving responsibilities without penalizing employees, and anti-discrimination measures to prevent bias against parents. Societal attitudes toward gender roles are also shifting, and we can observe the normalization of fathers taking active caregiving roles and using parental leave. More and more managers are challenging stereotypes that equate motherhood with reduced professional ambition or productivity. When both women and men are equally supported in their dual roles as professionals and caregivers, we can create a future where parenthood no longer dictates divergent career paths based on gender.

Self-Reflection 6.1: For Working Mothers

1. Do you feel like you have to choose between work and family?
2. How realistic is the ideal worker expectation in your organization?
3. Do you speak up if you hear others making negative comments about colleagues who use flexible work arrangements?
4. When you make decisions, to what extent do you take role models into consideration? Former YouTube CEO Susan Wojcicki (1968–2024) took paid maternity leave for each of her five children, sending a very powerful

message to younger parents in the organization that such a decision should not derail their careers.

6.2 Menopause: Are Hormones Hijacking Your Leadership?

Vignette 6.2: Rozana

Rozana, a seasoned executive, sat confidently in the board meeting as discussions about crucial funding decisions intensified. Suddenly, she felt a wave of warmth creeping upward—a hot flash that manifested in visible perspiration and a flush of color. Glancing around, she noticed her colleagues' concerned looks, realizing they might mistake her discomfort for disapproval.

Without missing a beat, Rozana smiled and said, "I'm just having a hot flash, definitely not objecting to the proposal!" Her candor drew warm laughter, and several colleagues nodded knowingly, recalling their own family members' experiences. Unruffled by this brief interruption, she proceeded to guide the conversation with her usual poise, demonstrating that a hot flash was no match for her leadership.

In a world that values youth, menopause is not often discussed openly, despite it being a normal part of women's lifespan. Currently, there are about one billion women worldwide who are postmenopausal, but the culture of youth makes women feel ashamed about menopause and try to hide or "fix" it.

Historically, women's value was narrowly tied to their reproductive role. However, as women continue to ascend to leadership positions in the twenty-first century, a significant demographic shift is occurring in the upper echelons of organizations. As menopause typically occurs around the age of 51 and the menopausal transition lasts for about seven years, at any point in time, a significant number of women employees will be going through this transition. The prevalence of menopausal women in leadership positions is a testament to their deserved career progression and the gradual dismantling of gender barriers in corporate hierarchies.

One of the most significant hurdles faced by menopausal leaders is the persistent stigma and misconceptions surrounding menopause in the workplace. Many people, especially men, lack awareness and understanding of menopausal symptoms and their potential impact on work performance.

This knowledge gap can lead to the misinterpretation of behavior or performance issues, potentially jeopardizing the career progression of capable leaders. Women find it difficult to speak up because they fear ridicule and because of the stigma of being perceived as not performing as well as in their earlier years, and therefore not deserving promotions (Greening, 2017). Without proper support and understanding, some women may choose to step down from leadership roles or exit the workforce entirely during this transitional period. This not only represents a loss of valuable talent and experience for organizations but also perpetuates gender imbalances in senior leadership.

On the upside, postmenopausal women may experience increased confidence as they feel more self-assured and less concerned with others' opinions. Only a small number of participants in a UK study (16.5%) thought the menopause had negatively influenced their managers' and coworkers' views of their competence (Griffiths et al., 2013). Interestingly, anthropologists have noted that humans share this extended postreproductive stage with only two other species: killer whales and short-finned pilot whales, raising the question of why these particular mammals continue to thrive well beyond their childbearing years. Research suggests that knowledge and experience contribute to an evolutionary explanation of the extension of these species' life cycle beyond reproductive years (Brent et al., 2015). Menopausal killer whales are twice as likely to be group leaders, particularly when food is scarce. Their wisdom fulfills the evolutionary goal through the transfer of knowledge and therefore increases the chances of survival.

Understanding Perimenopause and Menopause

Women and men experience physical, hormonal, and psychological changes throughout the lifespan. Middle age brings changes for both men and women, a stage called climacteric, in which sex hormone production decreases and reproductive capacity declines—and for women, ceases altogether (see Fig. 6.2). For women, this phase includes perimenopause, menopause, and postmenopause, and marks the gradual decline in ovarian function. Climacteric can begin in a woman's late 30s or 40s, but most commonly occurs in the mid-to-late 40s. The timing of each stage can vary significantly among women due to factors such as genetics, lifestyle, and health conditions.

Perimenopause is characterized by hormone fluctuations (especially estrogen) and symptoms such as irregular menstrual cycles and hot flashes. It

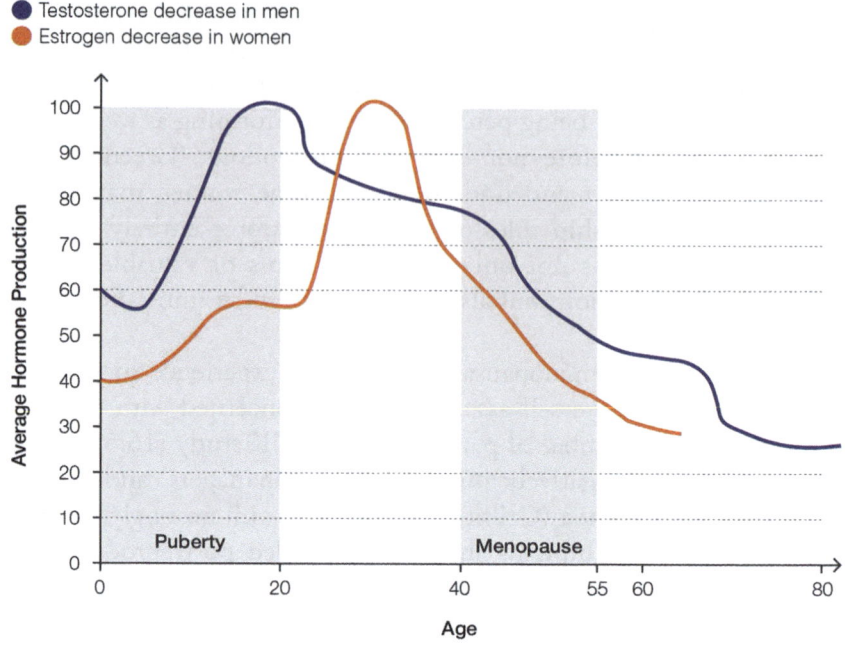

Fig. 6.2 Sex hormone production over the lifespan In middle age, testosterone and estrogen production decline respectively in men and women; however, the drop in testosterone is gradual compared to the steep drop in estrogen production during menopause. *Source* Gilli et al. (2020) (https://doi.Org/10.3389/fneur.2020.00616). Copyright 2020 by Gilli, DiSano, and Pachner

typically starts in the mid-to-late 40s but can begin as early as the mid-30s. It continues until menopause is reached.

Menopause is officially defined as beginning 12 consecutive months after the cessation of the menstrual period, typically occurring between the ages of 45 and 55, with an average around age 51 in many countries, and it can last 2–7 years. Menopause marks the end of reproductive capability.

Postmenopause refers to the phase of life after menopause has occurred. With life expectancy increasing, about a third of women's lives will be postmenopausal.

During menopause, women experience a mix of physical, emotional, and mental changes as a result of hormonal fluctuations. Not every woman will experience all of these symptoms, and their intensity can vary from mild to more severe. These symptoms include:

- Hot flashes and night sweats (vasomotor symptoms): The change in hormone levels affects how the body regulates temperature. Sudden bursts of heat in the upper body or all over are often followed by sweating and a flushed face.
- Changes in mood: Irritability, sadness, anxiety, or mood swings, as a result of fluctuating hormones, can make emotions feel more intense.
- Sleep disturbances: Women may experience difficulty falling or staying asleep, frequent awakenings, or restless sleep because night sweats or anxiety interrupt normal sleep patterns.
- Vaginal dryness and discomfort: Decreased estrogen levels reduce natural lubrication and thin vaginal walls. As a result, vaginal tissues become dry or less elastic, which can cause discomfort, pain during sex, or decreased libido.
- Urinary issues: Weaker pelvic tissues and decreasing hormones can affect bladder control, causing more frequent urges to urinate or mild incontinence (leaking urine when laughing or sneezing).
- Weight or body shape changes: Hormone reduction and natural aging slow metabolism and affect how the body stores fat, resulting in weight gain, especially around the belly, or changes in body composition.
- Cognitive symptoms: Sleep disturbances can affect mental clarity and lead to memory lapses, tiredness, difficulty concentrating, or feeling spaced-out.

There are no universal menopause symptoms, and for some women, menopause is a nonevent as it arrives unannounced. The most commonly reported symptoms are hot flashes, vaginal dryness, and sleep disturbances. One study in the United States reports that, on average, moderate to severe hot flashes continue for almost five years after menopause, and symptoms persist for 10 years in one-third of all menopausal women (Freeman et al., 2014). Hot flashes can lead to lower health-related quality of life, but only if the woman experiencing them finds the symptoms bothersome (Hess et al., 2012). Vaginal dryness is reported by 45% of menopausal women (Bygdeman & Swahn, 1996).

The effects of menopause vary among individuals. One study reports that around 25% of women surveyed experience severe menopause symptoms, which negatively influence their performance at work. This makes menopause a workplace issue (Steffan & Potočnik, 2023). Menopause symptoms can impact women's confidence as well. A study in the United Kingdom found that 39% of women reported lower confidence during menopause (Griffiths et al., 2013). Weight gain in particular, and changes in body shape, can make women feel less attractive, especially in cultures that value youth, and negatively affect their self-esteem. In reality, the average weight gain attributed to menopause is reported to be only about 1.6 kg or about 3.5 lbs, or 0.25 kg/ 0.6 lbs annually over the transition period (Hickey et al., 2024). Many women, however, perceive menopausal weight gain differently than what is scientifically reported. Although average total weight gain is minimal, the body fat distribution shifts toward increased abdominal fat. This change in shape can make the weight gain seem more noticeable or significant. The negative connotations associated with menopause may also contribute to the discrepancy between the modest measured weight gain and women's perception.

Some women experience reduced confidence in the workplace due to feeling less assured in their abilities, particularly when experiencing cognitive symptoms like memory lapses or difficulties concentrating. Again, research suggests something different: menopausal women's cognition might not be affected as strongly as people assume, and if they experience memory problems, they are minor and temporary (Maki, 2015).

Self-Reflection 6.2: Menopause Symptoms and Their Severity

If you have gone through menopause, reflect on the symptoms you experienced.
   Physical Symptoms:

- How frequently do you experience hot flashes or night sweats, and how intense do they feel?
- Are you having trouble falling or staying asleep? In what ways does this affect your energy and mood during the day?
- Have you noticed any joint or muscle pain that disrupts your usual routines or activities?
- Have you experienced changes in bladder control, such as needing to urinate more often or feeling an urgency?
- Do you experience vaginal dryness or discomfort during intimacy? How does this affect your well-being or relationships?

Psychological and Emotional Well-Being:

- Are you feeling more anxious, irritable, or emotional than usual? If so, in what situations do these feelings arise?
- Have you noticed shifts in your overall mood, such as feeling sad or depressed more often? What might be triggering these emotions?

- Do you find it harder to concentrate, remember details, or stay mentally alert? How does this affect your daily life?

Impact on Daily Life:

- Have your menopausal symptoms affected your ability to work, care for your family, or maintain social connections?
- Do you feel less confident or hesitant to participate in activities you once enjoyed? What factors contribute to these changes?

Health and Lifestyle:

- Have you modified your diet, exercise habits, or alcohol consumption to help manage symptoms? Which changes seem to be the most beneficial?
- Are you seeking regular medical advice or exploring treatment options to manage your symptoms if they affect your daily activities? How comfortable do you feel with this support?

General Well-Being:

- When comparing your current well-being to how you felt before menopause, what differences stand out the most?
- Which aspects of your life (physical health, mental well-being, or relationships) feel most impacted by menopausal symptoms?

Menopause as Liberation

While it's important to provide support and resources for managing menopausal symptoms, it's equally crucial to celebrate this transition and cultivate a more nuanced and positive understanding of this phase of life. Reframing the narrative empowers women to approach menopause with the mindset that it isn't an ending, but a gateway to a new life chapter filled with the potential for self-discovery and renewed purpose, instead of trepidation and anxiety. It's time to shift the conversation to reflect this empowering reality. Anthropologist Margaret Mead captured this spirit perfectly: "The most powerful force in the world is a menopausal woman with zest" (Brody, 1981).

The public discourse surrounding menopause often skews toward a negative narrative that predominantly focuses on symptoms and an alleged loss of femininity. Menopause is a natural biological process that marks a significant milestone in a woman's life. Rather than viewing it solely through the lens of loss or decline, it should be recognized as a normal developmental event that opens doors to a phase of life that can be a time of liberation and transformation. This period can bring about a deeper sense of self-awareness and confidence. Moreover, the postmenopausal years can be a time of enhanced creativity, leadership, and wisdom. Many women report feeling more assertive and self-assured, qualities that can significantly benefit both personal and professional spheres.

Different cultures offer alternative views of menopause. While some Western cultures treat menopause as a disability or a disease—another problem that needs to be fixed—other cultures take a more positive perspective. In some societies, postmenopausal women are revered for their wisdom and experience, assuming important leadership roles within their communities. In some Native American tribes, such as the Iroquois and Cherokee, the clan mother chooses and advises the chief (Wagner, n.d.). Among the Akan people of Ghana, postmenopausal women can attain the status of Queen Mother, a powerful leadership position that involves advising chiefs and settling disputes (Stoeltje, 2021). In Polynesian cultures, such as Samoa, older women frequently assume roles as healers, spiritual leaders, and keepers of traditional knowledge (MacQuoid, 1995).

Experts on gender in Western cultures have started contesting the negative perspectives that view menopause as a decline and deterioration. Camilla Quental and her coauthors argue that a new narrative has emerged as a result—one that emphasizes the positive aspects of menopause that have been overlooked (Quental et al., 2023). In their view, menopause brings biological liberation, where a woman's value is no longer linked to procreation. Distancing from the motherhood mandate presents women with the opportunity to claim their own personal space, reflect on life, and reevaluate their career progression. The authors argue that by ceasing to be viewed primarily as sexual beings, women can distance themselves from the "beauty mandate," shake off the anxiety about how others perceive their attractiveness, and embrace a more assertive and confident self. They conclude that there is evidence of the "zest" of menopause reflected in a surge of creative energy, based on maturity and wisdom.

Coping with Perimenopause and Menopause

Women are shamed for menstruating and then shamed for not menstruating.
Hickey et al., 2024, p. 954.

This quote highlights how societal attitudes unfairly stigmatize women at every stage of their reproductive lives, including menopause, a natural biological transition that should be normalized rather than stigmatized.

Framing menopause primarily as a hormone deficiency disorder requiring medical intervention reinforces negative stereotypes. Such medicalized discourse can result in unnecessary treatments and an excessive focus on menopause's adverse effects. Pathologizing menopause as an inevitable decline or decay contributes to negative expectations and fear among women approaching this phase. It is crucial to shift away from purely medicalized narratives toward a more balanced perspective, using clear medical terms alongside neutral and affirming language. This shift is particularly important because research has shown that women who have more negative attitudes prior to menopause report more symptoms during the transition to menopause (Ayers et al., 2010). A balanced approach facilitates open, stigma-free discussions while still acknowledging the significant impacts menopause can have on women's lives.

There are, of course, cases that might require medical help. Menopausal hormone therapy (MHT), which was earlier called hormone replacement therapy (HRT), is considered to be the most effective treatment for physiological symptoms like hot flashes, but it comes with a certain risk. It has been linked to an increased risk of breast cancer, stroke, uterine cancer, and blood clots. Epidemiological evidence suggests that "one additional case of breast cancer will occur for every 50 women taking combined MHT from age 50, and one in 70 taking estrogen-only MHT. There is no excess risk from vaginal estrogen (Lancet, 2024)."

Women sometimes feel self-conscious about visible menopausal symptoms in public, like hot flashes (Griffiths et al., 2013), because they worry these signs may reveal they are getting older. This fear reflects wider social attitudes toward aging and menopause, which can be seen in everyday language. In today's world, social media often encourages women to "fight" the signs of aging through methods like cosmetics or plastic surgery. This push isn't simply about vanity; it also stems from concerns about losing social status and facing age-related discrimination. Because hot flashes and changes in body shape can signal aging, these natural symptoms may become a source of anxiety or shame. Euphemisms such as "the transition period," "the hormone war," or "the change" may sound polite, but they trivialize women's experiences and imply these symptoms are shameful. By treating menopause as a taboo, such language risks undermining women's self-esteem and body image (Chrisler, 2011). As a result, some women may try to conceal or take control of the symptoms. They often suffer on their own by hiding the symptoms and trying not to draw attention to themselves. Some women leaders try to keep up an appearance, but others report using humor when dealing with hot flashes, just as Rozana did.

Research has revealed a remarkable finding: Self-perceptions of aging can impact longevity. The study matched data from the Ohio Longitudinal Study of Aging and Retirement, which measured self-perceptions of aging, with data from the National Death Index 23 years later (Levy et al., 2002). Results suggest that older individuals with more positive perceptions of aging, as measured up to 23 years earlier, lived an average of 7.5 years longer than those who held less positive views about aging. The researchers also discovered that this effect was partially explained by the participants' will to live. In other words, those with a more optimistic outlook on aging seemed to have a stronger desire to keep living and thriving in their later years. This is a powerful testament to the profound impact our mindset and self-perception can have on our health and lifespan. It suggests that cultivating a positive, accepting attitude toward aging may be just as important as maintaining physical wellness. After all, the way we think about growing older can profoundly shape the reality we experience. Nurturing a constructive, hopeful perspective on aging clearly correlates with health benefits and may be linked with living a longer, more fulfilling life. It's a reminder that our mental and emotional well-being deserve just as much attention and care as our physical health.

Organizations can also contribute to addressing menopause-related challenges by implementing supportive policies and fostering an inclusive culture that recognizes the needs of menopausal leaders. This may include flexible working arrangements, wellness programs, and education initiatives to increase awareness among all employees (Griffiths et al., 2013). In this way, companies can harness the full potential of their female leaders, benefiting from their wealth of experience and unique perspectives during this life stage. Each year, organizations in many countries use World Menopause Day, held on the 18th of October, to raise awareness, break the stigma, and share support for those who are going through menopause.

Seeking social support from supervisors and female colleagues is a good coping strategy that can buffer the negative impact of menopause symptoms. Connecting with others can help navigate this life change and alleviate negative thoughts. Women are taking initiatives such as Menopause Café and arts projects like Flesh after Fifty, which directly challenge negative beliefs about menopause. Digital technology empowers women to create informal support networks and successfully manage their menopause symptoms (see the URLs listed in the References section at the end of this chapter under Digital Resources).

Self-Reflection 6.3: Women in Climacteric

- Do you find yourself hiding or minimizing menopausal symptoms at work due to concerns about being judged or negatively evaluated?
- To what extent does how you think about menopause influence your confidence, ambition, or sense of professional value?
- Have you noticed any changes in how colleagues or managers interact with you since entering menopause, and, if so, how has this impacted your sense of belonging or value at work? How might fears around ageism or menopause-related stigma be affecting your interactions with them?
- How can you proactively seek resources or allies within your organization to navigate menopause confidently? Do you feel isolated and reluctant to speak up about your experiences?
- Do you worry that discussing menopause openly will lead others to perceive you as "a woman of a certain age"—less capable, productive, or promotable? What support might help you feel safer in speaking up?

Take Action 6.1: Plan Practical, Healthy Lifestyle Adjustments

Making healthy lifestyle changes benefits everyone, but many lifestyle changes can reduce symptoms and improve the quality of life during menopause. Below are some scientifically backed suggestions for lifestyle changes to promote health and well-being.
   Diet:

- Increase intake of foods rich in calcium, vitamin D, iron, and phytoestrogens (e.g., soy products, which may help with hot flashes (Clarkson et al., 2011).

Exercise:

- Engage in regular cardiovascular activity (e.g., walking, swimming), weight-bearing exercise to preserve muscle mass and bone density and protect against fractures, and Pilates to strengthen core muscles (Daley et al., 2014; Martyn-St James & Carroll, 2009).

Sleep hygiene:

- Try mindfulness or meditation before bed. Avoid looking at screens, such as smart phones and tablets, at least an hour before bedtime (Chang et al., 2015).

Social connections:

- Attend local events or classes to stay active and social. Share experiences and tips with others in virtual or face-to-face menopause support groups.
- Digital resources for information and connecting:
  - Menopause Cafe: https://www.menopausecafe.net/
  - Flesh After Fifty: www.fleshafterfifty.com/

- My Meno Plan: https://mymenoplan.org/
- Henpicked: https://henpicked.net/
- Women Living Better: https://womenlivingbetter.org
- Global Coalition on Aging: https://globalcoalitiononaging.com/

Relaxation and mindfulness:

- Set aside time each day to meditate or practice deep breathing to ease stress and anxiety (Cramer et al., 2012).

6.3   How a Therapist Can Help

Confidence: we all want more of it. But sometimes, our brains trick us into believing we are less capable, less valuable, or simply not good enough. In most cases, the techniques discussed in the previous chapters can provide sufficient support to manage negative thoughts and emotions. However, there may be times when professional help from a psychotherapist is needed. Psychotherapy can help quiet negative thoughts, challenge distorted self-perceptions, or dismantle unhealthy comparisons. You can think of well-trained therapists as personal trainers for your mind, and they are ready to guide you on your journey.

Psychotherapy is a method based on communication and interaction that diagnoses and treats dysfunctional thought patterns and behaviors that cause distress. Trained professionals can provide therapy face-to-face or virtually to individuals, couples, or groups. Psychotherapy provides a safe space for people to understand and process their thoughts, feelings, and past experiences to improve their emotional and psychological well-being. In addition, therapy can provide valuable coping skills for everyday challenges. It can also help address more serious issues like trauma, anxiety, depression, and psychological disorders, and explain how these issues affect behavior. The therapeutic journey involves examining how past experiences shape present behaviors and feelings, guiding clients toward healing and personal growth. This process is particularly beneficial for those facing emotional challenges or coping with psychological disorders.

There are many different types of psychotherapy, but we'll look at two therapies that are most commonly used for confidence issues: cognitive behavioral therapy (CBT) and psychodynamic therapy.

Cognitive Behavioral Therapy

Many researchers and practitioners argue that CBT is "the gold-standard of psychological treatment" since it is the most researched type of psychotherapy (David et al., 2018). As you read in Chap. 1, we often get stuck in a cycle of negative thoughts that seem to take on a life of their own. Imagine how different your life would be if you had the power to reframe those thoughts and transform them into positive beliefs. That's what CBT is all about. Unlike traditional forms of therapy that focus on analyzing the roots of the unconscious mind, CBT integrates approaches and techniques from cognitive and behavioral psychology to identify maladaptive thought patterns and help the person reframe these thoughts and change their behaviors to improve their emotions, behaviors, and overall mental well-being. The cognitive behavioral approach views our thoughts, feelings, and behaviors as interconnected, allowing for a more comprehensive approach to treating various psychological disorders.

CBT acknowledges the importance of past experiences, but it doesn't dwell on them; the primary focus is on current problems and how to solve them. CBT emphasizes a collaborative relationship between the therapist and the person receiving therapy, called the "client," rather than the "patient." Client and therapist work together to identify problems, set goals, and develop strategies to achieve those goals. The objective is for the client to become aware of their maladaptive thoughts, challenge them as they occur, and then reframe them to make them more accurate. For instance, a person grappling with confidence issues may constantly think, "I'm not good enough," "I'm inferior and I always fail," or "I'm worthless." A cognitive

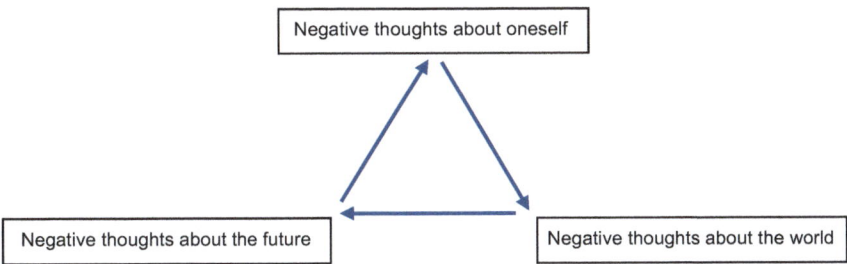

Fig. 6.3 The cognitive triad. Aaron Beck identified three negative, automatic, and spontaneous beliefs that are present in people with depressive disorders. The first one refers to negative views about the self (e.g., "I am a failure"). The second one reflects negative views of the world (e.g., "The world is a harsh place"), and the third one refers to negative thoughts about the future (e.g., "Things will never get better")

behavior therapist would help the client identify and challenge these maladaptive thoughts, and then replace them with healthier, more realistic
perspectives such as "I have the ability to learn and grow," or "Failure is
a part of everyone's journey."

Aaron Beck, often referred to as the "father of cognitive therapy," developed his approach in the 1960s while working with depressed clients. Beck
observed that these clients often had negative automatic thoughts that
contributed to their emotional distress. He formulated a theory called the
cognitive triad (see Fig. 6.3) that explains how negative beliefs about the self,
the world, and the future are at the root of depressive disorders.

Concurrently, Albert Ellis, whose ABC model you read about in Chap. 5,
developed rational emotive behavior therapy (REBT), which shares similarities
with Beck's cognitive therapy. Ellis believed that we should focus on what we
can control (e.g., our thoughts, actions, and reactions) and accept what we
cannot control (e.g., external events, the actions of others, etc.) and that our
emotional responses are shaped by our judgments and beliefs. In his view,
external events do not affect us; rather, it is our interpretation of those events
that causes distress (Epstein, 2001, p. 68). By changing our perceptions and
attitudes, we can achieve inner peace. Based on this philosophy, Ellis focused
on identifying and challenging irrational beliefs that lead to emotional distress.

You can think of CBT as a toolbox of strategies that helps identify and
challenge cognitive distortions, such as negative or inaccurate thoughts, and
replace them with more balanced and realistic ones. Common cognitive
distortions include all-or-nothing thinking, overgeneralization, catastrophizing, and others presented in Table 6.1 (Beck, 2011). Recognizing these
distortions can help challenge and reframe negative thoughts.

In addition to Ellis's ABC model, CBT uses techniques such as role-
playing and exposure therapy. Role-playing allows clients to practice new
behaviors and communication skills in a safe environment. It can be particularly helpful for improving social skills and preparing for challenging
situations. To help people who experience anxiety, CBT often uses exposure
techniques. Rather than avoiding the situations or objects that trigger fear
and anxiety, the client is guided through a series of steps to face them in a safe
and supportive way. As the client experiences each new level of exposure,
they gradually learn that these fears are not as overwhelming as they once
seemed. Exposure therapy can significantly reduce avoidance behaviors and
help the person feel more at ease.

CBT treatment is typically short-term, often lasting between 12 and 20
sessions. The duration varies depending on the person and their specific needs.

Table 6.1 Common cognitive distortions

Thinking error	Description	Example
All-or-nothing thinking	Viewing situations in black-and-white terms, with no middle ground	"My entire project was a waste of time, the client seemed not to like the color on page 15."
Overgeneralization	Making broad conclusions based on a single event or limited evidence	"I was turned down for this promotion; this means I'll never advance in my career."
Mental filter	Focusing solely on the negative aspects of a situation while ignoring the positive ones	"I received one criticism on my report, so it must have been terrible."
Discounting the positive	Dismissing positive experiences or achievements as unimportant	"I did well on my presentation, but it doesn't mean I'm competent; I just got lucky, there were no tricky questions."
Jumping to conclusions	Making assumptions without sufficient evidence, including:	"Everyone must think I'm incompetent because I made a mistake."
	Mind reading: Believing you know what others are thinking	"She didn't smile at me; she must be angry with me."
	Fortune telling: Predicting negative outcomes without evidence	"I'm going to fail the job interview."
Catastrophizing	Expecting the worst possible outcome in a situation	"If I make one mistake in my speech, it will be a disaster."
Emotional reasoning	Assuming that feelings reflect reality	"I feel anxious, so something bad must be happening."
"Should" statements	Placing unrealistic demands on yourself or others	"I should be perfect."
Labeling and mislabeling	Assigning negative labels to yourself or others based on a single incident	"I'm such a loser for missing that deadline."
Personalization	Taking responsibility for events outside of your control or blaming yourself for things that aren't your fault	"It's my fault that my colleague is upset."
Tunnel vision	Seeing only the negative aspects of a situation	"I got critical feedback on the project, which means I'm bad at my job and my career is doomed."
Magnification and minimization	Exaggerating the importance of negative events or minimizing the significance of positive ones	"I messed up the name of the researcher. My entire analysis was awful."

The sessions are structured, with specific agendas and homework assignments to reinforce learning outside of therapy. The homework typically involves practicing new skills, keeping track of thoughts and feelings, and confronting fears. CBT's structured approach to solving problems typically involves steps such as defining the problem, generating potential solutions, evaluating options, and implementing and reviewing the chosen solution. CBT often incorporates elements from mindfulness-based therapies, such as relaxation techniques and mindfulness exercises, to help clients manage stress and increase awareness of their thoughts and emotions. In close partnership with the therapist, the client is encouraged to take an active role in their treatment, applying the strategies learned in therapy to their everyday life.

The triple column technique

Using the principles of CBT, psychiatrist David Burns developed a tool called the "triple column technique, or Burns' 3-column exercise (Burns, 1981). The triple column technique is designed to help people identify, evaluate, and challenge their negative thought patterns or cognitive distortions. The three columns in this exercise are: automatic thoughts, cognitive distortions, and rational responses. See Table 6.2 for an example of the triple column technique.

Take Action 6.2: Applying the Triple Column Technique

Try the triple column technique yourself in Table 6.3. In the first column, write down any negative automatic thoughts you have exactly as they occur. These are the immediate, often irrational thoughts that pop into your mind in response to a situation.

Read each of your automatic thoughts and try to identify the cognitive distortion(s) present in these thoughts. Use Table 6.1 to label the distortions, keeping in mind that each thought might have more than one distortion. In

---

Table 6.2 The triple column technique

Automatic thoughts	Cognitive distortions	Rational responses
"I messed up the presentation in front of the CEO."	All-or-nothing thinking Overgeneralization	"Failing one presentation doesn't make me a complete failure. I've succeeded in other areas before, and this is just one setback. I can learn from this experience and improve my presentation skills."

Table 6.3 Applying the triple column technique

Automatic thoughts	Cognitive distortions	Rational responses

the second column, enter the cognitive distortion(s) you've identified. In the third column, challenge your automatic thought(s) and rewrite them as more logical, realistic, and rational responses. This last step involves critically examining the evidence for and against the automatic thought and considering alternative perspectives.

Incorporating the triple-column exercise into your daily routine maximizes its effectiveness. Some days, you may find that you are free from negative thoughts, eliminating the need for the exercise. On other days, you might experience numerous challenging thoughts, requiring multiple applications of the technique. Consistent practice of this method enhances your ability to recognize and confront negative thinking patterns. Over time, you'll develop the skill to mentally process the three columns without physically writing them down. This internalization of the technique allows for quicker, more efficient thought restructuring in real time.

As you become more adept at using this tool, you'll notice a gradual shift in your thought processes. The exercise will evolve from a conscious effort to an almost automatic response to negative thoughts, ultimately leading to improved emotional resilience and well-being. Remember, the goal is not to eliminate all negative thoughts but to develop a more balanced and realistic perspective. With patience and persistence, this technique can become a valuable asset in your mental health toolkit, helping you navigate life's challenges with greater confidence.

CBT and confidence

CBT provides strategies to boost self-esteem, such as setting and achieving realistic goals, practicing self-compassion, and enhancing self-awareness. You can significantly improve your confidence levels by changing how you think about yourself and how you interpret situations. Cognitive behavioral techniques can help you successfully deal with self-doubts, one thought at a time. It's important to note that progress in CBT doesn't always occur linearly, and setbacks can happen. However, with perseverance and the guidance of a skilled therapist, the path to improved confidence is achievable. One meta-study provides evidence that self-esteem (closely related to confidence) can be improved with the help of CBT (Kolubinski et al., 2018).

Let's consider some examples that illustrate how CBT can help individuals overcome confidence issues. Albert Ellis argued that self-esteem is the greatest sickness known to humankind because it's conditional. The goal of CBT is to reach a stage where the client can accept themselves unconditionally. Applying Ellis' approach, the dialog between the therapist and client might unfold like this:

> *Therapist*: "What are you telling yourself to make your confidence dissipate? You largely constructed your lack of confidence, it [the lack of confidence] wasn't given to you at birth. Therefore, you can dismantle it. What do you think you're telling yourself to make yourself this way?"
> *Client*: "I don't like my life . . ."
> *Therapist*: "Yeah, but that wouldn't cause you to feel a lack of confidence. What else are you telling yourself?"
> *Client*: "I shouldn't fail. I'm no good."

When the therapist hears the client's "shoulds," "oughts," and "musts," they work with the client to abandon these irrational demands. According to Ellis, the slogan is, "I will not should on myself today" (Epstein, 2001, p. 72). In his view, there are three musts that hold us back: "I *must* do well. You *must* treat me well. And the world *must* be easy."

Vignette 6.3: Janet

Janet is a young professional with debilitating negative thoughts. She continually tells herself, "I am a failure. I can't do anything right." Her therapist helps her identify these thoughts as "all-or-nothing" thinking, a common cognitive distortion. The therapist asks her to keep a thought record over the week, noting instances when she has these negative thoughts, the situations that prompt them, and how they make her feel and behave. Janet realizes that these thoughts often surface when she makes minor mistakes at work. Next, the therapist helps Janet challenge these distortions. They discuss whether the evidence truly supports her belief that she can't do anything right. They uncover situations where Janet has succeeded and demonstrated competence. Slowly, Janet learns to replace her maladaptive thought, "I'm a failure," with a more balanced thought, "Everyone makes mistakes; I'm still learning and growing." With time and practice, Janet's confidence improves. She stops treating minor mistakes as catastrophes and begins to view them as opportunities for learning and growth. By reframing her thought patterns, she is able to change her feelings and behaviors.

Since its inception, CBT has evolved significantly, integrating cognitive and behavioral approaches to create a powerful therapeutic tool. Its emphasis on the relationship between thoughts, feelings, and behaviors, its less intrusive nature compared to other therapies, and the link to rationality make it quite appealing to many people. Coupled with its time-limited and structured nature (e.g., standardized flow of sessions, application of worksheets, exercises, and homework), this has made CBT a popular choice among clinicians and clients alike.

CBT has been extensively researched and has been shown to be effective in treating a wide range of conditions. Numerous studies and meta-analyses have demonstrated its efficacy, often showing it to be as effective as or more effective than medication for certain conditions (Hoffman et al., Hofmann et al., 2012). As research continues to support its effectiveness, CBT remains at the forefront of evidence-based psychotherapy practices.

Psychodynamic Therapy

Psychodynamic therapy is a talk therapy that delves into unconscious conflicts and unresolved issues that may contribute to various mental health concerns, including a lack of confidence. The oldest and most famous form of psychodynamic therapy is psychoanalysis, developed by Sigmund Freud in the 1890s. According to the psychoanalytic approach, the sources of our feelings, thoughts, and behaviors are unconscious, and people tend to deny, suppress, or project them onto the therapist. The objective of psychoanalysis is to uncover those unconscious psychological forces.

Psychodynamic therapy focuses on exploring early life experiences, analyzing relationships and patterns, examining thoughts and behaviors, and fostering the development of self-awareness and personal growth. Psychodynamic therapists believe that by gaining insight into these deeper, unconscious issues, individuals can better understand why they feel inadequate or undeserving of their achievements, leading to greater self-awareness and personal growth. Psychodynamic therapists undergo extensive training, including participating in their own personal therapy, to become qualified practitioners. This rigorous preparation ensures that therapists are well-equipped to guide patients through the complex terrain of the unconscious mind.

The psychodynamic approach employs various techniques to uncover and address unconscious processes. Some examples of these techniques include:

- *Free Association*: A psychoanalytic technique in which the patient verbalizes thoughts spontaneously. The stream of uncensored thoughts may reveal unconscious conflicts.
- *Catharsis*: Emotional discharge that provides relief by consciously expressing suppressed feelings or memories.
- *Working Through*: The therapeutic process of repeatedly addressing unconscious conflicts to reduce symptoms and facilitate insight.
- *Dream Analysis*: Interpretation of dreams to uncover unconscious wishes, conflicts, or defenses.
- *Transference*: The projection of unconscious feelings or attitudes from past relationships onto the therapist during treatment.

This focus on the unconscious distinguishes psychodynamic therapy from other therapeutic approaches, like CBT, which concentrate primarily on conscious thoughts and behaviors.

In psychodynamic therapy, the primary goal of the initial interview is to determine if treatment is necessary and what form it should take. The focus of these initial meetings may range from addressing formal matters such as scheduling, confidentiality, or boundaries to delving into therapeutic content. While the initial interview varies depending on the therapist's approach, the therapeutic process typically begins with a comprehensive assessment of the individual's history, encompassing childhood experiences, family dynamics, and significant life events. In particular, the therapist pays attention to early relationships and experiences that may have contributed to the lack of confidence (McWilliams, 2011).

Following the initial interview, a series of 2–8 preliminary sessions typically occurs. During this period, the therapist conducts detailed diagnostic assessments, works to establish a sustainable therapeutic relationship with the patient, and determines the appropriate duration and cost of therapy. The duration and frequency of psychodynamic therapy can vary significantly.

Classical psychoanalysis, for instance, often extends over several years and requires one to five sessions per week.

The therapist establishes a safe, nonjudgmental environment, encouraging open exploration of thoughts and feelings (Gabbard, 2017). During the 50-min sessions, the client is invited to engage in free association, speaking about whatever thought or feeling comes to mind. This technique helps uncover unconscious forces related to self-doubt. For example, the psychoanalyst might search for unconscious conflicts potentially contributing to the lack of confidence, such as a tension between the desire for success and an unconscious fear of surpassing a parent. The psychoanalyst identifies and interprets defense mechanisms used to protect against anxiety or low self-esteem. One such defense mechanism might be repression, which blocks out any conscious memory of a failure, making the client unable to recall it even when asked directly.

The therapist pays close attention to the therapeutic relationship, observing patterns that may reflect interactions with significant others. For example, seeking excessive approval from the analyst might mirror the client's behavior with their parents. Dreams and fantasies are explored as valuable sources of insight into unconscious thoughts and feelings that might reveal beliefs or fears related to self-confidence.

Over time, the client gains an understanding of how their early experiences, particularly with caregivers, have shaped their self-perception and confidence levels. The psychoanalyst guides them in confronting and working through painful emotions or memories, offering interpretations to clarify the unconscious roots of their self-doubt. The psychoanalyst gently confronts resistance to exploring certain topics or making changes, recognizing it as an integral part of the therapeutic process. As the client develops insight and addresses unconscious conflicts, genuine self-esteem, based on a more realistic self-perception, is gradually built.

Throughout this journey, the psychoanalyst maintains a neutral but supportive stance, allowing the client to lead while providing guidance and interpretation. The ultimate goal is to uncover the root causes of low confidence, work through related conflicts and emotions, and foster the development of a more positive, realistic self-image. The psychoanalytic approach, grounded in both classical and contemporary theories, has shown efficacy (Shedler, 2010) in treating various psychological issues, including low self-confidence.

The cost of psychoanalytic treatment can vary significantly, influenced by several factors, including the therapist's expertise, credentials, and geographical location. In recent years, modern psychodynamic approaches have emerged, offering shorter durations due to patient expectations and insurance limitations.

In the United States, sessions typically range from $150 to $400, with prices in major metropolitan areas such as New York City or Los Angeles potentially exceeding $500 per session. To accommodate varying financial situations, many analysts offer income-based sliding scale fees. The United Kingdom sees a general price range of £50–£150 per session, with London commanding higher rates, often between £80 and £200 or more. Prices vary considerably across Europe, generally ranging between €50 and €150 per session. Switzerland stands out as one of the more expensive countries, with sessions costing from CHF 150 to CHF 250.

It's worth noting that in several European countries, certain psychoanalytic treatments may be partially or fully covered by national health services or insurance plans. This coverage can substantially reduce individual costs. In recent years, many insurance plans have begun to cover psychodynamic therapy, though coverage may be limited compared to shorter-term therapies. Research has shown that psychodynamic therapy can be effective for various mental health issues, including depression, anxiety, and personality disorders (Abbass et al., 2014). As we continue to understand the intricate workings of the human psyche, psychodynamic therapy remains a valuable tool in the mental health professional's arsenal. By offering a deep exploration of the unconscious and its influence on our thoughts, feelings, and behaviors, this approach provides a unique pathway to self-discovery and emotional healing.

Take Action 6.3: How to Find the Right Therapist

If you are dealing with serious confidence issues and have found that applying different techniques yourself has not worked, it's time to seek help. Taking the first step toward finding a therapist is a significant milestone in the journey toward improved mental health and a better quality of life.
   Here are some suggestions for starting this process:

1. Look for a licensed professional who has training and experience in CBT, including psychiatrists, psychologists, and social workers. The following organizations maintain directories of therapists:

- The Association for Behavioral and Cognitive Therapies (ABCT) https://www.abct.org/
- European Association for Behavioral and Cognitive Therapies (EABCT) https://eabct.eu/find-a-therapist/
- The American Psychological Association (APA) https://www.apa.org
- Psychology Today psychologytoday.com
- Shanghai International Mental Health Association: https://s-imha.com/therapists-list/
- International Mental Health Professionals Japan: https://www.imhpj.org/find-a-therapist-guide/

2. The International Psychoanalytical Association (IPA) (https://www.ipa.world) offers links to 52 national societies, each providing information about individual members and psychoanalysts in their respective regions.
3. Obtain referrals from your primary care physician, friends, or family members.
4. Many companies and organizations in the United States offer free and confidential counseling, referrals, and other psychological services through Employee Assistance Programs (EAPs) to their employees.
5. Arrange an initial consultation with the prospective therapist to ensure they are a good fit. During this meeting, ask about their experience, qualifications, and approach to therapy. Ask the therapist whether they specialize in treating the condition you are seeking help with.
6. The goal of the first meeting is to decide whether you can build a trusting, working relationship with the therapist. If the answer is no, expand your search to find a therapist with whom you think you could work. It's essential to feel comfortable with your therapist; the relationship between you and the therapist is a strong predictor of how successful therapy will be.

*   *   *

Confidence is not a gift bestowed upon a lucky few. It is a mindset and an evolving journey shaped by our experiences, environments, and beliefs. I hope the book leaves you with a challenge: to take what you have learned and apply it in your daily life, not just for yourself but for the next generation. As leaders, colleagues, mentors, and parents, we have the power to shape how confidence is understood and nurtured. We can teach our daughters to speak up without apology and our sons to value collaboration over competition. We can model vulnerability as strength and show that failure is not the opposite of success but an essential part of it. We can show that confidence is not about perfection, fearlessness, or fitting into predefined molds. It's about owning your voice, embracing your imperfections, and navigating challenges with resilience and self-belief. For women, this means rejecting the myths that have long held them back—myths that say they are too risk-averse, too emotional, or not "enough." For men, it's about recognizing the biases that perpetuate these myths and becoming allies in dismantling them.

Confidence is not something you wait for; it's something you build. By challenging the myths, breaking free from self-defeating behaviors, embracing authenticity, and stepping up to have those challenging conversations, you can redefine what it means to be confident, not just for women, but for everyone. Confidence isn't a myth; it's a legacy we pass on. Your efforts now will shape what society looks like tomorrow.

References

Abbass, A. A., Kisely, S. R., Town, J. M., Leichsenring, F., Driessen, E., De Maat, S., Gerber, A., Dekker, J., Rabung, S., & Rusalovska, S. (2014). Short-term psychodynamic psychotherapies for common mental disorders. *Cochrane Database of Systematic Reviews*, 7.

Ayers, B., Forshaw, M., & Hunter, M. S. (2010). The impact of attitudes towards the menopause on women's symptom experience: A systematic review. *Maturitas*, 65(1), 28–36.

Beck, J. S. (2011). *Cognitive Behavior Therapy: Basics and Beyond* (2nd ed.). Guilford Press.

Belsky, J., & Eggebeen, D. (1991). Early and extensive maternal employment and young children's socioemotional development: Children of the National Longitudinal Survey of Youth. *Journal of Marriage and the Family*, 1083–1098.

Brent, L. J., Franks, D. W., Foster, E. A., Balcomb, K. C., Cant, M. A., & Croft, D. P. (2015). Ecological knowledge, leadership, and the evolution of menopause in killer whales. *Current Biology*, 25(6), 746–750.

Brody, J. E. (1981, July 29). Personal Health. *The New York Times*, 17.

Brooks-Gunn, J., Han, W.-J., & Waldfogel, J. (2010). First-year maternal employment and child development in the first seven years. *Monographs of the Society for Research in Child Development*, 75(2), 7.

Budig, M. J. (2014). The fatherhood bonus and the motherhood penalty: Parenthood and the gender gap in pay. *Third Way*, 2.

Burns, D. D. (1981). *Feeling Good*. Signet Books.

Bygdeman, M., & Swahn, M. (1996). Replens versus dienoestrol cream in the symptomatic treatment of vaginal atrophy in postmenopausal women. *Maturitas*, 23(3), 259–263.

Chang, A.-M., Aeschbach, D., Duffy, J. F., & Czeisler, C. A. (2015). Evening use of light-emitting eReaders negatively affects sleep, circadian timing, and next-morning alertness. *Proceedings of the National Academy of Sciences*, 112(4), 1232–1237.

Chrisler, J. C. (2011). Leaks, lumps, and lines: Stigma and women's bodies. *Psychology of Women Quarterly*, 35(2), 202–214.

Clark, P. (2021, Dec 12). A work blunder teaches so much more than a triumph. *Financial Times*. https://www.ft.com/content/8a98b54c-9fa5-4ef1-8c62-cc16b09057cb

Clarkson, T. B., Utian, W. H., Barnes, S., Gold, E. B., Basaria, S. S., Aso, T., Kronenberg, F., Frankenfeld, C. L., Cline, J. M., & Landgren, B.-M. (2011).

The role of soy isoflavones in menopausal health: Report of The North American Menopause Society/Wulf H. Utian Translational Science Symposium in Chicago, IL. *Menopause*, *18*(7), 732–753. October 2010.

Cohen, C. F. (2021). Return-to-work programs come of age: Companies can benefit from hiring mid-career professionals who've taken a break. *Harvard Business Review*, *99*(5), 49.

Cramer, H., Lauche, R., Langhorst, J., & Dobos, G. (2012). Effectiveness of yoga for menopausal symptoms: A systematic review and meta-analysis of randomized controlled trials. *Evidence-Based Complementary and Alternative Medicine, 2012*, (1), 863905.

Cukrowska-Torzewska, E., & Matysiak, A. (2020). The motherhood wage penalty: A meta-analysis. *Social Science Research*, *88*, 102416.

Cunningham, C. R., & Murray, S. S. (2005). Two executives, one career. *Harvard Business Review*, *83*(2), 125–131, 150.

Daley, A., Stokes-Lampard, H., Thomas, A., & MacArthur, C. (2014). Exercise for vasomotor menopausal symptoms. *Cochrane Database of Systematic Reviews (11)*.

David, D., Cristea, I., & Hofmann, S. G. (2018). Why cognitive behavioral therapy is the current gold standard of psychotherapy. *Frontiers in Psychiatry*, *9*, 4.

Ely, R. J., & Padavic, I. (2020). What's really holding women back. *Harvard Business Review*, *98*(2), 58–67.

Ely, R. J., Stone, P., & Ammerman, C. (2014). Rethink what you "know" about high-achieving women. *Harvard Business Review*, *92*(12), 20.

Epstein, R. (2001). The prince of reason: An interview with Albert Ellis. *Psychology Today*, *34*(1), 66–76.

Freeman, E. W., Sammel, M. D., & Sanders, R. J. (2014). Risk of long-term hot flashes after natural menopause: Evidence from the Penn Ovarian Aging Study cohort. *Menopause*, *21*(9), 924–932.

Gabbard, G. O. (2017). *Long-term Psychodynamic Psychotherapy: A Basic Text* (3rd ed.). American Psychiatric Association Publishing.

Gilli, F., DiSano, K. D., & Pachner, A. R. (2020). SeXX matters in multiple sclerosis. *Frontiers in Neurology.*, *11*, 616.

Greening, J. (2017). *Menopause transition: Effects on women's economic participation*. Government Equalities Office. Retrieved from https://www.gov.uk/government/people/justine-greening

Griffiths, A., MacLennan, S. J., & Hassard, J. (2013). Menopause and work: An electronic survey of employees' attitudes in the UK. *Maturitas*, *76*(2), 155–159.

Harlow, P. (2014, December 17). Women run banks differently: They are aware of "collateral damage." [Video] CNN Business. https://edition.cnn.com/2014/12/09/business/jane-fraser-citi/index.html

Heilman, M. E., & Okimoto, T. G. (2008). Motherhood: A potential source of bias in employment decisions. *Journal of Applied Psychology*, *93*(1), 189.

Hess, R., Thurston, R. C., Hays, R. D., Chang, -C.-C. H., Dillon, S. N., Ness, R. B., Bryce, C. L., Kapoor, W. N., & Matthews, K. A. (2012). The impact of menopause on health-related quality of life: Results from the STRIDE longitudinal study. *Quality of Life Research, 21*, 535–544.

Hickey, M., LaCroix, A. Z., Doust, J., Mishra, G. D., Sivakami, M., Garlick, D., & Hunter, M. S. (2024). An empowerment model for managing menopause. *The Lancet, 403*(10430), 947–957.

Hideg, I., Krstic, A., Trau, R. N., & Zarina, T. (2018). The unintended consequences of maternity leaves: How agency interventions mitigate the negative effects of longer legislated maternity leaves. *Journal of Applied Psychology, 103*(10), 1155.

Hofmann, S. G., Asnaani, A., Vonk, I. J., Sawyer, A. T., & Fang, A. (2012). The efficacy of cognitive behavioral therapy: A review of meta-analyses. *Cognitive Therapy and Research, 36*, 427–440.

Hutchinson, J., & Cassidy, T. (2022). Well-being, self-esteem and body satisfaction in new mothers. *Journal of Reproductive and Infant Psychology, 40*(5), 532–546.

Kolubinski, D. C., Frings, D., Nikčević, A. V., Lawrence, J. A., & Spada, M. M. (2018). A systematic review and meta-analysis of CBT interventions based on the Fennell model of low self-esteem. *Psychiatry Research, 267*, 296–305.

Ladge, J. J., Humberd, B. K., & Eddleston, K. A. (2018). Retaining professionally employed new mothers: The importance of maternal confidence and workplace support to their intent to stay. *Human Resource Management, 57*(4), 883–900.

Ladge, J. J., & Little, L. M. (2019). When expectations become reality: Work-family image management and identity adaptation. *Academy of Management Review, 44*(1), 126–149.

Lancet. (2024, March 9). Time for a balanced conversation about menopause. [Editorial]. *The Lancet, 403*(10430), 877.

Levy, B. R., Slade, M. D., Kunkel, S. R., & Kasl, S. V. (2002). Longevity increased by positive self-perceptions of aging. *Journal of Personality and Social Psychology, 83*(2), 261.

Lombardi, C. M. (2023). Early maternal employment and children's school readiness: Changing associations over time? *Journal of Child and Family Studies, 32*(4), 1032–1047.

MacQuoid, L. P. (1995). The women's mau: Female peace warriors in Western Samoa. [Unpublished master's dissertation]. Manoa: University of Hawai'i.

Mainiero, L. A., & Gibson, D. E. (2018). The kaleidoscope career model revisited: How midcareer men and women diverge on authenticity, balance, and challenge. *Journal of Career Development, 45*(4), 361–377.

Maki, P. M. (2015). Verbal memory and menopause. *Maturitas, 82*(3), 288–290.

Martyn-St James, M., & Carroll, S. (2009). A meta-analysis of impact exercise on postmenopausal bone loss: The case for mixed loading exercise programmes. *British Journal of Sports Medicine, 43*(12), 898–908.

McWilliams, N. (2011). *Psychoanalytic Diagnosis: Understanding Personality Structure in the Clinical Process*. Guilford Press.

Mercer, R. T. (2004). Becoming a mother versus maternal role attainment. *Journal of Nursing Scholarship*, *36*(3), 226–232.

Ottesen, K. K. (2022, March 15). Activist Reshma Saujani: "Women are in the worst state that we've ever been." *The Washington Post*. https://www.washington post.com/magazine/2022/03/15/activist-reshma-saujani-women-are-worst-state-that-weve-ever-been/

Quental, C., Rojas Gaviria, P., & Del Bucchia, C. (2023). The dialectic of (menopause) zest: Breaking the mold of organizational irrelevance. *Gender, Work & Organization*, *30*(5), 1816–1838.

Shedler, J. (2010). The efficacy of psychodynamic psychotherapy. *American Psychologist*, *65*(2), 98.

Silveira, M. L., Ertel, K. A., Dole, N., & Chasan-Taber, L. (2015). The role of body image in prenatal and postpartum depression: A critical review of the literature. *Archives of Women's Mental Health*, *18*, 409–421.

Slaughter, A.-M. (July–August 2012). Why women still can't have it all. *The Atlantic*. https://www.theatlantic.com/magazine/archive/2012/07/why-women-still-cant-have-it-all/309020/

Steffan, B., & Potočnik, K. (2023). Thinking outside Pandora's Box: Revealing differential effects of coping with physical and psychological menopause symptoms at work. *Human Relations*, *76*(8), 1191–1225.

Stoeltje, B. J. (2021, March 25). Asante Queen Mothers in Ghana. *Oxford Research Encyclopedia of African History*, Retrieved 27 Mar. 2025, from https://doi.org/10.1093/acrefore/9780190277734.013.796

Tinsley, C. H., & Ely, R. J. (2018). What most people get wrong about men and women: Research shows the sexes aren't so different. *Harvard Business Review*, *96*(3), 114–121.

Van Scheppingen, M. A., Denissen, J., Chung, J. M., Tambs, K., & Bleidorn, W. (2018). Self-esteem and relationship satisfaction during the transition to motherhood. *Journal of Personality and Social Psychology*, *114*(6), 973.

Villamor, I., Hill, N. S., Kossek, E. E., & Foley, K. O. (2023). Virtuality at work: A doubled-edged sword for women's career equality? *Academy of Management Annals*, *17*(1), 113–140.

Wagner, S. R. (n.d.). How native women inspired the women's rights movement. *National Park Service*. https://www.nps.gov/articles/000/how-native-american-women-inspired-the-women-s-rights-movement.htm

Waldfogel, J., Han, W.-J., & Brooks-Gunn, J. (2002). The effects of early maternal employment on child cognitive development. *Demography*, *39*(2), 369–392.

Wiese, B. S., & Stertz, A. M. (2023). Mothers' regrets of having (or not having) returned to work after childbirth: Longitudinal relationships with organizational commitment. *Applied Psychology*, *72*(2), 451–476.

Yu, W.-H., & Hara, Y. (2021). Motherhood penalties and fatherhood premiums: Effects of parenthood on earnings growth within and across firms. *Demography*, *58*(1), 247–272.

Index

© The Editor(s) (if applicable) and The Author(s), under exclusive license to Springer Nature Switzerland AG 2025
G. Toegel, *The Confidence Myth*,
https://doi.org/10.1007/978-3-031-97305-5

GPSR Compliance

The European Union's (EU) General Product Safety Regulation (GPSR) is a set of rules that requires consumer products to be safe and our obligations to ensure this.

If you have any concerns about our products, you can contact us on ProductSafety@springernature.com

In case Publisher is established outside the EU, the EU authorized representative is:

Springer Nature Customer Service Center GmbH
Europaplatz 3
69115 Heidelberg, Germany

Batch number: 09137403

Printed by Printforce, the Netherlands